Managing the
Difficult Patient

Managing the Difficult Patient

Robert E. Hooberman, Ph.D.
Barbara M. Hooberman, M.D.

PSYCHOSOCIAL PRESS
Madison   Connecticut

Library of Congress Cataloging-in-Publication Data

Hooberman, Robert E.
    Managing the difficult patient / Robert E. Hooberman, Barbara M. Hooberman.
        p.   cm.
    Includes bibliographical references and index.
    ISBN 1-887841-08-3
    1. Physician and patient.   2. Psychotherapist and patient.
3. Medicine and psychology.   I. Hooberman, Barbara M.   II. Title.
    [DNLM: 1. Physician-Patient Relations. 2. Patient Acceptance of
Health Care.   3. Mental Disorders—psychology.   4. Patients-
-psychology.   5. Transference (Psychology)   W 62 H776m 1997]
R727.3.H63   1998
610.69'6—dc21
DNLM/DLC
for Library of Congress   97-19686
                                                                  CIP

Manufactured in the United States of America

TO: JESSICA HOOBERMAN
JOSH HOOBERMAN

THE LIGHTS OF OUR LIVES

Contents

Preface

Throughout the course of our marriage, many dinnertime discussions have taken place about our respective work and of our struggles and successes. From our long association, we have gained both knowledge and appreciation of the work that each of us does. Our respective fields of psychology and medicine allow us to have a particular perspective into the interaction between mind and body that we hope is transmitted in this work.

Our intent is not to produce a technical workbook. Rather, we believe that knowledge and understanding of patient motivation will lead to increased comfort for the health care practitioner. Consequently, we have endeavored to mix both practical and useful suggestions with material that leads toward a greater level of psychological sophistication. Knowledge often reduces anxiety and leads toward greater mastery of material that is threatening and bewildering. We hope that an appreciation of the forces that create and motivate personalities will result in calmer and more satisfied practitioners. Satisfaction with one's work is a crucial and attainable goal for all of those who work.

Much of the discussion in the ensuing chapters is about the practitioner-patient relationship. Humans are raised within relationships, and it is inevitable that difficulties that arise in the professional encounter will be the result of relationship difficulties. Conflict between individuals is not always perfectly resolvable, but understanding the sources of the difficulties can lead toward more satisfying relationships and a reduction in interpersonal difficulties. Although this book is aimed toward health care professionals, the issues and concepts are applicable to all. Interpersonal interactions are unavoidable, despite the wishes of those who find such interactions so difficult.

Any work that entails interacting with people is bound to be difficult because of the complexity of individuals and society. To label a patient or person as "difficult" may be unfair, one-sided, and simplistic. In many ways, it is the interaction between people with the attendant strong emotions that creates a sense of the difficult. Assigning responsibility to the patient for patient-practitioner problems does not do full justice to the manner in which people, both patients and practitioners, uncannily create and re-create dramas that ensnare those involved. We hope that we have taken a balanced approch, but we recognize that this view is written from the perspective of the practitioner.

We would like to thank Drs. Errol Soskolne, Alexander Gotz, Leslie Walker, and Dan Cahill for their generosity in sharing their personal and professional experiences as physicians.

1

Introduction

Discussions with physicians indicate that a substantial amount of their time is spent on addressing problems unassociated with physical illness. The effects of psychosocial difficulties are apparent to all. The local or national news is replete with a litany of murders, suicides, family difficulties, personal despair, and interpersonal conflict. It is only to be expected that these difficulties will manifest themselves in the consulting rooms of health care professionals. Patients want to be able to turn to their health care providers for advice and counsel during times of stress and confusion. Unbeknownst to the provider, the patient may have a hidden agenda that has little, if anything, to do with physical disease. Consequently, the physician, perhaps to his or her dismay, becomes identified as the problem solver for emotional and behavioral difficulties.

Example

Mrs. S. requested an appointment with her family physician but refused to inform the receptionist of the nature of her problem. The physician expected to hear about the woman's gastric difficulties, a problem for which she had previously been treated. Instead, he was overwhelmed by the extremely painful story of the patient's husband's infidelity and of Mrs. S.'s distress and depression. Unprepared, and mindful of the potential for schedule disruption, the physician was curt and unsympathetic, and the patient left feeling further distressed.

1

EXPECTATIONS

Health care professionals, like others, have particular expectations about the nature of their work that do not always match the reality of everyday life. In the preceding example, the doctor may have had the expectation that his practice would consist solely of treating physical complaints, and he is dismayed that his patients bring so many personal and interpersonal complaints to his office. Not only are his expectations unmet, but he is also unskilled in and uneducated about dealing with such problems, resulting in feelings of inadequacy that cause him to react angrily toward his patient. For this particular physician, any patient with emotional difficulties is a difficult patient.

Example

A beginning psychotherapist believes that treatment is progressing well with her depressed patient. She has referred her for medication, and the rapport with the patient is well established. The patient then informs the therapist that she has something difficult to discuss and proceeds to describe the symptoms of a dissociative disorder. At times the patient has episodes in which she feels detached from herself, experiences a sense of loss of self, and has a frightening waking dream wherein she imagines herself on a stage in costume with a number of strangers. The therapist says little, feeling overwhelmed by the bizarreness of the story. In the following session the therapist informs the patient that she felt overmatched by the patient's difficulties and wishes to refer her to the therapist's supervisor. The patient becomes quite disturbed, feels rejected, and never returns.

In this instance, the therapist expected the patient to have relatively uncomplicated problems that were responsive to medication and to the level of treatment that the therapist felt competent in handling. Under the circumstances, the therapist acted quite appropriately and ethically by not trying to treat a disorder that she felt ill prepared for managing. It is impossible to know whether this particular therapist had her own emotional difficulties that precluded her from being effective or whether she mostly needed further training. At this point, it is safe to say that this was a difficult patient for this particular therapist. When one is working in the health care field one must be prepared for any eventuality, and the variety of patient problems and pathology is amazingly complex and unpredictable. Those that expect patients to meet their expectations are bound to be disappointed.

SUGGESTION. Practitioners can be more comfortable if they maintain realistic expectations for themselves and for their patients.

It is not only in the area of health care that clients exhibit troublesome characteristics.

Example

An individual was suing another man for injuries suffered in a car accident. Throughout the trial the plaintiff talked out of turn, muttered to himself, and loudly disputed testimony being presented. Despite a strong case, the jury found for the defendant because they were so alienated by the plaintiff's behavior. The attorney had some sense of his client's propensity to act inappropriately but assumed that he would behave once the trail began, which was a serious miscalculation that cost him the case. If the attorney had a better grasp of his client's difficulties and had been able to prepare him appropriately, the outcome might have been different. Unfortunately, the attorney was not trained to deal with such difficulties.

Everyone must deal with difficult and unreasonable people. In fact, everyone behaves unreasonably from time to time. People like to think that *they* are perfectly normal and it is only someone else's behavior that is odd. Many patients who seek out psychotherapy wish to prove that their problems arise from external issues and do not originate within themselves or arise purely as a response to the external. Married people often believe that they would be happier if their spouse would just shape up. Of course, the spouse feels similarly.

Oftentimes it is not a simple question of abnormal behavior that creates discomfort in others. Individual and cultural preferences account for some behavior that is considered strange.

STRANGERS

Example

"Personal space" refers to the physical space between interacting people that each culture deems appropriate. In the United States, a person who violates another's personal space is reacted to very negatively. We are very territorial, and in such instances act as if the person has trespassed on our property. There are many other cultural differences that create strong feelings of dislike and derision in those unfamiliar with a minority culture. Dietary differences can create revulsion. In many parts of Africa, a wide range of insects are considered an essential and valued part of diet. There are few Americans who would be glad to partake in such a meal, and some would find such preferences "disgusting."

Treating individuals from other cultures can be daunting for the health care professional, in part because the former may envision professional relationships in a different fashion than do patients in the United States. If the professional feels that he or she is not communicating well with a patient from a different culture, it would be helpful to ask about patient expectations and explore cultural differences.

Example

A Chinese woman sought help from a psychologist because of depression. She appeared to be a very shy and private person who complained about an emotionally abusive husband. The treatment did not seem to progress well, and it only moved forward when the therapist became aware that the patient felt she could only divulge information asked for; she was unaware that her therapist had the unexpressed expectation that the patient be an active participant in the process. The patient expected more of an authoritarian model. The therapist and the patient were both required to alter their expectations of each other.

Cultural differences could and perhaps should invite curiosity by others. Unfortunately, this is not always the case. Humans organize themselves into groups: families, religions, regions, countries. Infants go through a period of "stranger anxiety," beginning at approximately 9 months old, when they suddenly become afraid of strangers. They have become more aware of their separateness from their parents and have developed a stronger identity with the family unit. Strangers begin to feel threatening and dangerous. This phase represents the strengthening of the sense of security within the sameness of the family. Those that are family members are viewed as safe; those outside are frightening and different. As the child grows, the sense of the identity within the family and within the culture continues be strengthened. One advantage of school is to introduce children to others with different backgrounds and to encourage them to learn and appreciate different cultures. Some families, however, instill distrust of those that are different. Persons belonging to a different group are often viewed with suspicion and sometimes hatred. Ethnic warfare throughout history is evident. A major source of these conflicts is the tendency to assign to the "other" negative qualities. Scapegoating is the desire to (unfairly) blame others. It is a way of maintaining a positive sense of self regardless of the reality of the situation. Those prone to scapegoating are insecure and cannot tolerate responsibility for their own situations. The insecurity arises from excessive blaming and hostility within the individual's family of origin. A child punished severely for a misdeed may come to feel so negatively about himself or herself that the feelings become intolerable, and the child looks for others to whom to assign this sense of "badness." The child thinks, "It's not me who is bad and naughty, it is that person over there who looks different than I do, the stranger." Scapegoating and blame are ubiquitous, and function to maintain a sense of security and positive self-regard for those within the "in" group. In this light it becomes evident that those who present themselves as different can be viewed as odd or difficult.

Example

A 16-year-old girl tragically died in a car crash after returning from an unauthorized visit to her boyfriend in college several hundred miles away. Apparently, she fell asleep after the long drive and lost control of her car a scant 20 miles from home. There was an outpouring of support and concern from many who knew her or her family, but there was considerable criticism of her parents for not having kept a tighter rein on her, and the young girl was blamed for being foolish for having gone on the trip. The horror of the tragedy that is every parent's nightmare caused people to find ways to distance themselves via criticism. It is as if they are saying, "This cannot happen to my child since I am a better parent." They are trying to deny the possibility of something similarly tragic happening to them. The reality is, of course, that their children are also vulnerable to unforeseen situations. Scapegoating and blaming such as this are designed to protect oneself and to maintain illusions of safety and control.

At times, strangers can be frightening. People feel secure in their own environs, where they are familiar with their own customs. Foreignness can be equated with dangerousness. There are a considerable number of people who do not venture out of their own neighborhood, let alone out of their own country. This may not be chauvinistic in the sense of an insistence that their country or group is the only good one. Some children become very concerned with being lost or abandoned. Oftentimes this is in response to past relationships in which parents and/or other caregivers were not available or consistent. On occasion children have been left to fend for themselves at an inappropriately early age, resulting in a lifelong fear of abandonment. Additionally, children may develop the belief that their unacceptable thoughts and behavior will result in parental abandonment should they be exposed. People who have experienced actual parental abandonment tend to imagine that it is because of some misbehavior. Having to fend for oneself is a terrifying prospect for a child, and being in a strange locale brings up concerns generated from early fears of abandonment.

Example

In the course of treatment, Mrs. O. informed her therapist that whenever she traveled she was terrified of being lost. She felt ill equipped to follow a map, and even if she had traveled a route a number of times she was always concerned about losing her way. She worried about being lost and also about being kidnapped and tortured. She was a woman who greatly feared abandonment because of what she perceived to be an inattentive mother. She also feared strangers, particularly those who dressed or wore their hair in fashions that were not in the mainstream, such as those with pierced body parts or brightly colored hair. Interestingly enough, this woman had been abused and terrorized by her siblings. The therapist pointed out to her that those who had looked similar to her were the ones who had hurt her the most in her life. Her need to view herself and her family as "good" and strangers as "bad" was very strong.

It is important to remember that health care professionals are not immune to biases and prejudices. Similarly, many have difficulty with those that are different because of personal idiosyncrasies or cultural differences. Patients' strangeness or foreignness, or the practitioner's need to see others as "bad," are reasons why those in the helping professions label a person as troublesome. Most of the time, however, patients are considered difficult when they present behavioral and emotional problems that seem out of the professional's level of expertise. The earlier example of Mrs. S. discussing her husband's infidelities is a good example of this dynamic. Certainly, most medical personnel gravitate toward that field because they wish to work with people with physical disorders. Treating psychological problems is not part of their expectations. Similarly, attorneys, architects, and other professionals may be uninterested and certainly unprepared to deal with those individuals with psychological problems.

SUGGESTION. Practitioners need to be aware of their prejudices and of their attempts to view those who are different as odd or pathological.

Definition. *A difficult patient is a person who presents to the caregiver behaviors and emotional difficulties of a severity significant enough to impact adversely on the treatment or on the provider.*

Examples

A patient presented herself to her gynecologist complaining of menstrual irregularities and pain. The patient was so tense that she suffered from vaginismus (involuntary contraction of the muscles surrounding the vagina), which prevented the examination. The patient explained that she had never been able to have an examination, felt disgusted about her genitalia, was terrified of the idea of intercourse, was planning to be married within the year, and could the doctor please cure her difficulties, quickly.

A patient suffered a heart attack, and his cardiologist recommended that he lose 30 pounds, begin an exercise program, stop smoking, and participate in a stress-management program. The patient refused to follow any of the recommendations and became furious with the physician when confronted about his noncompliance.

A woman suffering from chronic schizophrenia is brought to the hospital emergency room after suffering a fall at the rooming house where she resides. Upon her arrival, she begins to scream uncontrollably and is combative and threatening.

A man visits his dentist, where it is discovered that he is grinding his teeth during the night, resulting in teeth damage and jaw pain.

A parent visits a pediatrician with her son. She is concerned about his academic difficulties and insists that the doctor put him on medication for hyperactivity despite the obvious fact that the family is in great turmoil and the child is most likely responding to the discord.

The examples could be endless. Professionals who work intensively with people are going to have to contend with patients or clients who manifest difficult behaviors. Of course, it is always easy to point a finger at others. It is important to remember that all people have difficult aspects, which may impact others. The most intolerant people are those who struggle the most with their own sense of inadequacy. Those more comfortable with themselves can tolerate their own dysphoric affects without needing to displace them onto others and are also tolerant of others' inadequacies.

EXPLANATORY MODELS

In medicine there exists a predominant "theory" that explains the functioning of the human body and of disease processes. Medical schools throughout the country essentially teach the same curriculum and use the same explanatory models. Chiropractors and practitioners of alternative medicine differ from traditional medicine in some of their conceptions of disease and treatment, but there is still far more agreement on causality and treatment of physical disease than there is regarding emotional and behavioral disorders. The physical body is a concrete reality that can be directly examined and dissected to the microscopic level. If a person is diagnosed with cancer, it is most likely discernible through imaging or biopsy techniques. With regard to the mental disorders, consensus regarding diagnosis, causality, and treatment does not exist. The brain is a physical reality; the mind is not. A pathologist could dissect brain tissue and know little, if anything, about most people's emotional life and level of functioning. Certainly, chronic alcoholics might show neurological deficits, cellular and biochemical changes in the liver, and other physiological changes. Some theorists would argue that schizophrenics have neurological differences as well, but this assertion is still hypothetical, and, in any case, the fact of physiological changes in some mental and behavioral disorders would still not address causality. Even if actual changes are found in brain tissue of those suffering from mental disorders, a case can be made for the position that the psychological disorder has an effect on the brain, as opposed to the notion that brain disorders cause mental disorders. More importantly, knowing solely a person's psychiatric diagnosis tells very little about him or her other than the symptom picture and a general notion of traits. The person's essence, his or her individuality, remains elusive.

Through the years a number of explanations have arisen to explain the existence of various emotional disorders. Each of these theories has cohesiveness in the sense that the treatment recommended follows the theoretical explanation. One who believes that schizophrenia is biochemically/genetically based is going to emphasize a medication-oriented treatment, and any psychotherapeutic treatment prescribed will be designed to help the patient manage symptoms caused by a medical disorder. Sometimes it seems that there are as many theoretical approaches to emotional disorders as there are practitioners. To simplify matters, it may make sense to speak of the predominant models adhered to today. Biologically-based theories, cognitive-behavioral theory, and psychodynamic models encompass the approaches of most practitioners. It is important to remember that these are rough approximations and that many practitioners adhere to more than one model for different people and for different disorders. Furthermore, within each theoretical model there exist many variations, which may be in opposition to each other. Yet these variations do have much in common and can be examined under specific rubrics.

The Medical Model

Biologically-based explanations for emotional disorders postulate a physiological cause for mental disorders. Proponents would not claim that all disorders have a biological base, but they look toward that etiology whenever possible. Their prescribed treatment would be medication, sometimes combined with psychotherapy, usually from a supportive and problem-solving perspective.

Example

A patient who is exceedingly anxious and who has trouble sleeping and relaxing is referred to a psychiatrist for evaluation and treatment. The psychiatrist diagnoses an anxiety disorder that he determines runs in the patient's family, and indicates to the patient that the difficulty is treatable with tranquilizing medication and relaxation techniques.

The implication is that the anxiety disorder is biologically based, essentially "hardwired" in the patient's brain or genes, and thus is not curable although it can be managed medically. Many patients suffering from major depression are informed that they are suffering from a chemical imbalance that is genetically caused and that medication is the necessary and sufficient treatment. From this perspective, psychotherapy is designed to assist the patient in adjusting to his or her disease and is not viewed as being potentially curative. It is an adjunct to the main pharmacological treatment. Typically, patients are initially seen weekly until the psychiatrist completes the assessment and the patient becomes stabilized on the medication. Thereafter visits are less frequent, sometimes on an "as needed" basis or perhaps every month, 6 weeks, or even every 6 months. The prescribing psychiatrist is mostly interested in symptoms and will adjust the medication based on the symptom picture. "For practical purposes our definition of what constitutes a psychiatric illness is simply a medical illness with major emotional and behavioral aspects . . . the study of medicine in the literature divides its presentation of illness and disease into a definition, epidemiology, signs and symptoms, etiology, and treatment" (Winokur & Clayton, 1994, p. xiii). Consequently, medically-oriented psychiatrists will order lab tests and look for biochemical markers, seeing the treatment of mental disorders through the lens of the medical model.

Example

A patient is referred to a psychiatrist because of persecutory delusions. He believes that his best friend is trying to kill him and that the threat of Armageddon is imminent. He also indicates that he is afraid of being homosexually assaulted. The psychiatrist's main interest is in ascertaining the severity of the symptoms and their alleviation. The reason for the development of the disorder is of secondary importance, as is an attempt to ascertain the particular meanings of the delusions. In other words, the psychiatrist may have little curiosity as to reason for the content of the specific delusions or on the precipitants of the development of the disorder.

Some disorders cannot be considered to have a physiological base. For instance, a victim of sexual abuse will have difficulty with his or her emotions because of the assault. A clinician who is primarily medically oriented will still emphasize alleviation of the dysphoric affects through the use of medication. If so inclined, he or she may try psychotherapy to help the patient with the aftereffects of the trauma or may refer the patient to a therapist skilled in working with trauma victims. Regardless, medication-oriented practitioners are symptom-oriented. That is, it is the alleviation of primary symptoms that is the focus, not exploration of underlying personality aspects.

Cognitive-Behavioral Therapy

Cognitive behavioral therapy is often used in conjunction with medication, but certainly can stand on its own. Cognitive-behavioral therapists usually do not become embroiled in controversies over hidden motivations. Rather, they focus on thoughts (cognitions) that accompany emotional disorders and teach their patients methods to alter maladaptive thoughts and behaviors. They typically emphasize short-term treatment, tend to focus more on behavior instead of personality change, and have a solution-oriented perspective.

Example

A patient is referred by his prescribing psychiatrist to a cognitive-behavioral therapist for treatment of his recurring depressive symptoms. He describes a family history of rejection and physical and emotional abuse. His marriage is "on the rocks" and he is doing poorly on the job. The therapist assists the patient in identifying the thoughts that he has when he feels depressed and helps him to identify concrete steps he can take to alter his marital situation and to improve his job performance. He role plays with the patient in order to practice the new behaviors learned.

In this model, the cognitive-behavioral therapist focuses on the patient's thoughts when he is feeling depressed. The theory suggests that the patient feels the way he does because of the maladaptive thoughts, beliefs, and "schemas" that he developed. The therapist believes that there are alternative ways of responding to a given situation and assists the patient in exploring these alternatives, with the expectation that a more rational assessment will result in a lowering of the dysphoric affect. This orientation suggests that emotional difficulties result from faulty information processing.

> First of all the individual is helped to distinguish between thoughts and feelings—for example, that they were feeling anxious about coming to therapy and thinking that they might be asked upsetting questions. They then note the situation and the stream of thoughts that immediately preceded or occurred coincidentally with the emotional response (i.e. the automatic thoughts). Intervention begins by helping the individual come up with alternative responses to the automatic thoughts by examining the inferences made when emotionally upset. (Twaddle & Scott, 1991, p. 72)

Cognitive-behavioral therapy is typically quite structured and relatively straightforward. Some theorists would point to faulty childhood learning processes and/or to biological factors underlying the etiology of the various emotional disorders, but the treatment of the disorders does not necessarily depend on intensive exploration of childhood factors. Cognitive-behavioral therapy, like medication models, is symptom-oriented, but it delves more into internal processes, particularly the faulty core beliefs (cognitions) of the patient, with some focus on their development.

Example

Mrs. G. has been working with her therapist on her depressed feelings. She describes an incident when she was at a party and her best friend ignored her in order to talk to another person. The friend apologized for her apparent rudeness but the patient was very upset, certain that she had been snubbed, and she became tearful and despondent. The patient insisted that the friend's behavior meant that she did not really care for her, which reinforced her feelings of being unloved. The therapist questioned her on her specific thoughts when she was feeling upset, and the patient indicated that she would say to herself that she was worthless. The therapist examined with the patient whether there could be alternative ways of understanding the friend's behavior. The patient, after some hesitancy, acknowledged that the friend's behavior could reflect thoughtlessness rather than indicating some personal attack. This becomes a stimulus for examining other instances of faulty information processing that result in self-condemnation. The patient recognized that she is often thin-skinned because she feels so negatively about herself. With the therapist's assistance she examined the rationality of these thoughts and was helped to replace these thoughts with more rational ones. The therapist also assisted the patient in considering what she could say to her friend to convey the thoughtlessness.

Cognitive-behavioral theorists describe four levels at which faulty information processing can occur. The levels are organized by the degree of accessibility to the patient. "These levels are hierarchically arranged. Voluntary thoughts are highly accessible and easiest to modify. Automatic thoughts may seem to occur without awareness but clients can be quickly taught to identify these cognitions. Modifying these thoughts is associated with immediate symptom reduction. At the third level are assumptions and values. . . . At the deepest level are the schemas which organize information and operate outside awareness" (Gluhoski, 1994, p. 594). Cognitive-behavioral therapy is designed to alter the faulty information processing at the level which causes the patient difficulty.

In cognitive-behavioral therapy, the therapist will often be very directive with the patient, offering direct suggestions and giving tasks for the patient to work on between sessions. Treatment is considered short-term, with weekly sessions being typical; treatment rarely lasts longer than 6 months.

Psychodynamic Theory

"Psychodynamics" as a term represents a variety of psychological theories that are explanatory both of personality development and functioning and of psychological treatment. A proponent of psychodynamic psychotherapy views an individual's thoughts and behaviors as being determined and meaningful. They are determined by aspects of the person's personality functioning, exist for a reason, are understandable, and have a logic, even if that logic is not readily apparent.

Example

Consider the patient mentioned earlier with the delusion that he was in danger of being homosexually attacked. A psychodynamic therapist would be very interested in the nature of the delusion and would help the patient to come to understand the reasons underlying the formation of a delusion and the content of the delusion. The therapist would also focus on the present-day circumstances of the patient in order to understand the events precipitating the psychotic episode.

Psychodynamic theory is a theory of personality and proposes a very complex system. It is based on psychoanalytic formulations originated by Freud in the early part of this century. Psychodynamics is not synonymous with psychoanalysis, in the sense that psychoanalysis as treatment has very specific parameters while psychodynamic therapy refers to a more generic treatment based on psychoanalytic principles. Psychodynamic therapy subsumes a number of like-minded theoretical perspectives with common characteristics. These characteristics are the acceptance of the notion that the mind has both conscious and unconscious aspects and that unconscious processes are extremely important in driving emotions, thoughts, and behaviors; that behavior is meaningful and can be understood, and that knowledge of one's motives leads toward greater levels of mental health; that emotional disorders tend to have their origins in childhood (a developmental perspective); that psychotherapy can be curative; that difficult feelings are at the bottom of emotional disorders, in contrast to cognitive-behavioral therapy's emphasis on thoughts; that the nature of the relationship between patient and therapist is of crucial importance in understanding and treating a patient; that the expectation is that the patient will do most of the talking and that the therapist will provide interpretations of the patients thoughts, feelings, and behaviors, which will alleviate distress; that psychological disorders are difficult to treat and generally require treatment that is intensive and long-term; that the function of the therapist is to promote independence and autonomy, such that decisions about life events are left to the patient's discretion, and that the treatment tends to be exploratory as opposed to directive. Additionally, most psychodynamically-oriented therapists emphasize the quality of interpersonal relationships as a crucial component in emotional well-being.

Example

Mrs. L. was referred to a psychodynamically-oriented therapist after being suspended from her job, apparently without just cause. A lawsuit on her behalf had been initiated. She presented to the therapist as a tearful, distraught, and bewildered woman who was in a panic over her predicament. She could not sleep or eat. Her reactions were not unusual under the circumstances. Nevertheless, she gradually worsened, becoming overly suspicious, with increasing preoccupation with religion, and was convinced that she was being punished by God for some unknown transgression. Exploration uncovered evidence of childhood sexual abuse. Despite being a victim, she felt terribly guilty for the abuse, and the present situation brought back feelings of abuse, concomitant guilt and panic, and terror, as she had felt when originally abused. She was helped by the therapist to explore and understand her present situation in the light of the past abuse. Furthermore, she was assisted in understanding how the abuse had molded other aspects of her personality and had contributed to her having married an abusive man. The therapist and patient met twice weekly for a period of about 1 year, until the patient felt that her problems were sufficiently resolved.

The psychodynamic orientation does focus on present difficulties but looks at them in the context of the patient's past life. People exist in a continuum of time, such that the present cannot be adequately comprehended without an understanding of the past. In the preceding example, it becomes apparent that the patient has reacted to her predicament in the same fashion as she did when she was sexually assaulted as a child. Despite having a strong case and competent attorneys, she felt overwhelmed and confused, which is similar to what a child would feel under extreme duress. The insight that the patient developed helped put her present experience into perspective and enabled her to operate much more effectively. She mounted a vigorous defense of her position, which resulted in vindication and a reasonable monetary settlement for being wronged. Prior to the treatment, she had not thought much about her childhood sexual abuse, and it was only in the context of the present abuse that it became salient. Treatment not only assisted her in dealing with her present-day problems, but exploration of the past abuse helped her to understand herself and her propensity to put herself into abusing situations. If she had continued in treatment, the focus would have been to continue to help her identify for herself the ways in which her past has influenced her present-day functioning.

This kind of insight does not occur in a sterile fashion. Rather, it is hoped that the realizations achieved come about in an emotionally laden and meaningful fashion. Furthermore, psychodynamic treatment teaches the patient a great deal about the functioning of his or her mind and elucidates decision-making processes, such that future decisions become more grounded in rationality. The psychodynamic model incorporates a developmental perspective with several ramifications. As mentioned, the patient is viewed within a time continuum, with the primary orientation being present-day functioning but with an eye on the past and also a push toward the future. It is assumed that the patient has goals in his or her life and that the therapist is assisting in the accomplishment of those goals. The developmental approach also proposes that traumas and difficulties in a person's childhood will interfere with adequate adjustment as an adult.

Example

A 55-year-old man entered psychotherapy complaining of psychosomatic difficulties, depression, and a general dissatisfaction with life. Exploration of his history uncovered a history of significant interpersonal losses: his father's prolonged absence during the war, his father's alcoholism, resulting in neglect, and his father's, aunt's, and grandfather's death during the patient's 12th year. Consequently, he avoided interpersonal relationships throughout his life in order to avoid potential further hurt, which resulted in a rather empty and depressing life. Troublesome and unresolved events in his past created difficulty in his adulthood.

Psychodynamic treatment aims to look at an individual through a microscope. It is not enough to know that the individual described in the example is depressed because of childhood losses. This understanding alone is not curative. The therapist strives to understand, in the most specific way possible, how the patient experienced the loss, what he thought and felt, what fantasies, conscious and unconscious, he developed about his father's absence, what it was like for him to grow up without a father, and how those experiences have created the present-day adult. For a psychodynamic therapist, there is never too much data.

The developmental perspective also suggests that difficulties in managing normal childhood developmental events will cause gaps in the ability to function adequately later in life. It is, of course, a normal event for children to have siblings. Some children, outward appearances notwithstanding, have tremendous difficulty with the arrival of a new child in the family. They may feel displaced or perhaps question how well loved they are. They often develop distorted ideas about the power of feelings and thoughts.

Example

Mr. F. was in psychotherapy because he never felt successful in life. He was bright and capable but always seemed to be thwarting himself. Intensive treatment uncovered a significant problem in an assertion that was tied in to early feelings about his sister's birth. He felt tremendous resentment about it and wished for something terrible to befall her, yet he felt tremendous guilt because of these feelings. He was afraid that having angry feelings could actually hurt his sister, whom he also loved. This guilt was reinforced by his family's disapproval of angry feelings. As he grew up, each act of assertion represented aggression to him, which felt forbidden, resulting in a diminution in his ambition and resultant self-defeating behaviors.

Psychodynamic theory places significant emphasis on family relationships. Those raised in healthy families tend to become healthy and well-functioning adults. Those with significant family problems are likely to have difficulties throughout their life. However, it is important to view individuals as in charge of their own destiny. What is crucial is how people respond to the environment that they find themselves in. Throughout life, people make choices and have to understand and accept responsibility for their choices, even if these choices were made as a result of childhood problems. Another crucial component of psychodynamic theory is the fact that children have difficulty understanding and processing events that seem obvious to adults. In the aforementioned example of the boy who resented his sister, it is not true that his parents wanted to have another child because they did not love him. This was a distortion. Nevertheless, this is what be believed, and it was the interplay of this belief, his angry feelings, and his parent's disapproval that combined to cause him difficulty. Childhood distortions tend to become unconscious and ingrained. They are a source of psychic distress and are a significant reason for the necessity of intensive psychotherapy.

Psychodynamic theory is complex and attempts to explain much of human behavior. Unlike the other models mentioned, it is a comprehensive personality theory. Proponents of different perspectives within psychodynamics promote their views vigorously, which creates a continuously evolving theory. The psychodynamic perspective is what we will be using to explore difficult patients and to elucidate the etiology of emotional disorders. It offers a perspective that is comprehensive and explanatory. Since psychodynamics is both theory and technique, there is a cohesiveness that is helpful in developing methods to deal with problematic patient behaviors. In the following chapters we will be elucidating further psychodynamic concepts that are essential in understanding people. Additionally, we will be looking at a variety of psychological disorders that can negatively impact treatment. Different medical disorders evoke some typical reactions from patients, and thus we will also be concentrating on some specific disorders and the difficulties that they may generate within the provider-patient relationship. Another emphasis will be on the emotional difficulties that providers themselves may have and how they impact upon treatment.

VIEWS OF THE PATIENT

Physicians, of course, have organized their study of the human body through the various medical specialties. Divisions are through organ systems (cardiology, gastroenterology), age (pediatrics, geriatrics), and gender (obstetrics-gynecolgy), by disease (oncology), diagnostic versus applied, and so on. Within each speciality, patients can be apprehended by readily observable techniques (visual appraisal, palpation), or through microscopic or other artificial imaging techniques (X-ray, magnetic resonance imaging [MRI]). There are also many different ways of viewing patient behavior and personality. In order to properly assist a patient in need of psychological help, appropriate diagnosis is essential. Psychological tests are available but are infrequently used, particularly by psychodynamic therapists. They rely on the initial evaluation period, wherein psychological assessment occurs through the interview, but also consider the ongoing therapy as a diagnostic process. This suggests that diagnosis is continual and that the therapist is not seen as omniscient. *The premise of this book is that the psychodynamic approach to understanding patients and their behaviors and emotions can be very useful to those who treat patients with physical disorders.*

The intricacies of psychological diagnosis go beyond the scope of what we are attempting to convey. However, there are some techniques that could be useful for physicians and other providers to consider. The psychodynamic therapist attends to many cues, verbal and nonverbal. Patients have many things to tell the therapist, but unfortunately do not always have the ability or knowledge as to what to convey.

Example

A patient on his initial visit to a psychologist keeps his eyes downcast throughout the initial interview. His description of his presenting problem is sparse, other than indicating that he is very unhappy, socially isolated, and depressed. The therapist, noticing his indirect gaze, questions the patient, who indicates that he is not aware of that tendency. The therapist continues to gently probe into his feelings about his downcast look, and the patient begins to talk at length about his sense of shame, which has plagued him for most of his life. Until the therapist questioned him, he never really had put together his unhappiness and social isolation with his shameful feelings. Without observing the patient's demeanor, an incorrect diagnosis could have been made, with the focus being on the patient's depression, which, in actuality was a reaction to his lifelong shame and social isolation.

The patient's facial expression creates a strong impression for the therapist and is used diagnostically. Implicit in psychodynamic treatment is the notion that the patient is not always able to tell the provider the actual nature of his or her distress. Consequently, the therapist or medical practitioner must use other techniques to ascertain the actual source of the patient's discomfort. Analogously, a physician may have to use laboratory tests or imaging techniques in order to make a correct diagnosis. Psychodynamic concepts can be useful in assisting the medical practitioner in making assessments as to the nature of the patient's distress.

Examples

A patient calls an internist's office for an appointment but refuses to tell the office staff the presenting complaint. The physician is informed of this and is thus prepared for the patient to tell her something that is extremely sensitive and perhaps embarrassing. The patient is obviously anxious but only talks about a tendinitis problem that has been previously discussed and treated. Mindful of the patient's unwillingness to tell the receptionist of the nature of her complaint, the physician asks the patient if anything else is bothering her. The patient says that everything is fine except for some minor gastric distress. The doctor informs the patient that she is aware of the patient's reluctance with the receptionist and wonders if there is something else concerning her. The patient finally begins to talk about her marital problems and her wish for a referral to a marriage counselor.

Mr. P., who had been in psychotherapy for several weeks, brings several dreams to the session. He tells them very rapidly, one upon the next. His speech is pressured and labored. The therapist is listening carefully and tries to understand the dreams in order to ascertain what the patient is trying to convey, yet feels overwhelmed by their quantity and by the rapidity of their telling. The content of the dreams are of some help, since they are repetitive of waterfalls and turbulent seas. Eventually the therapist comes to realize that the patient is feeling overwhelmed by his turbulent feelings, which is conveyed not only by the content of the dreams, but also by the manner in which the dreams are recounted. The therapist interprets that the patient seems to feel overwhelmed, and in response the patient is able to calm down and talk about what is troubling him in his life.

Throughout the psychotherapy session, the therapist is again having difficulty figuring out what is troubling Mr. P. The patient seems scattered, with each subject presented seemingly having no connection with the one prior. Since the session was the first one after a vacation break, the therapist wonders if the patient felt the interruption to be difficult, resulting in a sense of disconnection. The disconnection was apparent to the therapist by the scattered and disconnected way that Mr. P. presented the material. After the therapist made his interpretation, Mr. P. was then able to talk about the distress he felt by the break and how isolated and alone he has felt in his life because of significant interpersonal losses.

The therapist and the medical practitioner need to "read between the lines" in order to ascertain the true nature of the patient's difficulty. The phrase "listening with the third ear" has been coined to describe the therapist's mode of listening. In the last instance, the therapist is listening to the "form" of the patient's associations, not to the content. The patient had no other way available to tell the therapist what was bothering him, and thus he needed to demonstrate it. All those who work in helping professions need to be able to use all the information available in order to understand their clients. Limiting oneself only to literal and concrete information will result in valuable data being missed.

SUGGESTION. Being aware of nuances and the unspoken can provide significant information that can be useful in understanding and working with those struggling with emotional difficulties.

Doctor-patient relationships are often long-lasting, sometimes spanning years. Like any other relationship, each participant will know more about the other as the relationship endures. Despite this, there can be surprises.

Example

After 13 years of a long psychotherapy, a patient tells the therapist that she was sexually abused at age six or seven. This information, which the therapist never suspected, helps explain a number of perplexing patient characteristics, including her feelings of being overwhelmed in situations that seemed benign.

In medical practice, the patient will communicate more about himself or herself as time goes on, as long as he or she feels comfortable with the practitioner, is confident that he or she will be accepted and understood, and senses that the practitioner has a genuine interest in hearing more.

Being open and interested will allow the medical practitioner to learn more about the patient but will also result in the practitioner understanding the patient in a deeper way. People's psychological problems are enduring and permeate their personality. Emotional difficulties tend to remain constant without some sort of psychotherapeutic intervention. After years of medical care, physicians can be fairly certain how their patients will react to their disorders. There is a predictability to people. Even very chaotic and hysterical people are predictable in their reactions: One may not be able to predict the exact nature of their overreaction, but an overreaction is to be expected.

Example

After years of taking care of Mrs. D., the physician knows that she will always need to schedule an extra-long appointment for her. Mrs. D. always has a lot of concerns on her mind and will call the doctor at night if her concerns are not addressed doing the appointment time. If a longer appointment is not scheduled, the patient is dissatisfied and the doctor suffers through after-hours phone calls.

Each time a patient comes for psychotherapy he or she has a task, an issue, an "adaptive context" (Langs, 1976) in mind. "This refers to the main event—inner and outer experience—that the patient is responding to" (Langs, 1976, p. 19). There is some issue that the patient wants to address or some problem that he or she wants solved within the session. It is useful to try to break these tasks down into that which is achievable during the time available. For instance, it is not possible to cure a patient of depression in one session. It may be possible to provide the patient with a sense of being understood within the one session, with the expectation that the larger issues will gradually be addressed. In medical practice as well, it is important for the practitioner to assess what the patient is struggling with at that particular time.

SUGGESTION. Helping the patient to identify the adaptive task within the interaction helps the patient and provider to structure the interaction and to create realistic expectations.

Example

A patient visits her gynecologist for her yearly examination. Physically, the patient is fine, and after the examination the doctor asks the patient if there is anything else of importance that should be discussed. The patient tearfully recounts a long story of family problems. The physician wonders what, if anything, can be done, but decides just to listen. The patient pulls herself together, profusely thanking the doctor for listening. On her next visit she again tells the doctor how much she appreciated her listening.

In this situation, the physician intuited that there was not much that she could concretely offer the patient and decided that it would be most beneficial to quietly listen. Keeping in mind that each patient has a goal in mind for each appointment or interaction can be quite useful in framing the treatment, in putting a structure on it. This is particularly useful with more disorganized and fragmented patients, whose goals may not be readily apparent, even to themselves. Every patient, within every discipline, wants to leave the experience with some result. They have something that they want to take from the interaction. Unfortunately, they cannot always get what they desire, but an attempt should be made to provide some satisfaction or understanding to the patient with each visit.

Example

Throughout the psychotherapy session, the patient seemed to ramble on. The therapist had difficulty in understanding what the patient was trying to get at. Eventually, the therapist disclosed this difficulty to the patient, who confirmed that he did not really know what was bothering him but that he knew that something was. The task initially was to ascertain that something was troubling the patient. The patient and therapist then were able to discover that the patient had a worry in the back of his mind about his wife's fidelity; this concern was available for discussion only when they were able to understand the defensive rambling.

That which is achieved within each visit may seem rather insignificant. Keeping this concept in mind can yield excellent results, since it relieves the practitioner of his or her own high expectations and makes treatment more grounded within the reality of the patient's life and present situation.

SUGGESTION. Providing the patient with some result during the encounter helps him or her feel more satisfied and confident in the physician.

CONCLUSION

Psychological assessment by the physician can be extremely helpful in anticipating patient reactions to disease. Information can be broached in particular ways and tailored for the individual patient, and the physician will be more comfortable if he or she allows himself or herself to think of patients from a psychological perspective. The psychodynamic model offers a comprehensive approach to understanding patient behavior and offers insight for the physician and other professionals in working with those with psychological disorders.

SUMMARY

1. All professionals, including those in the health care professions, must contend with difficult people.
2. Difficult people are those whose behavior and emotional difficulties interfere with the treatment and are aversive to the provider.

3. Provider expectations for patients may be unrealistic, resulting in dissatisfaction and anger.
4. Scapegoating is a psychological maneuver designed to maintain one's feelings of self-regard.
5. Psychodynamic theory provides comprehensive explanations for people's behavior and emotions and has a developmental perspective.
6. Patients do not always know what is bothering them or how to communicate it to the provider.
7. The central adaptive context or task is that issue that the patient is concerned with during any given encounter.

2

Working Alliance and Transference

The relationship between the physician and patient is perhaps the least investigated aspect of the healing process in traditional medicine. "Physicians have opportunities to make important interventions in the emotional lives of patients. There are numerous accounts of incidents in clinical practice where such interventions make dramatic changes in the lives of patients" (Kagan, 1984, p. 209). Within the psychodynamic perspective, the relationship between therapist and patient is of crucial importance in the curative process.

Example

Mrs. N. was referred for psychotherapy because of numerous psychosomatic complaints, including gastric distress and headaches. Her background consisted of a rather cold, depressed, and withdrawn mother and a distant and authoritarian father. It was quite clear that she had never been listened to and relished the opportunity to talk freely with the therapist. Quite rapidly her gastric difficulties and tension headaches abated, even though she had not yet achieved any insight into the origins of her difficulties.

The psychotherapeutic relationship, in and of itself, was ameliorative. This is not to suggest that her problems were permanently resolved. It does indicate that a positive relationship

27

between patient and provider greatly enhances the probability of successful treatment, and this includes treatment of physical disorders.

Since a positive relationship can be ameliorative, it obviously behooves practitioners and patients to establish a cooperative working relationship. Within this relationship each participant should understand the purpose of the interaction, the goals, the methods employed to reach the goals, and the roles of each party. This relationship has been referred to as the *working alliance* (Greenson, 1965). It is an agreement, explicit or not, as to the rules and regulations of the encounter. The working alliance is a recognition that each participant has a vested interest in the success of the interaction and implies a cooperative partnership. A patient has certain expectations as to how he or she will be treated and that the experience will result in the desired outcome—the alleviation of the symptoms for which he or she requested treatment. Within medical practice, the patient should expect to be a participant in the process, arriving on time, informing the staff of his or her symptoms, and cooperating with the examination. The medical office, for their part, should be interested in providing the patient with good service in an efficient and timely manner.

Example

Mr. J., after years of seeing his family physician, is aware of the ground rules of the practice. He knows that he is expected to be on time, to check in with the receptionist upon his arrival, and to pay for the service before he leaves. He has chronic hypertension and knows that the nurse will be taking his blood pressure and will be asking questions about his diet and blood pressure readings he has taken between appointments. He understands that he will have about 15 minutes with the doctor unless there is some urgent concern. The doctor understands that Mr. J. is a moderately anxious man and that he needs to be realistically reassured about his condition and to have the opportunity to have his questions answered. The doctor also realizes that his patient values his own time and thus tries to be on time and not keep him waiting. After the examination, the doctor reviews his findings and discusses treatment options with Mr. J., and they jointly agree upon a future course of action. The patient leaves satisfied. The doctor is also satisfied and wishes that all of his patient interactions were as pleasing.

In the preceding example, the purpose of the visit, the goals, the means to achieve the goals, and the roles of each party are consensual. Unfortunately, interactions between people rarely proceed as smoothly as the participants would wish. Expectations of one or both parties within the interactions may not be realized, resulting in frustration and anger. The working or treatment alliance never gets established, or, once established, becomes disrupted.

Example

A patient arrives at his physician's office already quite anxious about the ringing in his ears. When he approaches the reception area, no one is visible, but he hears laughter in the back. The receptionist eventually greets him, still laughing, and tells him to have a seat, that the doctor will be with him shortly. The waiting room needs a good cleaning and the magazines are old and torn. He is kept waiting 45 minutes past his scheduled appointment time, with no explanation from the receptionist. The doctor is harried and hurried, treats the man's symptoms in a dismissive way, and seems generally uninterested in the patient's concerns. The patient has had considerable family stress of late and feels rather fragile, and hoped to be able to at least mention it to his physician. Unfortunately, the doctor must attend to his next patient and the present patient's distress is not addressed. Upon leaving, the patient is told that the doctor no longer bills the insurance company for his services and that it is the patient's responsibility to submit the bills for reimbursement. The patient leaves feeling angry and uncared for.

It is not likely that this patient feels satisfied. It is also unlikely that the physician is finding much pleasure in his work. The working alliance, the sense of cooperation between doctor and patient, has become greatly diminished by the encounter just described. The disorder in the office, the rude manner in which the patient was treated, and the alteration in the payment rules contributes to a disruption in the sense of trust and cooperation. Clearly, a more organized and professional office would impart a dignified sense of competence, which would be beneficial to both staff and patient. Those in charge set the tone for the office. A sense of disorganization will permeate the office and result in staff who feel scattered and who act unprofessionally. An atmosphere that is consistent and structured will be anxiety-relieving to those whose condition makes them feel vulnerable and afraid. This observation can also apply to the helping professionals, who are under great stress from difficult jobs and from their own personal difficulties.

Donald Winnicott (1960), a British pediatrician and psychoanalyst, coined the phrase *"the holding environment"* to describe the atmosphere that is helpful when patients are confronting painful emotional issues. The holding environment is an artifact of the early mother-infant relationship, whereby the infant feels safe and emotionally "held" by the nurturing mother while struggling with the storms of its own emotions or by the fright of an incomprehensible world.

Example

A patient who was raised in a very chaotic family environment was in long-term psychotherapy with a psychologist. She presented with a history of physical, emotional, and sexual abuse. All of these issues held great emotional power and were extremely difficult for her to discuss. After some period of time, the patient was aware of how consistent her therapist was. He was always on time, he was well groomed, and he always listened carefully to what she said and was never judgmental or critical. This atmosphere greatly contributed to the patient's sense of safety, such that she could address her difficult and painful issues.

This therapist provided a holding environment for the patient that enabled her to feel relatively safe and secure. Patients struggling with physical and emotional problems also need to be "held" in order to feel safe. Without this, emotions can run rampant and distress both patient and providers. Winnicott also referred to the importance of the patient's emotions being "contained." Those most vulnerable tend to feel most scattered and disorganized. Order, continuity, and consistency help such patients feel that their feelings are "contained," and not out of control and overwhelming. Consequently, organized and consistent health care providers are essential in assisting the patient who is beset with intense emotions. The physician whose office is clean and runs efficiently is likely to help patients feel contained and safe. Furthermore, physicians who are explicit in their expectations of their patients and in their recommendations tend to engender confidence and a sense of security.

Example

Dr. R. was very careful not to present himself as authoritarian. He preferred to present treatment options to patients when possible, highlighting pros and cons and encouraging patients to make informed treatment decisions. Mrs. M. brought her son in for an examination because of chronic tonsillitis. Dr. R. raised the possibility of a referral to a specialist for further evaluation and discussed with the mother the potential diagnoses and treatment options. Mrs. M., already rather anxious, became more agitated, upset, and angry. She was a woman who was overly worried about her son's health and felt even more overwhelmed by the burden of making a choice of treatment. The doctor, seeing her agitation, realized that it would be most prudent for him to take charge, and made the suggestion that an appointment be made with an ear, nose, and throat (ENT) physician. The patient calmed down and was able to become more realistic.

Many patients do welcome a less authoritarian stance and feel comfortable in a cooperative relationship. Others, however, become anxious without a firm structure, and ambiguity causes them distress. In the preceding situation, the doctor was able to use his intuition to understand what the mother needed, and he functioned as a "container" for the patient's uncomfortable feelings, enabling a working alliance to be maintained.

SUGGESTION. Providing structure through consistency, orderliness, a confident demeanor, clarity, and sensitivity creates a "holding environment" that diminishes patient anxiety and promotes the maintenance of the working alliance.

TRANSFERENCE

There are many times when the practitioner operates with consistency and structure and yet a rupture in the working alliance still occurs. The concept of transference can be used to understand these ruptures and to explain many patient (and provider) difficulties. Transference is a concept developed by Freud and occupies a central place in psychodynamic theory and practice. Freud varied his concept of transference through the years, but a consensus as to its definition exists today.

Definition. *Transference is the tendency to relate to those in the present based on past experiences and relationships.*

Example

A patient visited her gynecologist, who performed a routine examination. The doctor informed the patient that all was well and that the patient would be called if the Pap test findings were abnormal. Later in the day the physician received a frantic phone call from the patient. It seems that the doctor seemed preoccupied and worried to the patient, and she became convinced that something was seriously wrong with her that the doctor was keeping from her. The doctor reassured the patient that the examination revealed no abnormalities.

There are many ways of understanding the patient's concern. For the present discussion, it will be looked at from the perspective of transference. This patient's mother was severely depressed and was continually worried about some unspecified and never-realized impending disaster. This caused the patient to be constantly worried that some disaster was about to befall her or her family. Her mother never did tell the patient what she was worried about, and the patient often felt that important information was being withheld. The doctor may have been preoccupied during the examination or the patient may have misread a pensive look. Regardless, she was misinterpreting the meaning of the doctor's demeanor in the light of her past relationship with her mother. She was relating to the doctor as if she were her mother. This is the essence of transference.

The presence of transference is not always easy to ascertain, yet an appreciation of its occurrence can greatly facilitate understanding of interpersonal relationships and conflict. People "transfer" continuously. That is, they relate to others in ways that reflect past relationships. The way the world is seen is based on how individuals were treated in the past. Those who have been treated kindly tend to see the world in a more positive way, to see themselves similarly, and to relate to others in a more optimistic, trusting way. Conversely, those whose past relationships have been hurtful tend to bring that sense of hurt into everyday relationships.

Example

Mr. W. reluctantly made an appointment with a psychologist because of distress over the breakup of a long-term relationship with his girlfriend. He was devastated by the dissolution of the relationship and could not understand the reasons for being rejected. It quickly became apparent to the therapist that Mr. W. was an extremely sensitive, easily hurt, demanding, and a rather mean person. Exploration showed that Mr. W. had been raised by a very difficult father who could be demeaning and cruel upon occasion. The relationship between Mr. W. and his father was being reenacted with his girlfriend through a reversal of roles.

In this example, the present became infused by the past. Mr. W. viewed the world and relationships through the lens of his past experiences.

From the moment a patient is provided with a practitioner's name, a transference develops. The patient, even if he or she knows nothing about the provider, develops expectations and mental images. The patient may develop a small fantasy about the first encounter, which will reflect the patient's hopes or fears. For instance, some patients may imagine their physician to be very understanding and sympathetic. Others who have had negative experiences with authority figures may anticipate an unhelpful response. Some may minimize the importance of their difficulties and imagine that they will be dismissed and not taken seriously by the physician. Consequently, the patient may be angry before he or she has even met the doctor. The past experiences of the patient will reflect the expectations that will develop prior to the first appointment. It is quite common to conjure up mental images of others prior to a first introduction. Inevitably, this mental image never matches reality, resulting in some minor disappointment. Since transferences will vary tremendously from patient to patient, the physician has no way of anticipating a new patient's reaction.

It is important to remember that transference reactions do not only reflect problematic relationships. In the majority of doctor-patient interactions, transference reactions are minimal and cause little, if any, problems. The transferences are positive and benign. Yet some patients have very strong feelings, both positive and negative, and never give any indication to the physician of their existence.

Transference reactions are commonly referred to as "positive" or "negative" depending on the valence of the emotion. For example, a patient angry at his physician is said to have a negative transference. Similarly, a patient who has fond feelings toward his or her doctor is said to have a positive transference. The patient's overt emotion is not always a direct indication of the true, perhaps underlying, emotion.

Example

A patient who had recently been diagnosed with breast cancer was exceptionally rude and belligerent with her oncologist. He questioned her about her hostility, and she told him that she was angry with his uncaring and cold attitude. He was perplexed since he had always prided himself on his empathy and warmth. As the relationship progressed and the patient became aware that her life was not in immediate danger, she seemed less angry and hostile. She began to realize that early in her treatment she was frightened and angry about having cancer and that it was these emotions that were being expressed toward the doctor. It was much easier for her to be angry than to be frightened.

It is not especially helpful to label transferences as positive or negative, since it is the underlying feeling that is most telling and important. Labeling transferences as either positive or negative creates a value system wherein positive transferences are encouraged and negative ones are frowned upon. As the preceding example shows, the overt emotion does not always reflect the real issue. An oversensitive physician might have gotten angry and defensive in response to the patient's anger, and then never would have been able to assist the patient with her fearfulness. In addition, expecting patients to have only positive, pleasant, and benign feelings is unrealistic and is uncharacteristic of the nature of people, particularly when they are stressed. Furthermore, it does not always make sense to look at transferences in such a dichotomous way.

Example

> An obstetrician was puzzled that her patients continued to call her at all hours and inform her that they were in labor prior to going into the hospital. She had requested that patients go into the hospital without calling when their labor pains were of particular duration and intensity. She became irritated by the constant interruptions, day and night. She discussed this with her colleagues and discovered that they all had similar experiences.

In this instance, the patients have developed a transference reaction. They have a need to "touch base" with the doctor, just as a child feels the need to do with the mother in difficult times. This understanding helps the physician not to feel so disregarded by her patients and diminishes her anger.

Transference reactions are often benign and pleasant and enable treatment to flow smoothly. In these circumstances, the working alliance between patient and doctor is not impinged upon by difficult emotions and both participants experience a sense of cooperation. The positive and benign transference is of great assistance when dealing with difficult medical problems. The patient trusts his or her doctor, which enables the patient to withstand and comply with unpleasant treatment regimens. In a sense, any transference is unrealistic since it imposes on a person in the present attributes from another in the past. However, these benign transferences are beneficial to both participants and do no harm.

SUGGESTION. Being aware that transferences impinge upon and affect treatment can be helpful in understanding puzzling patient behavior and can reduce angry responses to some patient behaviors.

In psychodynamic psychotherapy, transference reactions are often the focus of the treatment. The transference, the way the patient views and behaves toward the therapist, provides a window into the patient's psyche. Instead of discussing the patient's difficulties in an abstract, removed way, the difficulties get played out in the therapist's consulting room. The patient may relate to the therapist as if he or she were a significant person from the patient's past, or the patient may project an aspect of himself or herself onto the therapist, providing valuable information as to difficulties of which the patient may be unaware. Thus, transference not only refers to past relationships that impinge upon the present but also reflects a vehicle between the unconscious and conscious parts of the mind.

Example

Mr. Q. was describing a situation to his therapist in which his wife was mad at him, presumably for not paying the charge card bill on time. He became quite anxious and indicated that he had slept poorly the night before and was reluctant to come to that session that day. In fact, he described himself as being very anxious and filled with dread. The therapist asked the patient to ponder his feelings of dread and to think about any possible reasons for those feelings to emerge that day. The patient began to talk about the punitive and unforgiving father of his childhood, and it soon became apparent that he expected the therapist also to be angry at him for his mistake. Further discussion elicited the degree of self-hate the patient felt toward himself for this and for other mishaps. This led to a memory of hitting his sister while both were children, resulting in severe reprimands and punishment by his parents.

Prior to the session, the patient was not really aware of the scale of his self-criticism. He tended to ascribe his difficulties to what he characterized as a "bitchy" wife. During this session, he became more cognizant of his own difficulties and of some of their precipitants, of which he was unaware.

Freud postulated that the mind can be viewed in a topographic fashion, like a cross-section of the earth's strata. Deepest and inaccessible is the unconscious, more accessible is the preconscious, and most evident is the conscious part of the mind. The preconscious part of the mind is what is available to one's awareness should attention be focused there, like an idea "at the back of one's mind." The unconscious is not normally retrievable but exerts tremendous influence on one's behavior. Unconscious transference reactions are what typically cause disruptions in the doctor-patient relationship.

Example

A father visited the pediatrician with his young daughter. Rather than being examined by the doctor, the child was scheduled with a nurse practitioner. The father became enraged, fearing that his daughter would be inadequately examined. His child was healthy, and the visit was for a routine examination, yet he reacted as if his daughter was endangered by an incompetent nurse. In reality, the father was beginning a new career and was concerned about his own competence, and this concern was displaced onto the nurse. He was aware of his anxiety about his job but not of the extent of his worry.

Although transferences may refer to internal aspects of the mind, they manifest themselves mostly within relationships. Every relationship is tinged with transference. People relate to others in ways that reflect how they were treated or wished they had been treated in the past. In the preceding example, the father had not felt that he was respected and valued as a child and, as a consequence, doubted his own professional abilities, which was then expressed as doubts about the nurse's abilities.

People create fantasies in order to understand feelings and as a way of dealing with difficult and overwhelming situations. Children have difficulty in understanding their feelings, their reactions, and the reactions of others. Thus, transferences reflect past actual relationships along with wishes for solutions and imagined causes for difficulties. Wishes and distortions caused by immaturity can result in later emotional difficulties.

Example

Children experience myriad difficulties related to parental divorce. It is commonly recognized that children may blame themselves for the divorce, and more sensitive parents take pains to reassure their children that the divorce had nothing to do with the child. Many children cannot seem to accept that and do end up blaming themselves. Children tend to be egocentric, and want to view everything that occurs within the family as having some connection to them. In angry times, some children may have wished for their father or mother to leave, and when the marriage does dissolve they may begin to believe in the potency of their wishes. In other instances, the children may have engaged in some behavior that they view as being wicked, and therefore they see the divorce as punishment for their sins.

Children tend to exaggerate and imagine that their sins are great and that punishment will be horrendous. As the child grows older, these conceptions and beliefs become repressed, and thus outside of conscious awareness. Unfortunately, they can continue to exert considerable influence on the child's behavior. The child may grow up guilt-ridden, avoiding relationships lest someone discover his or her "crimes." Although it may seem ludicrous for a grown person to hold such beliefs, the power of the unconscious with its fantasies and fears is considerable. One reason for this is that the unconscious is not really altered by experience or by the child's growth and maturity. It remains encapsulated, preserved and unmodified by time and experience.

Patients do not usually realize that they are being unreasonable or that they are under the sway of unconscious process and fantasies. Their demanding behavior may appear to them to be normal and reasonable. Even if they might be aware that they are being extreme, they experience little control over their anxiety. They expect their doctor to be able to absorb their anxiety and to neutralize it, just as a parent does for his or her child. In a certain sense patients experience their own feelings to be foreign and perplexing, almost toxic. The provider's function may be to provide a holding environment to help patients to "detoxify" their feelings and to calm down. Certain patients who have not had adequate parenting have great difficulty in soothing themselves and look to the physician for comfort.

Example

A psychologist was called in for an urgent consultation in a hospital emergency room (ER). A patient with a history of mental illness had been brought in after having been found bleeding and semiconscious on the street. Once in the ER, the patient became belligerent and seemingly incoherent, and the staff was frightened and angry and wanted to forcibly place the patient in restraints. The psychologist suggested that the staff acknowledge to the patient that they knew that he was probably frightened and ask him what else might be bothering him and how else they could assist him. The patient did calm down somewhat, and the staff was able to do a more thorough assessment of what turned out to be rather superficial abrasions.

Some physicians (and others) get overly concerned when patients get upset. They feel uncomfortable with the emotions expressed and feel that they must *do* something. Medical personnel tend to be action oriented and are trained to physically respond to a medical problem. Emotional reactions may require the physician to restrain himself or herself from overreacting. Truly listening to the patient while trying to understand his or her distress can be very helpful. In the preceding example, the patient was frightened and benefited from the emotional "hold" offered by the staff. It should be pointed out that not all patients will respond to such interventions. Some are so frightened, angry, or psychotic that no amount of understanding and soothing is going to make an impact on them.

Some patients do not only look for soothing and nurturance, but want their doctor to absolutely cure them of all of their ills, even if it is beyond the realm of possibility. Patients, particularly at the beginning of any treatment, expect to be fully restored to perfect functioning, and some become enraged at the limitations of physicians. Their unconscious fantasy is reminiscent of a young child's expectation that their parents are all powerful and omniscient. Recognizing one's own limitations and helping the patient to express his or her disappointment can relieve both patient and doctor of considerable distress.

SUGGESTION. Providing a holding environment helps patients to contain distressing feelings and helps them to maintain a reality orientation in times of stress and vulnerability.

Because of vulnerability, patients tend to watch the physician very carefully, interpreting every look and behavior as significant. These reactions are idiosyncratic to the person and are varied and surprising. As mentioned earlier, many physicians have received frantic calls from their patients after an examination in which the patient was certain that a certain expression on the physician's face indicated some dire problem. People in vulnerable states distort reality, sometimes slightly and sometimes considerably. Oftentimes the physician has no idea that the patient was upset. If the patient seems puzzled or seems to have unexpressed feelings or concerns, it is best to question him or her. It should be remembered however, that patients may not be able to tell the doctor the specifics of their concerns, though they may be able to talk about some sense of disquietude.

To the psychotherapist, the development of transference reactions is desirable, as they function as a movie projector of the patient's personality. Transference reactions operate with great subtlety and usually beyond one's awareness. Some examples of transference might help elucidate the concept.

Example

A couple visits a marriage counselor because of continual conflicts. The wife accuses the husband of being "controlling." He denies this vehemently, indicating that his wife is misinterpreting him and that he is only concerned for her welfare and safety. As the session comes to an end, the husband seems reluctant to leave, trying to prolong the session. After several such incidents, the therapist points out their occurrence and suggests that the husband is trying to control the time at which the session ends and that this is very similar to what the wife is experiencing. With the therapist's gentle prodding, the husband is able to acknowledge this behavior and realize that he is overbearing with his wife. Further exploration reveals that he has been very afraid of his wife's newfound independence and is afraid that she will leave him if she is not dependent on him. This led to a discussion about his sense of inadequacy and his lifelong sense of being powerless in important relationships.

The therapist, via the transference, is able to help the husband and wife understand how the husband's difficulties have become manifest within their relationship. A more complete treatment would lead to further exploration of his difficulties, using his past history to help him understand the origin of his "controlling" behavior. Marriages are fertile ground for transference reactions to develop. Unconsciously, people hope that their marriage will undo or repair past hurts. They hope that, this time, they will choose someone to love them, rather than someone who will hurt or betray them, as has happened in the past. Unfortunately, these plans often do not reach fruition.

Example

A patient visited a psychotherapist for pervasive feelings of dissatisfaction and depression. He had a number of psychosomatic complaints, including stomach ailments and erectile difficulties. The psychotherapy seemed rather sterile, and the patient did not seem to improve, yet he seemed committed to the process. His history indicated that he had suffered a number of significant personal losses as a young child. It became quite clear that he had become fearful of establishing close relationships and that this had become manifest in the psychotherapy, where he did not allow himself to become attached to the therapist, resulting in an empty and detached feeling. This was reminiscent of his childhood experience, when he felt terribly abandoned, and he had made the unconscious decision to never become too involved with anyone for fear of reexperiencing that sense of loss.

In psychotherapy, the relationship between therapist and patient is of crucial importance both diagnostically and therapeutically. A patient who does not form some sort of relationship with his or her therapist is avoiding emotional interaction, and this indicates that fear of emotional involvement is a significant problem. Additionally, the therapy will be made more difficult since the therapist does not have that venue as a source of information available. In medical practice, the absence of a relationship between doctor and patient also eliminates a source of important information for the physician. Additionally, it removes a significant source of satisfaction for both doctor and patient.

SUGGESTION. The relationship between doctor and patient is a significant source of satisfaction for both participants and provides important information for the doctor.

People feel compelled to repeat difficult and troublesome aspects of the past by bringing them into the present. This is referred to as the *repetition compulsion*. The fact that transference exists is an example of the repetition compulsion, since it reflects past events being brought into the present.

Example

Mrs. B. entered psychotherapy because of several failed relationships. She would fall madly in love very quickly and would later discover that these men were quite unsuitable for her, being either abusive or untrustworthy. Her history showed that she was raised by a single mother after her father was killed in a car accident. She had been exceptionally close to her mother since they had only each other. She had never known her father, and yet fantasized that he was a wonderful, caring, and thoughtful man. Her propensity to involve herself in unsuitable relationships reflected several difficulties. She had suffered much pain because of the loss of her father. She imagined that she could not tolerate her mother's distress over being left alone if she happened to meet a man that she could love. Unconsciously, she was still searching for her father, and unsuitable men left her available, should he magically return. Finally, in some sense, she viewed her father's death as being abusive and an example of his being untrustworthy. His death was a recurrent ache that directed her life.

The language of loss and abandonment is the language that she was raised with and is what she understands. Those who have suffered disappointments want to change the past, and this can only occur if the participants have characteristics similar to those from the past. People also want to repeat the past in order to feel more in control of situations in which they felt overwhelmed.

Example

Ms. A. was a young woman who had suffered terrible physical and sexual abuse as a child. As she grew older, she became involved in a series of abusive relationships. She seemed to become a perpetual victim, which mirrored her past traumatic situations. However, there were several important distinctions. First of all, despite being abusive, these relationships were consensual to some extent. In this sense she was more in control than in the original abuse. Second, in her mind she was able to imagine herself triumphant, since she imagined that it was her provocation that caused the abuse. Third, her lifestyle involved criminal behavior, such that others were being victimized instead of herself. Although her lifestyle was extremely painful, her desire to work out her traumatic past caused her to repeat the past, but with her imagining that she was in control this time.

The repetition compulsion is not voluntary, nor is it conscious. Those in its grip are not aware that they are acting out a drama that is ages old and the ending of which is foreordained. Physicians and other professionals can unwittingly become participants in these dramas.

Example

Ms. T. was a 16-year-old who made an appointment with a male therapist because of being terribly unhappy and confused. She had had several boyfriends in the last $1^1/_2$ years and seemed to be promiscuous. She seemed to like the therapist and was able to talk about painful issues regarding her parents and her feelings of being unloved. Gradually, she began dressing seductively during the sessions, and the atmosphere became sexually charged. The therapist became aware of the emotion in the consulting room and questioned the young woman. She became uncomfortable but acknowledged having romantic and sexual feelings toward the therapist. With great distress, she divulged the incestuous relationship that she had had with her father.

The patient felt compelled to repeat within the therapeutic relationship the abusive relationship. An insecure and disturbed therapist could have participated with the patient in a repetition of a terribly destructive relationship, which would have been to his and to his patient's detriment. The transferential relationship draws the practitioner into the patient's emotional life. Once embroiled, it may be difficult for the doctor to extricate himself or herself. In the preceding example, the therapist paid close attention to the affective quality of the interaction and used it to identify a significant problem area. Therapists often use their own feelings as a way of identifying issues that are not being articulated.

SUGGESTION. Practitioners can use their own affective reactions to understand patients. It is important to remain objective and to not become a participant in patients' lives.

DEFENSES

The nature of the doctor-patient relationship promotes the establishment of transference. Patients are seeking medical care because of a medical problem, a vulnerability that can be akin to the vulnerability of childhood. Having little knowledge of anatomy or physiology, they may have distortions and misconceptions about their disorders. They are dependent on the practitioner, which may replicate parent-child relationships. Power differentials exist between the doctor and patient because of the nature of the relationship. This also mimics early childhood relationships. Some patients may view the physician as having higher social status as well. Consequently, patients are at a decided disadvantage. In times of stress, people use a variety of mechanisms to try to maintain their sense of equilibrium and safety and to maintain a stable sense of self. These mechanisms are referred to as *defenses*. Defenses are used to protect an individual from experiencing feelings and thoughts that would feel dangerous to his or her sense of well-being. The doctor-patient relationship offers many opportunities for such difficulties to develop.

Example

A patient visits a gastroenterologist complaining of severe gastric pain. She informs the doctor that she has consulted with numerous physicians in the past and none has been helpful. She has received many recommendations about this doctor and is sure he can help her. The doctor is flattered, performs a thorough examination, and cannot find any abnormalities, but since the patient is in pain, he orders some blood tests and prescribes an antispasmodic. The patient is effusive in her praise and leaves quite satisfied, even though nothing of significance has occurred. Over a period of time, she continues to visit the doctor, with her complaints increasing. She becomes quite vituperative in her unhappiness. Gradually, her view of him has changed from the most wonderful to the worst.

There are some patients who view themselves and others in black-or-white fashion, either all good or all bad. Initially, they tend to overidealize their caregivers and are unrealistic in both their praise and in their expectations. The practitioner may feel quite gratified in having a patient who recognizes his or her unique talents, especially if he or she secretly wants to agree with the patient's assessment. This is potentially a dangerous situation. Such patients tend toward a self-concept that is not well integrated. They lack perspective into their own capabilities. They may view themselves as either inordinately successful or as abysmal failures, neither of which likely reflects reality. Their wish for fantastic success is a defense against feelings of failure. They are plagued by feelings of inadequacy and failure and as compensation fantasize themselves as being wildly famous and well loved. These individuals have suffered profound disappointment in their lives, which they have trouble tolerating. Their defense against these feelings is to develop grandiose beliefs and expectations about themselves.

Example

The patient with the gastric problems (see preceding example) experienced a serious failure at her job. She had neglected to finish a project on time, resulting in a reprimand from her boss. Her gastric pain increased, and she made an appointment with her doctor. He was his usual warm and engaging self and was more than willing to hear her out and to try to assist her. However, she was rude to him, castigating him for his supposed incompetence. He was shocked by her attacks and also disappointed, since he had enjoyed the praise that she was so lavish in providing. The physician wondered what had happened to the pedestal that he had been on.

The doctor has not done anything to warrant the reversal of the patient's opinion. Rather, it is the patient's own sense of incompetence that gets placed onto the physician. The sense of failure and inadequacy that she cannot tolerate gets directed outward onto the doctor.

SUGGESTION. Physicians should be wary of overidealizing patients and should encourage a realistic attitude by acknowledging fallibility and patient responsibility for a good or bad outcome.

Those prone toward projection are those who cannot process and integrate their own sense of inadequacy. *Projection,* a defense mechanism, is the attribution to someone else of one's own feelings and beliefs. The patient's own sense of badness feels overwhelming and, in this case, stimulates a psychosomatic response and an accusation of incompetence. The patient is trying to protect herself from profound feelings of hurt and disappointment. Developmentally, this person and those like her were subjected to hurtful and excessive feelings that were overwhelming. As a consequence, they cannot contain or process such feelings and feel the need to rid themselves of the intolerable affect by projecting it onto another. In fact, these people, as children, were subjected to excessive projections themselves. That is, the significant persons in their lives, their parents, could not contain their own feelings and projected them onto their children. The children, as projective containers for their parent's disappointments, feel forever like a disappointment, and they learn to not be able to tolerate disappointment.

Example

An adolescent girl sought out psychological treatment because of family conflict. The therapist felt it to be very unusual that the 16-year-old called and made the appointment herself and that parental input seemed minimal. The girl complained of her mother being extremely judgmental, condemning, and rageful toward her. The therapist met with the young woman and found her to be intelligent. From all accounts she was performing well in school, academically, athletically, and socially. Unfortunately, family conflict was serious. The therapist requested a consultation with the parents. Only the mother came, since the father was uninvolved with the children. The parents were in the process of divorcing, and the mother was very bitter about how her life had turned out. The therapist was surprised to hear the hatred with which the mother described the daughter, attributing to her a malevolence that was at odds with the therapist's evaluation. No degree of intervention would soften the mother. She hated her daughter and thought she was a "terrible person." She refused to pay for further treatment, yet the therapist continued to see the young woman for a nominal fee in order to help her work through and understand her mother's hatred so that she would not fulfill the mother's prophecy. The patient also needed help in learning to process her own disappointments so as to not be prone toward projective defenses herself.

Presumably, the mother had herself experienced a harsh and unforgiving background and thus could not contain her own sense of failure. Undoubtedly, the girl, like most teenagers, could be provocative and did not always adhere to parental rules. Nevertheless, the degree of hostility present indicated a pathological process operating within the mother.

It is not essential, realistic, or even desirable for parents to be perfect. Rather, it is expected that they be "good enough" (Winnicott, 1960). They need to understand or, at least, to try to understand their children and to help them sort out and tolerate their feelings. Recent research by Daniel Stern (1985) and others has shown that it is essential that parents be "attuned" to their children; they need to read their infant's moods, feelings, and behaviors in order to help the child calm himself or herself and to be able to understand and contain their feelings. When parents are deficient in this, they misinterpret their children's moods and project their own moods onto the child. This occurs because the parents themselves are feeling overwhelmed by life's events, by their own feelings, and sometimes even by their children's feelings. These parents are themselves rather fragile and have trouble tolerating their children's distress. It is not uncommon to see an unfortunate cycle wherein a crying child stimulates an emotional outburst from a parent, resulting in further crying and eventuating in emotional or physical abuse. The parent feels overwhelmed by the child's dysphoric emotions and consequently directs blame toward the child. Sadly, most of these children are usually only asking for nurturance and affection. The result of this is that all the participants end up feeling inadequate and blamed.

Similarly, it is not expected that physicians be perfect. Rather, they too need to be "good enough." If a patient becomes accusatory, it is more helpful to encourage the patient to articulate his or her disappointment with the doctor and, if possible, to try to make a connection with any outside life difficulties. It may be that the patient is aware of the outside stressful event, knows the hurt involved, but is having difficulty making the connection between the outside events, the physical problem, and dissatisfaction with the doctor. Such difficulties offer the physician an opportunity to assist the patient in making connections between transferential feelings, outside events, and psychogenic disorders.

SUGGESTION. Making explicit that which is not quite conscious is very helpful. Making connections between outside stressors, psychosomatic disorders, and feelings toward the physician can alleviate considerable distress.

Projective identification is a variant of projection, but the affect of being disowned is more intense and the patient retains some ownership of the projection. Instead of just recognizing the patient's discomfort, the physician becomes uncomfortable as well. People who are prone toward projective identification are more disturbed and are commonly described as borderline personalities. Those with this disorder are notoriously difficult to work with and, as a consequence, a later chapter is devoted to those so diagnosed.

Borderline personalities have difficulty in discerning boundaries between themselves and others and are often very demanding. A borderline patient may accuse a doctor of incompetence, which is a projection of his or her own sense of inadequacy. However, with projective identification the doctor begins to feel uncomfortably anxious and distraught. The patient projects and the doctor then accepts the feeling being projected.

Example

A patient diagnosed as a borderline personality would become extremely upset when her therapist would go on vacation. Rather than being solely angry and lonely, the patient would become disconsolate, extremely anxious, and demanding of the covering therapist and of physicians she was consulting. She would induce in her treaters the panic she felt. Additionally, she would create such havoc that her providers were, in essence, recipients of her hostile feelings. She had been hurt by her therapist leaving, and she was turning the tables by hurting her other caregivers. The covering therapist was able to articulate to the patient what was occurring, resulting in a decrease in the patient's (and providers') distress.

Projective identification is a form of communication for a person who has no other avenue of expression available. The patient in the example does not have the words to articulate her distress. The original trauma that the therapist's vacation reevoked may have related to preverbal parent-child separations and disruptions. Consequently, the patient has no words available to describe her distraught feelings. Additionally, this patient's family was so chaotic and unattuned that she was never helped to sort out, understand, or label feelings. Her only available mode of communication is by creating those same feelings in another person. One only needs to think of the common phrase "he makes me feel guilty" to recognize the ubiquity of projective identification.

Practitioners do not appreciate being recipients of either projections or projective identifications. These defenses are uncomfortable and tend to engender defensiveness and angry reactions from the practitioner. This is counterproductive, since patients will react against the practitioner's defensiveness. Rather, the physician needs to be able to absorb the patient's projections, "contain" them, and maintain his or her professional manner. If it is recognized that the patient is reacting out of anxiety and despair and that accusations represent a difficulty in processing disappointment, the physician can maintain an attitude of equanimity. This will serve to help the patient calm down and to help both the patient and the practitioner to address the patient's distress. It is not expected that practitioners will not have a reaction to patient projections. Perhaps the physician can use the presence of uncomfortable feelings to understand the patient's distress and to help the patient articulate concerns that are not quite conscious. Much occurs in psychotherapy that initially puzzles the therapist. It is essential that the therapist maintain a curious attitude in order to encourage the patient to explore his or her feelings and thoughts. A condemnatory attitude is sure to stifle treatment. Therapists who are secure within their own abilities are not easily threatened by patient accusations and are able to look beyond the projection for useful information. A sense of humor is helpful in working with such strong feelings.

SUGGESTION. A tolerance for patients' expression of uncomfortable affect is essential in helping patients to tolerate and understand their own strong affects. Projections provide the physician with important information about the patient. A curious attitude is particularly helpful.

People are often accused of *denial,* another defense mechanism. It has entered the popular lexicon and, as such, has lost some of its meaning. Defenses are typically thought of as operating unconsciously. An accusation of its presence is not useful because the person may not be aware of its existence. Denial is the inability to see or the refusal to acknowledge that which is true or obvious. It is a negation of reality. It operates at all levels of consciousness.

Examples

A patient visited his internist, who asked him about his alcohol intake. The patient minimized his intake and insisted it was not a problem. The patient knew that he had a drinking problem but did not feel that he wanted to or could reduce the amount he drank, and was embarrassed to admit his problem.

A man was in psychotherapy for about 1 year. He liked his therapist, felt that he was being helped, and looked forward to his sessions. After every vacation interruption, the patient would be late for the next session and would find it difficult to talk freely. The therapist wondered if the patient had a reaction to breaks in the sessions. The patient's initial reaction was to deny that it had any impact. As treatment progressed he became aware of how he avoided intimacy and was able to see how that was manifested in the therapy, such as by not allowing himself to see the painful impact of canceled sessions.

People deny that which is too painful to admit. Accusing a patient of denying the obvious is never helpful. On the other hand, colluding with the denial is equally unhelpful. Some practitioners tend to take their cue from the patient and wait until the patient brings up problems. Generally, it is most helpful to gently question and probe a patient if the physician suspects a problem. Typically, this will occur in the areas of substance abuse, physical and sexual abuse, and eating disorders, and in noncompliance. Each of these issues will be addressed in later chapters.

SUGGESTION. Gentle probing and careful confrontation can help patients address that which they are denying. Practitioners need to be careful not to collude with patients in their denial.

The tendency to collude with patients is strongest with those patients toward whom the practitioner feels fondness. Practitioners want to believe the best of patients who are most like themselves, and then tend to deny or overlook obvious pathology or self-destructive behavior.

Enactment refers to the fact that both parties in a relationship can become embroiled in a troublesome drama that recreates issues unresolved from their respective pasts.

Example

> A doctor finds himself becoming attracted to a patient. Initially, he tells himself that he should put such thoughts out of his mind because they are inappropriate and dangerous. After some time his feelings of attraction become overwhelming, and he begins to tell himself that it is really harmless because the patient feels unloved and would benefit from his attentions. He convinces himself that he is helping her. The patient feels flattered that this busy and powerful man is attracted to her, particularly since her husband is so critical and unaffectionate. She succumbs to the seduction and a sexual relationship ensues.

In reality, the doctor, of course, is not being helpful to her; he is abusing her with his power and position. Despite his success, he had always felt rather inadequate and overwhelmed. These feelings were not predominant, but mostly existed as nagging doubts that he would quickly deny. He had always had difficulty with women, who often rejected him because of his subtly abusing manner. In point of fact, he had always felt dominated and controlled by women. Throughout his younger years he had been barraged by feelings of masculine inferiority. The patient in the example is a victim of childhood sexual abuse, of which she has told no one and for which she blames herself. She has had difficulty in responding sexually and has always felt herself to be unattractive and unworthy. In this situation, each participant is enacting unresolved troublesome incidents from their own past. They are working in concert, albeit unconsciously. Both are attempting to feel better about themselves and to work out unresolved feelings and conflicts.

Traumatic incidents leave an imprint on a person. The person feels plagued by them and seeks resolution. The nature of trauma is to overwhelm, and the person retains that sense of being overwhelmed and confused. Consequently, he or she continues to repeat and to reenact the trauma in order to understand and overcome it. In the preceding example, both participants are doomed to repeat their traumas. The patient is again in an abusive and exploitative relationship wherein she is being used to satisfy a man's power needs. The doctor is behaving inappropriately and abusively in order to feel more masculine and in control. Any sense of masculine competence is illusory because it occurs only in the context of a violation of professional boundaries. He is not being appreciated because of himself, but because of his position.

Countertransference refers to the transference of the practitioner. When a doctor or health care practitioner reacts to the patient in ways that reflect unresolved issues from his or her past, it is referred to as countertransference. Throughout this book, countertransference issues will be addressed. The doctor's exploitative behavior in the preceding example illustrates countertransference. At times, doctor and patient become embroiled in a enactment, a transference-countertransference dyad. For sophisticated practitioners, countertransference feelings can provide helpful information about the patient's issues and projections, and about the practitioner's own difficulties. Countertransference becomes a problem when it is acted out in an inappropriate fashion.

SUGGESTION. Physicians and other health care professionals must be careful to always maintain a professional manner. Psychological help should be sought if the professional is concerned about the appropriateness of his or her behavior.

Some patients engender very strong reactions in others. Practitioners have their own likes and dislikes and respond better to some patients than to others. Most often, physicians are able to tolerate a wide range of personalities without difficulty. At times, one particular patient will interact with a practitioner in a way that the practitioner cannot tolerate. Several things can eventuate. The doctor can "grin and bear it" and manage to remain professional despite his or her intense feelings. On, the other hand, the doctor's feelings may somehow become evident. The patient becomes hurt or angry and acts out his or her feelings in some maladaptive way, or the patient finds another doctor. Physicians and other professionals usually feel bad when they react negatively to a patient. They want to be objective and be able to treat the disease regardless of the nature of the patient. This is an unrealistic expectation. No one can be successful and comfortable with all patients, and recognition of one's limitations is important. Talking to patients about such difficulties is very hard to do but can be very helpful to both doctor and patient. It can give each participant an opportunity to air their differences in an attempt to resolve the problem. If a patient willfully refuses to follow the doctor's instructions such that his or her care is compromised, it is perfectly within the physician's purview to terminate care. Otherwise, the physician might compromise his or her ability to provide quality care because of resentment. Similarly, if the physician believes that the patient is harboring negative feelings it is best to inquire about them as soon as possible lest they build up and create greater problems in the future. Consultation with a colleague can assist the practitioner by giving him or her an opportunity to articulate difficult feelings, and feedback can be helpful to normalize the physician's feelings. In some cases, it is most appropriate to refer the patient elsewhere if the physician cannot be comfortable with his or her feelings toward the patient.

There are some patients that, unfortunately, nobody seems to like. They engender negative feelings from almost everyone that they encounter. Doctors and nurses tend to avoid such a person, who ends up feeling unappreciated and uncared for. If he or she was demanding and irritating before, rejection increases such behavior, perpetuating a cycle. Such individuals have mostly known rejection in their lives and know no other way of interacting. The medical staff become unwitting participants in the patient's drama.

Example

An 8-year-old boy was brought to his pediatrician for consultation. In speaking with the mother, it became apparent that the boy was dreadfully unhappy. He was picked on in school and seemed to be liked by no one. Interestingly enough, his behavior seemed to provoke the other children. He tattled on others, was somewhat socially awkward, would try to boss other children and, at times, would have temper tantrums in school. His parents were having marital difficulties and had little time for him. His school problems were causing his parents to attend to him, and although he received unpleasant attention in school, he was getting some recognition.

A child like this has not developed the social skills necessary to be successful. His sense of himself as being odd and out of sync with the rest of the children will likely become internalized, and he is likely to continue to act out this unpleasant role. Those with this propensity can be very difficult patients. Practitioners may unwittingly play the role of tormentor. The patient expects the doctor to react negatively and, in fact, tries to induce such a reaction. Physicians need to be careful to not allow themselves to be pulled into these detrimental and destructive interactions. Patients who induce such feelings require extra patience and understanding in order to break the rejecting cycle.

SUGGESTION. Open communication of interpersonal difficulties with patients is most beneficial. Physicians need to be careful not to be rejecting and hostile despite the provocation. Referral of patients that the practitioner cannot tolerate is recommended.

CONCLUSION

The relationship between doctor and patient can greatly facilitate or can enormously interfere with successful treatment. Practitioners' awareness of the factors influencing the doctor-patient relationship can assist in maintaining a positive relationship. The transference concept can assist practitioners in understanding difficult patient behaviors and can provide an avenue toward the maintenance of a positive working alliance. Physician difficulties can also be understood through the transference-countertransference model.

SUMMARY

1. The establishment of a working alliance is of paramount importance.
2. An organized office and a consistent practitioner is of great value in maintaining patient confidence and comfort.
3. A sense of calm efficiency imparts a holding environment.
4. Transference is the tendency to relate to those in the present based on past experiences and relationships.
5. Disruptions in the working alliance often relate to difficulties within the transference relationship.
6. Transferences are often unconscious and operate very subtly.
7. The repetition compulsion fuels the transference, and physicians need to be very careful not to become embroiled in patients' dramas.
8. Patients use many defensive maneuvers to protect themselves from painful memories, feelings, and thoughts.
9. Practitioners need to be careful not to act out their own transferences (countertransferences).

3

Noncompliance

The impact of psychological factors impinging upon medical practice is clearly seen in the phenomenon of noncompliance. "Estimates of non-compliance with medical regimens are staggeringly high (30-60%)" (Cameron & Gregor, 1987, p. 671).

Definition. *Noncompliance can be defined as the patient's refusal to follow prescribed treatment recommendations, large and small.*

Antibiotics are not finished, other medications are often taken incorrectly, dressings are not properly changed, and recommended lifestyle alterations are routinely ignored. In fact, only a minority of treatment recommendations are followed to the letter.

Examples

A patient had had pulmonary difficulties as a young man and, consequently, one lung had been removed. He went to his pulmonologist, complaining of shortness of breath and wheezing. He admitted to smoking marijuana frequently, yet refused to curtail its use despite the obvious dangers.

A woman diagnosed with lymphoma refused further chemotherapy after three treatments because of the unpleasant side effects. The doctor counseled against this action, but the patient was adamant.

The examples above are obvious and representative of some common instances of patient nonadherence to physician recommendations. Noncompliance also operates in very subtle and surprising ways.

Example

A patient was prescribed an antibiotic for a sinus infection. Unfortunately, he did not seem to improve. His doctor, concerned, prescribed a different antibiotic with the same result. He questioned the patient as to whether he was taking the medicine as prescribed. He indicated that he was, but that he was taking only one-half a pill per prescribed dose since he did not feel that his condition was that serious.

In psychodynamic psychotherapy, the patient is requested to say whatever comes to mind without censure. Patients almost always agree to this and then invariably do not tell the therapist everything that comes to mind. They tend to tell themselves that the thoughts are not important or revealing or that they are *too* revealing and embarrassing. In fact, saying what comes to mind without inhibition is extremely difficult, and most patients are able to accomplish this only after considerable experience. The practice of psychodynamic psychotherapy often consists of helping the patient to explore and understand the reasons for his or her reticence. Those feelings and thoughts avoided are of crucial importance. Patients seem to insist on putting their own unique twist on medical or psychological treatment, often to their detriment and to the practitioner's frustration.

It is not just in the helping professions that noncompliance is a problem. It occurs in every area of life. Appliance manufacturers struggle to find ways to get customers to read the instruction manuals that are provided with the machines. If instructions are not followed, the machines have a greater probability of malfunction, resulting in increased warranty cost and decreased customer satisfaction. This chapter looks at noncompliance, examines the possible reasons for its existence and ubiquity, and offers some suggestions to decrease the frequency and impact of nonadherence on the practitioner.

THE PRACTITIONER AND NONCOMPLIANCE

In general, the relationship between doctor and patient will set the tone for a cooperative treatment. "The relationship between the patient and health care provider can be the key factor in adherence" (Francis, 1991, p. 34s). Lange, Heins, Fisher, and Kopp (1988) tried to identify professional behavior that would facilitate compliance with treatment regimens. They list six physician behaviors: becoming better acquainted with the patient, becoming more aware of the patient's lifestyle, providing clear instructions, inquiring about the patient's feelings, being appropriately self-disclosing, and being able to accept negative feelings from the patient.

These six factors, as well as the importance of not creating an authoritarian atmosphere, emphasize that the physician-patient relationship is of crucial importance. However, it is not being suggested that the physician become friends with or in some way intimately involved with his or her patients. Rather, it is being suggested that benefit accrues to both patient and practitioner when an honest and authentic relationship is established and endures.

Knowing the Patient

A relationship cannot be established without personal knowledge being shared. Information in relationships is shared in many ways.

Example

A new patient arrived at the therapist's office. He was rather disheveled and seemed depressed, yet was quite articulate. He was obviously intelligent and thoughtful, although his education stopped at high school. He had consulted with several therapists before and had not been able to establish a working alliance. He felt discouraged and somewhat hopeless. As the therapist and patient discussed his situation, it was clear to both of them that there was a sense of connectedness between them, a sympathetic understanding. Both felt that they could work well together and did.

The therapist went beyond the obvious facts of the patient's life history and of his external characteristics. The sense of connectedness between the two participants provided crucial information that the therapist could use both diagnostically and prognostically. That is, the therapist had the sense that outward appearances notwithstanding, that the patient probably did function at a relatively high level and that there was a good likelihood that they could work together with a positive outcome. Pertinent facts about the patient and his life were disclosed later in the relationship.

One's sense of a patient as a person provides significant information as to the probability of a successful interaction.

Example

A patient began her relationship with an obstetrician by informing her that she was in the process of interviewing doctors about their delivery practices so that she could make an informed choice as to which obstetrician to see. She had a number of requirements that the doctor felt uncomfortable with, and the adversarial demeanor of the patient was off-putting. The obstetrician felt that taking care of this patient could possibly result in a conflict over her sense of proper medical practice. Additionally, she felt at odds with the woman and knew that a positive working relationship would be difficult to achieve. She gently suggested that other doctors would be more appropriate for the patient.

Most practitioners do not like to turn away prospective patients. At times, however, one should recognize one's own personality inclinations and not work with those individuals who are obviously going to be problematic. In the preceding example, the physician used her first impression of a patient to make a decision that was probably beneficial for both of them in the long run. One's intuitive sense can be a valuable tool in understanding patients.

As the doctor-patient relationship develops, it is important to take a genuine interest in patients, inquiring about their life, family, and other interests. Patients know when their doctor is genuine and interested and will react positively to the concern. Physical illnesses often require patients to be emotionally strong. A compassionate physician can assist patients in marshaling their inner resources for the battle ahead. This means that considerable energy must be extended in nurturing the doctor-patient relationship, just as in all relationships. Practitioners must be prepared to spend considerable time with patients in order for an attachment to be formed.

Example

Ms. E., a 20-year-old woman, had been referred to a specialist in adolescent medicine for evaluation and treatment of possible anorexia. The patient later reported to her gynecologist that the specialist had been helpful in the sense of referring her to a nutritionist who gave her useful advice about her diet and her calorie intake. Unfortunately, the doctor had kept her waiting for $1^1/_2$ hours and then had seen her very briefly, conveying little interest or concern. This behavior would be problematic with any patient, but particularly with an adolescent with possible anorexia. Anorectics by their nature are noncompliant, and a positive relationship is crucial for successful treatment. Anorectics tend to feel overcontrolled and react very negatively to behavior that conveys a lack of regard.

The physician lost an opportunity to establish a positive relationship with the young woman that could affect compliance.

Many doctor-patient relationships endure over some period of time. Patients are more likely to want to follow difficult treatment regimens if they feel understood and cared for by their physicians. At times, physicians will take care of several family members, which provides interesting and useful perspectives that can enhance treatment.

Example

A obstetrician/gynecologist took care of several sisters and their mother. The family relationships were quite intense, and the doctor came to know the intricacies of the family's interactions. This gave her insight into the family's dynamics, and her knowledge of

and involvement with the family gave her a credibility that enhanced the treatment relationship and thus compliance with treatment regimens.

SUGGESTION. Patients are more likely to follow treatment recommendations when they feel that they have a personal relationship with the doctor.

Health care providers come in contact with a wide range
of differing lifestyles. It has already been mentioned in Chapter
1 that it is of crucial importance for the practitioner to remain
open-minded and not to treat those of a different culture in a
discriminatory way. Additionally, it is very helpful to become
as acquainted as possible with the patient's lifestyle and family
heritage. Obviously, it is important for physicians to be knowledgeable about patients' diet, tobacco use, and alcohol and
drug use. This information is notoriously difficult to accurately
obtain since people routinely deny or underestimate problematic eating behaviors or substance use. Yet a person whose family history is replete with overeaters is going to have difficulty
in maintaining weight control.

Example

Several members of the J. family have trouble with their weight
control. The family did not encourage physical fitness and seemed
to reinforce notions that the women were singularly unathletic.
Those that were within normal weight boundaries were viewed
with some displeasure. The mother would buy fattening sweets for
her children despite their weight problems. One son would request that she not buy him such treats, but she disregarded his request.

In this family, one was considered a true member of the family
if one adhered to dietary preferences that were antithetical to
good health.

It is going to be very difficult for any family member to
maintain a healthy lifestyle when family pressures operate that
negate the influence of the physician. People are very tied to

their family's rituals, which are a source of family identity. Asking a person to lose weight in a family where eating great quantities of food is part of the family culture may be akin to asking him or her to betray the family. Individuals in such families may be afraid of being estranged from the family should they adopt more healthy eating habits. A doctor familiar with family pressures can approach the patient gently and can enlist the entire family in efforts toward better health. It is essential that the physician not become impatient with the individual and his or her struggles, since it should be recognized that healthy behavior may come at great psychological cost to the person.

Identification and Autonomy

By encouraging healthy behavior, the health care practitioner may be, in essence, encouraging the patient toward independence and autonomy. Yet, the need to belong is very strong and sometimes operates to undermine growth and maturity. It is obvious that infants are dependent on their parents for their essential needs to be met. This dependency and the intense emotions between parent(s) and child(ren) creates a very strong sense of identity within the family. Children often want to grow up to be just like their parents, and most parents take great pride in that. However, parents also need to let their children become independent and make choices that they may not always agree with. The maturational process consists of gradual separation and individuation from parents, with the hoped-for result of a competent and independent adult. This is an ideal, and the degree of independence that people achieve is varied. Some families discourage independence and autonomy, and the children become overly dependent and unable to separate in order to make independent choices. Under the stress of physical illness, there is a tendency to fall back upon old modes of behaving and to become more dependent. Consequently, they may feel drawn to the family's behavior patterns, which may not support healthy lifestyle choices.

Example

Mrs. E. had struggled for years with feelings of inadequacy and insecurity. Her weight problem had been serious for a number of years but she maintained relatively good health, regardless. She was diagnosed with breast cancer and underwent lumpectomy and excision of several lymph nodes. From all indications she was clear of any further malignancy, but the healthy lifestyle that she had worked so hard to develop deteriorated. She gained further weight and became involved in some destructive relationships. The strain of the disease caused her to become reidentified with a family ethic that emphasized poor health and dangerous behaviors. In some way she felt comforted with this family connection, even though it was detrimental to her well-being.

A patient such as this has difficulties that are of sufficient severity to warrant a referral to a mental health professional. Consequently, the physician may very well feel frustrated seeing patients become so self-destructive. Patience and understanding are most beneficial. A positive relationship with the physician can partially mitigate the preceding process because the patient may psychologically identify with the physician. This sense of identity can supplant the old identificatory patterns that are maladaptive. Consequently, it is important that the physician model healthy behaviors. Doctors who smoke are not going to be particularly successful in getting their patients to stop smoking. More importantly, a positive doctor-patient relationship increases positive identification and can be helpful in maintaining healthful behaviors, including compliance with treatment regimens.

The positive transference can also be helpful in enhancing adherence. The patient identifies the doctor with the beloved parent of his or her past, and the same desire to please and to be cooperative is activated.

SUGGESTION. Knowledge of the patient's lifestyle and family culture can give important clues to reasons for noncompliance. A positive doctor-patient relationship enhances compliance through identification and because of the patient's desire to feel positively connected with the physician.

Many families are ignorant of anatomy and physiology and may develop their own theories as to how their bodies work, theories that are often rooted in fantasy. Family advice and instructions are often given in the light of these misconceptions. The sense of identity within families is exceptionally potent and intense and can be problematic in helping patients to maintain adherence.

Examples

A patient was in long-term psychotherapy and would often talk about her angry reactions toward others. Exploration suggested that the patient was experiencing intense feelings of jealousy and competitiveness. She reacted very negatively when the therapist suggested that she was jealous. Later she was able to realize that jealousy was an emotion whose existence was denied within her family, with two results. One, she felt self-criticism should she feel jealous, and, two, she was never able to come to grips with her rather normal feelings since they had to remain secret.

Some families, particularly from backgrounds of poverty, believe that being overweight is a sign of health and prosperity. Such families may become very critical of those members trying to lose necessary weight, and may put considerable pressure on a family member of normal weight to eat more and to gain weight. This can be very dangerous for those who need to lose weight or to decrease fat intake for health reasons.

Those from such families may feel overcontrolled yet powerless in interactions with their families. The patients want to be healthy and follow prescribed treatment recommendations, but they also want to be approved of within the family. This sets up a dilemma for the patient and for the doctor. It can develop into a power struggle with the patient in the middle, feeling pulled in two directions. It is not useful for the practitioner to become a participant in such a drama. If the doctor is able to spell out for the patient the conflict that the patient is experiencing, the patient can feel more in control and can then make appropriate decisions. Often the patient knows that he or she is uncomfortable and is finding it difficult to comply with treatment recommendations but does not understand the underlying reasons.

Those who find it difficult to make independent choices can be considered the product of *enmeshed* families. These are individuals who have, either overtly or covertly, been discouraged from being strong and independent. They function as an extension of the parents rather than as separate individuals. Those enmeshed have difficulty pulling away from family expectations. They feel entangled within the family and experience independent action as being somehow damaging to the parents or to the family unit. The sense of being entangled or enmeshed is amazingly potent and can directly affect compliance.

Example

A patient was seeing a psychologist because of extreme emotional distress and depression. She was diabetic, had Crohn's disease, and was morbidly obese. Obviously, her eating habits were seriously detrimental to her physical well-being. Her family history indicated that both parents were obese and that she was not encouraged to develop independent interests. Being a good girl meant following family health habits, which were obviously detrimental. The patient had never married and was frightened of developing intense relationships outside of the family. One of her sisters had not been overweight until after she had married, when she started to gain weight. Prior to that she had tried to be more independent from the family. As she gained weight, she seemed to have more interest in being more involved in the family.

Here is a patient with serious health problems that are exacerbated by her need to stay attached to the family.

A child's greatest fears are loss of love and loss of relationships. In healthier families, the child understands that independence is valued and will not result in loss of love or in estrangement. He or she then feels freer to form new attachments and to maintain healthy lifestyles. In enmeshed families, the individual is very insecure and greatly fears abandonment and loss of love; he or she will maintain unhealthy behaviors if it signifies security and attachment. Direct confrontation of this issue by the physician is not likely to result in success.

Example

In the preceding example, the therapist initially established a working alliance by exhibiting concern for the patient's distress. The patient indicated that she had tried several therapists previously but that she had always terminated after getting angry for not making progress. This was further confirmation to the therapist that the patient had mixed feelings about resolving her difficulties, since it is unlikely that all of the rejected therapists were incompetent. The present therapist informed the patient that she would probably feel that way toward him at some point in the future, and said that if that happened she should please inform him so they could try to understand her distress in order to resolve it. In the beginning of the treatment, the therapist said little about the parent's family. He understood the enmeshment pull and knew that he would threaten the treatment if he pushed her about her attachment to the family. A major initial emphasis was to help the patient to become psychologically stronger in order to be able to tolerate discussion about the need for independence. It was only considerably later that the therapist brought up her eating habits and was able to have her look at their origin without feeling threatened or anxious.

A physician treating this patient is not going to have the time for or the capability of addressing her issues in this fashion. Nevertheless, being aware of the patient's family situation can provide considerable information to the physician that can be useful. The doctor will have to understand that any alteration in her eating habits is likely to be resisted and that patience and understanding will be essential. The physician can point out to the patient that she is putting herself at risk and can identify that she is following family traditions. In recognizing the difficulty in altering problem behaviors, the doctor can help the patient set small achievable goals that will reinforce independent behavior. Fortunately, that this patient is in psychotherapy provides hope that her emotional difficulties can be addressed, with a resultant reduction in her problem behaviors.

SUGGESTION. Patients in enmeshed families will have difficulty with compliance if it represents separation. This issue must be broached gently because of the intensity of the issue. Setting small, achievable goals reinforces a sense of independence.

Clear Instructions

Providing clear and direct instructions is welcomed by patients. Most are quite anxious about their physical condition, and the stress of the situation may cause regression, which results in an impaired ability to process information. At times health care practitioners may not realize the lack of sophistication of their patients, and that what seems obvious to the practitioner may not be so for the patient. It is never a mistake to underestimate the level of a patient's knowledge and understanding. A patient's ability to process information is compromised under the stress of illness. Instructions may need to be given more than once. Written instructions can be very helpful as well. Unfortunately, even written instructions are misunderstood or ignored. It is of vital importance that health care workers provide patients with ample opportunity to ask questions and that these questions be truly welcomed. Patients know when they are being patronized or thought stupid and will not ask questions if they feel embarrassed.

SUGGESTION. Clear instructions are essential for promoting compliance. An atmosphere that welcomes questions enhances adherence.

The Patient's Feelings

Those doctors and health care professionals who are interested in their patients' feelings are going to be rewarded with patients who are more likely to comply with treatment recommendations. Encouraging patients to discuss their feelings about their life, about their disease, and about their treatment can be very beneficial. In psychotherapy, it is a well-accepted fact that patients will, even in the best of circumstances, develop negative transferences. That is, they will have unpleasant and angry feelings toward their therapists, deserved or not. For psychotherapy to be successful, these unpleasant feelings must be addressed. If they are not attended to, the patient is not going to be able to identify important issues. Furthermore, unanalyzed negative transferences can result in acting-out behaviors that are detrimental to the patient and that can result in premature termination.

Example

Mr. K. was an outwardly compliant psychotherapy patient who suffered from depression and a considerable number of psychosomatic complaints. The psychologist's evaluation suggested that the patient was very angry, which manifested itself as conflict with his son and wife. Apparently, he was very short-tempered and would get in screaming matches with his teenage son. From the patient's history, the therapist knew that he had suffered a number of disappointments and losses at an early age and that, in some ways, he felt himself to be a failure. The anger he expressed at his son for his son's inadequacies was representative of his own level of self-criticism. He was able to understand this but his argumentativeness continued. The therapist understood that the patient was now displacing his anger from the therapist onto his son, and that helping him redirect his anger would improve the family situation and would enhance the intensity of the treatment. The patient went to great lengths to disavow any feelings of dissatisfaction toward the therapist. However, it was noted by the therapist that Mr. K. often did not tell the therapist what was on his mind, preferring to mull his thoughts over before disclosing them. This was contrary to the therapist's instructions. It was through this behavior that the therapist and patient were able to get access to his rebellious defiance. This led to important information regarding the patient and how his angry feelings had become self-destructive, as he continued to smoke and overeat despite his physician's recommendations.

The therapist actively sought out the patient's negative transference, which resulted in a diminution of the patient's family conflict. Furthermore, it enhanced compliance because the patient was able to see that his censoring himself, his continued smoking, and his overeating were designed, in part, to thwart his doctors. He felt angry about being out of control over certain aspects of his life and, in a sense, wanted his doctors to experience that feeling. Additionally, his sense of incompetence and inadequacy caused him to try to project that feeling onto his practitioners as an attempt to lessen his negative feelings. It was crucial for the therapist to assiduously look for hostile and unpleasant feelings and to help the patient to accept their presence and to understand their origins. Similarly, medical practitioners have to be alert to the presence of negative feelings and should not be hesitant in addressing them with the patient.

Example

A 53-year-old man was put on antihypertensive medication by his physician. He was a new patient, and the doctor did not have much of a sense of him as a person. He did know that the patient had recently been widowed and seemed to live a very solitary life. He was not particularly communicative with the physician, yet seemed agreeable to the treatment. On the return visit, he informed the doctor that he had discontinued the medication. In discussing the situation the patient was angry and sullen. The doctor encouraged him to talk about his dissatisfaction, and the patient talked at length about his loneliness, isolation, and depression. He felt cheated by life and saw no reason to maintain his health. He felt angry toward the doctor for prescribing medication with side effects. As the patient described his unhappiness, he seemed to brighten slightly. The doctor suggested that they try another medication and was supportive and sympathetic to the patient's distress. The patient experienced some sense of relief and felt more committed to the treatment.

The physician was able to tolerate, to "detoxify," the patient's feelings, resulting in a diminution of negative affect and greater cooperativeness. Patients need to feel comfortable in venting the full range of feelings that they may have, including angry and frustrated ones. A patient such as the one just described would probably benefit from a referral to a mental health professional. However, that referral would probably be better made after a stronger relationship with the patient is established. The doctor can intuitively understand that this patient is rather resistant to interventions and is probably not going to respond positively to a referral. Furthermore, a sensitive patient such as this may experience a referral to a mental health professional as a message from the doctor that he does not want to deal with his strong emotions, and may experience it as a rejection.

SUGGESTION. Tolerating the patient's negative and frustrating feelings is important in increasing compliance. Unacknowledged hostile feelings can result in acting-out behaviors by the patient.

At times, those in the helping professions do not want to hear such complaints, fearing being blamed or not wanting to feel powerless. It is inevitable that patients will be unhappy. Sometimes this feeling is directed at the health care practitioner and sometimes it relates to the realities of their disease or of their life in general. One aspect of being in the helping professions is that one is going to encounter considerable patient distress, which at times is manifested through accusations of incompetence. At other times, distress, anger, and feelings of frustration are expressed in a less accusatory fashion. In both instances, allowing and even encouraging the patient to express his or her feelings is likely to lead to a better result.

The Doctor's Attitude

The manner in which health care practitioners relate to their patients can have a significant effect on compliance. Most patients welcome doctors who are genuine and sincere in their manner and who are appropriately self-disclosing. Self-disclosure does not necessarily mean sharing personal details with patients, although that can be one aspect. It also means sharing with the patient one's personality. It means letting patients see that one feels for and with them, that one empathizes with their situation. *Empathy* refers to the ability to "stand in another's shoes." It means to experience what someone else is experiencing without being judgmental or critical. The physician may, at times, feel comfortable in sharing with the patient facets of his or her own life that match that of the patient. This is really a matter of choice and is not crucial. It is most important that the doctor show the patient that he or she is also a person who knows what it is like to be ill, to suffer, and to be scared.

Example

A patient was very reluctant to continue her chemotherapy regimen, which had terrible side effects. The oncologist empathized with the patient and let her know that she could appreciate the difficulty of the regimen. She encouraged the patient to talk at length about the pain and discomfort as well as the embarrassment she felt from the hair loss and general incapacitation. She told the patient that she knew that she was frightened and tired of being ill and that she herself would feel similarly if in the same situation. The patient could tell that the physician was genuinely concerned for her and that she appreciated her pain. This knowledge enabled her to feel that she could continue the treatments, at least for awhile.

The physician, through years of experience, knew what kind of privations the patient was enduring. She was genuinely concerned for the patient, in fact, liked her a great deal, and these feelings came through to the patient.

Patients may feel overwhelmed by their affects in general and particularly when faced with physical problems. Oftentimes allowing patients to express themselves openly and emotionally can be very helpful. However, some health care practitioners are very uncomfortable with emotions and may try to quiet the patient. At times, the doctor may leave the room or encourage the patient to talk to the nurse, or prescribe tranquilizing or antidepressant medications. Extreme emotional response may require mental health referral and/or medication, but the initial response should be to try to offer support and nurturance, and to encourage emotional expression. Those with physical disorders *should* be upset and should be encouraged to articulate their distress.

SUGGESTION. Empathy refers to the ability to emotionally appreciate another's situation. Empathy is of crucial importance in making patients feel cared for, which promotes a sense of well-being as well as adherence to treatment regimens.

Being effective as a physician requires a great deal of intuition, which one develops with experience. Using tact when confronting patients is of great value.

Example

Mrs. G. was seeing her internist for a checkup. She seemed unusually quiet and thoughtful. She was tearful, and yet insisted that all was well in her life. The doctor was certain that something was wrong but had no idea what it could be. He encouraged the woman to continue talking, gently asking questions about her family and work. After a period of time, he could see that she would get more upset when speaking about her husband. The doctor asked her if she were having marital problems. The patient broke down in tears, acknowledging that her husband was having an affair.

Patients need to feel safe in order to be able to divulge very difficult, painful, and embarrassing information. They need to feel certain that any secrets divulged will be handled gently and in confidence. People will often deny problems if asked directly. It is more fruitful to encourage people to talk about their lives in a broad fashion rather than curtly asking if they have any problems and taking their denial at face value. If problems are suspected, patients should be encouraged to call back or to come back when they feel more ready to talk. Sometimes, thoughts and emotions need to "percolate" to the surface, and people need time to become comfortable in disclosing difficult material.

Authoritarian versus Authoritative Manner

Patients want their health care providers to be authorities on disease and its treatment and rarely want a cold, distant, and authoritarian practitioner. Most people respond positively to kindness and warmth and can become rebellious and resentful of those who are aloof and condescending. One should always have respect for patients and for their right to make choices.

Example

> Mr. V. sought out marital therapy for himself and his wife. One issue that seemed to bother him was that his wife was an attorney, and he felt inadequate because he was "only" a high school teacher. He had enrolled in a Ph.D. program but had not been able to complete his dissertation. The therapist became rather derisive, challenging the patient to finish his requirements. This did seem to propel him, and he did finish his degree. Unfortunately, several other issues went unaddressed, resulting in a marriage filled with conflict that caused terrible problems for the children they had and that ended in an acrimonious divorce. The authoritarian stance ignored many other difficulties. A more empathic, comprehensive approach may have been able to address his educational difficulties while still addressing the other issues.

Health care professionals do need to confront patients on noncompliance or on behaviors that are self-destructive. Rarely is it helpful to be angry and disapproving. In psychotherapy, interpretations made about a person's behavior can be made to emphasize the positive or to accentuate the negative. Interpreting on the side of the positive is almost always the best choice.

Example

> The patient had neglected to get her husband a present for his birthday. The husband had been upset, and the patient indicated that she had forgotten the birthday, which seemed unlikely. The therapist was able to ascertain that the patient had been angry at the husband for being rude to her at a party and that her angry feelings caused her not to buy him a present. The therapist, being aware of her pattern to act out grievances, could have emphasized her vindictive nature. He chose to first emphasize her hurt feelings as motivating the behavior. This is more palatable and is probably more to the point than her vindictiveness. The vindictiveness will need to be addressed at some time, but can be approached in terms of hurt feelings so that the patient will feel less threatened.

With problematic behaviors in the office, it is always better to take the high road.

SUGGESTION. Patients respond negatively to cold, aloof, and authoritarian practitioners. It is most helpful to look at motivation from a more positive, less critical perspective.

Anger and Hopelessness

There are times in every health care professional's career when he or she will become furious with patients. Patients bring all of themselves into the examination room, and this includes their infuriating side. Some are rude and belligerent; others blithely ignore treatment recommendations and put themselves at risk; still others will take advantage of doctors by missing appointments, by not paying bills, or by calling in the middle of the night for specious reasons. It is not expected that practitioners will not get angry. In fact, in many instances, they should get angry. What is important is how the angry feelings are processed and dealt with.

Example

Mr. Y. seemed willfully provocative with his internist. He ate what he wanted, drank alcohol to excess, smoked cigarettes, and generally ignored his doctor's recommendations. To add insult to injury, he was accusatory and rude with the doctor and blamed him because his gastric difficulties were not improving. When he spoke with the doctor, he mimicked his mannerisms and was snide and sarcastic. The physician felt enraged with his patient's behavior and became snide and sarcastic in return. Their encounter degenerated into a shouting match with the patient leaving the office in disgust, screaming profanities. The physician was extremely upset, as were patients and staff in the office.

The doctor lost his sense of professionalism when provoked by the patient. He was understandably very angry but should have handled it differently. It would have been better if he had told the patient, even in an angry tone, that he did not appreciate nor would he tolerate being abused and that if the patient could not be more considerate, he would have to find another physician. It is helpful to help the patient by being a "container" for the patient's feelings, yet one should not allow oneself to be abused.

Some patients are angry and frustrated because their life or their physical condition is or seems hopeless. Those in the health care professions always confront pain and suffering, and outcomes are not always positive. It is important to allow patients their frustration. Physicians can become defensive when confronted with angry patients complaining of their poor health. Defensive doctors do many things to ward off accusations, including becoming angry and accusatory toward patients. It is important for health care professionals to recognize the limitations of their abilities and to accept that all patients cannot be cured in the optimal manner. Within this reality is the fact that all patients potentially can be helped in some fashion, even if the eventual outcome is death. Their suffering may be able to be relieved or, if not, perhaps their journey can be eased by a sympathetic, genuine, and caring physician.

SUGGESTION. Angry and frustrated feelings are acceptable for health care professionals as long as they are expressed in a reasonable fashion. Providing hope and concern even for those with poor prognoses can be helpful to patients and rewarding to the physician.

THE PATIENT AND NONCOMPLIANCE

People act and react rather consistently, but not always rationally or reasonably. Illness, physical traumas, and bodily changes are stressful and tend to have a regressive pull on those experiencing the difficulties. *Regression* means a retreat to some earlier developmental period and tends to occur in response to stress. Situations that could often be coped with comfortably create difficulties when the person is feeling overwhelmed by other factors.

Example

Mr. S. functioned well prior to his father's death. He was a successful executive, had a reasonably happy marriage, and was a good and involved father. After the sudden death of his father he went into a tailspin, performed poorly on the job, began drinking, and became less interested in his wife and children. Reluctantly, he sought out the services of a psychotherapist. Together they discovered that he had harbored very intense feelings toward his father, which created emotions that were so overwhelming that he could not function as adequately as he had previously.

The press of emotional distress caused this patient to regress. He could not function at the same level of capability as he had prior to his father's death. Different people have different levels of coping ability. Some are able to withstand intense experiences and still remain relatively calm. Others feel overwhelmed at the slightest change in routine. The level of coping ability can be considered a measure of one's *ego strength*. Several variables interact and combine to determine a given patient's ability to comply with treatment recommendations. One is the patient's ego strength, a rough measure of his or her emotional well-being. The second would be the quality of their interpersonal relationships. Another is the level of physical distress and its seriousness. A third is the level of stress that the person is contending with in his or her life. A final variable would be the symbolic meaning of the physical problem. The level of stress and the extent of the seriousness of the illness can be considered external factors, that is, nonpsychological. Ego strength and the symbolic meaning of the disorder are internal psychological factors. These variables create a fascinating mélange that can result in a cooperative and pleasant patient or in an exceedingly difficult one, along with every possible variation in between.

Ego Strength and Relationships

In psychodynamic theory, the ego represents that part of the mind that is a mediator. It mediates between internal desires, wants, and prohibitions and external reality constraints. A person with significant ego strength is one who can navigate the world successfully, who can set goals and achieve them, who is able to be assertive and yet is sensitive to others. It is a definition that implies strength of character. Strong individuals are able to tolerate pain and deprivation without significant regression. Typically, those with significant ego strength have had positive childhood experiences where they have been encouraged to be strong and independent and where parents have not projected themselves into the child. They have been raised with kindness, concern, and sensitivity. They have been treated fairly and have been encouraged to understand that they have choices and that their choices have consequences. Since ego strength arises out of positive relationships, those with positive levels of ego strength tend to have good interpersonal relationships. Such relationships are enormously important in one's level of satisfaction in life and are helpful in coping with the adversities of life. The physician can get a sense of the patient's coping abilities and qualities of interpersonal relationships through the personal history. A comprehensive history along with an ongoing relationship will give the physician a good idea of how the patient has coped with adversity and his or her level of satisfaction with life. Ego strength is not an all-or-nothing proposition. People vary along a continuum.

Examples

Mrs. H. was at a party when she realized that the glass that she was drinking from was chipped. She immediately panicked with the concern that she had swallowed a piece of glass that could greatly damage her internal organs. She was reassured by a physician who was present and was able to calm down.

Mrs. W. discovered a lump in her breast. She was understandably distraught and worried about the diagnosis. Nevertheless, she carried on with her activities and took care of her children and the rest of her life while she went through the diagnostic procedures. She had a good relationship with her husband and several close and supportive friends.

The first woman could barely tolerate an insignificant occurrence, while the second was able to cope with a problem of potentially far greater magnitude. These examples illustrate two very different levels of ego strength.

Level of Physical Illness and Level of Stress

Of course, a serious illness is going to greatly increase stress in the patient's life. However, some people who become ill are already contending with considerable stress in their life that could make coping with their illness and complying with treatment even more difficult.

Example

Mrs. H. (see preceding example) had significant marital problems, which caused her considerable distress. Her reaction to gall bladder difficulties was extreme, and she reacted as if her life was in danger. She became insistent and demanding and, since she did not get along well with her husband, had no one to turn to in her distress. Although not seriously ill, the absence of a positive relationship along with poor coping ability created a very uncomfortable situation for the patient.

SUGGESTION. An assessment of the patient's ego strength, quality of interpersonal relationships, and external stressors will give the physician an idea of the capability of a patient to deal with the rigors of a given treatment.

Symbolic Meanings

Disorders often have symbolic meanings for patients. That is, they evoke feelings, thoughts, and unconscious fantasies. For instance, a patient who is plagued by a sense of guilt may view a disease as a punishment and consequently be resistant to treatment regimens because of a need to suffer. This would not be a conscious belief but would still exert tremendous influence on the patient.

In psychosomatic disorders, the organ system involved has psychological significance. Psychodynamic theory suggests that symptoms develop for specific reasons and that the body part involved has meaning.

Example

A patient suffered gastrointestinal upset over a period of many years. Her physician could offer little relief but did make suggestions as to some over-the-counter medications that could be used. The patient consistently refused to try them. Further inquiry showed that this patient had a mother who was inappropriately intrusive and demanding with her bowel movements when the patient was a child. Consequently, the patient experienced the doctor's suggestions as being intrusive and controlling and felt the need to resist. The patient was in psychotherapy and expressed bewilderment about her resistance. The resistance disappeared once the connection between her early experiences and the present was made.

One might question why the patient made such a big deal out of something that happened many years ago and seems to be of such little significance. With this patient, toilet training was just one of many battlegrounds for autonomy and independence. The patient often experienced her parents as domineering and had to resist them in order to maintain her sense of separateness and autonomy. The resistance occurred surreptitiously because of her fear of being punished. The resistive quality became characterological. That is, in many areas of her life she could be quite stubborn in ways that were not obvious. The physician, as a transference object, represented her controlling mother, with whom she struggled to maintain her sense of integrity and identity. The developmental perspective suggests that people's level of functioning represents both successes and failures at childhood developmental tasks. The aforementioned patient had conflicts in the period of her life where her sense of independence and autonomy developed, and these issues were unresolved and carried over into adulthood.

Resistance

Resistance is a term that refers to an individual's reluctance to acknowledge certain realities. The patient in the preceding example resisted the treatment recommended by the doctor. Resistance is really another label for noncompliance. It is a psychodynamic/psychoanalytic term, and it has the unfortunate aspect of having a rather pejorative quality. Patients do not generally resist or noncomply in order to be difficult or contrary. Rather, they resist because they know no other way of reacting. Patients resist as an attempt to avoid emotional pain.

Example

A patient, Mr. Z., was in long-term psychotherapy because of his dissatisfaction with himself, since he was painfully shy and lonely. He was hyper-self-observant and self-conscious, constantly afraid of criticism and ridicule. Treatment went very slowly since every observation or comment that the therapist made that was not complimentary was felt by the patient to be a criticism. Consequently, he could not learn from the therapist since he accepted no feedback. His fear of being criticized and of being embarrassed were all-encompassing and caused him to freeze up in social situations. He took no initiative in his relationships for fear of being rejected. He insisted that he had no feelings toward the therapist other than frustration for not being helped sufficiently.

This patient was highly resistant to the treatment. He would not really immerse himself in the relationship for fear of being hurt. He had been so hurt by an overintrusive, controlling, and contemptuous mother that he felt unable to make any moves. Criticism represented something very threatening to him. He frustrated the therapist, creating in him the same bind that the patient felt. He too could never do anything right. The patient was so invested in being right that he always needed to make the therapist wrong. The only way change was going to occur was for the patient to feel safe enough to look at himself and others in a different way. His resistance to treatment was not consciously purposeful. He knew no other way. This is the same with patients who are noncompliant in medical practice. Seriously noncompliant patients are likely to have had childhood experiences in which they did not feel particularly in control of themselves. They were overcontrolled, were not particularly understood, were subject to their parent's externalizations, and were probably, in some crucial way, neglected.

SUGGESTION. Noncompliant or resistant patients are trying to avoid emotional pain, even at the cost of further suffering. They are rarely aware of the reasons for their resistance.

Neglected Patients

Those patients who have been neglected in their lives offer a special challenge for the physician. Some of the people with such histories have learned to fend for themselves and have difficulty in allowing themselves to become dependent on others for advice. They have told themselves that they are able to handle any problem that comes along and often resist treatment. Their sense of competence is very important to them, and they may view illness as a way of succumbing to a weakness.

Example

An obese woman had a number of health problems, including diabetes. She had significant heart disease in her family, yet absolutely refused to participate in any weight reduction programs. She was intelligent and capable and essentially ran her present family, with little input or assistance from her husband. She had pretty much been neglected as a child and essentially had to learn to fend for herself, including preparing her own meals at an early age.

Here we have an extremely capable woman who resolutely refuses to comply with treatment recommendations. Her obesity indicates that she was not really as capable as she believed. Her pose of competence is designed to protect her from long-suppressed fears of reexperiencing frightening, confusing, and upsetting feelings from those times when she was left on her own as a child. For her, to accept the doctor's recommendations meant to become incompetent, weak, and terrified. The resistance to the treatment protects her from painful feelings.

With this patient, the physician can only take a less proactive stance while trying to make sure that the patient has a sense of control over her treatment. Presenting her with options and choices and encouraging her to make sound decisions will have the greatest probability of success.

This patient was greatly benefited by her high level of intelligence, which enabled her to cope with life in a moderately effective way, her obesity and resistance notwithstanding. Other people who are products of neglect are not so fortunate. The neglect may have been more severe or their ability to cope with it compromised, such that they are not able to negotiate life very effectively. Furthermore, like children, they do not see themselves as having much control over their lives, may expect magical cures from the physician, and may become enraged when they are not forthcoming. Under the stress of physical illness, those from backgrounds of severe neglect regress, sometimes to very poor levels of adaptation.

Example

Mrs. C. was an obese woman who had been psychiatrically hospitalized numerous times. She had worked effectively in psychotherapy and had been able to achieve much more satisfying levels of adaptation. Nevertheless, in some ways she was still very disturbed and very noncompliant. She took her psychiatric medication in ways that were not prescribed and abused other medications as well. She was enormously needy and demanding, making endless phone calls to the therapist, to the prescribing psychiatrist, and to her other physicians. She threatened suicide or threatened to mutilate herself, which she had done in the past. She rarely heeded any treatment recommendations and was extremely frustrating to her health care professionals. Any physical illness would cause further regression.

Beyond her provocativeness, one could see the neglected, frightened, abused, and abandoned child who felt that she could only maintain relationships with others by being abusive and demanding. Within the professional relationships, she was replicating her early childhood experiences. Fortunately, she was being helped by an extremely competent therapist who was assisting her in her distress. Her treating physicians tended to become caught up in the traumas of her life, themselves becoming upset and angry at the patient. Even though this woman was reacting in a fashion that represented a developmental failure, it was important to remember and to remind this patient that she was able to function at a higher level, that she was an adult, and to insist that she treat them with respect. Furthermore, it would be helpful to enlist her cooperation in an adult way by explaining treatment options clearly and by insisting that she had the capability to make necessary decisions about her life. Enlisting her ego strength can help shore up her defenses.

SUGGESTIONS. Patients who were neglected and/or abused as children present special problems. They often feel out of control and may try to control treatment by not complying. Appealing to their adult side by emphasizing and encouraging choices is helpful.

Patient Manipulation

Some patients can be blatantly manipulative, and this can be seen in noncompliant behaviors. The way a patient treats the medical staff is often reflective of how he or she treats others and, most importantly, how the patient was treated in the past. This behavior is indicative also of a patient's self-concept.

Example

A patient who was scheduled for a cesarean section told her obstetrician that she needed to have the operation on a particular day and time since her psychic adviser told her that it would be more opportune for her and the baby. In reality, this was more convenient for her husband. The obstetrician felt quite put out by this manipulation, felt that her control over the case was being compromised, and did not feel comfortable with the situation. The patient was informed of the doctor's discomfort, and she precipitously sought out obstetrical care elsewhere, resulting in care with a new physician who had little knowledge of the patient or of her condition.

We can infer from this situation that the patient has not always been treated courteously or with consideration and was probably manipulated. Furthermore, it is unlikely that this

woman was able to form very intense and meaningful relationships because of the manner of disregard with which she
treated the physician. Understanding such behaviors does not
always enable the practitioner to feel better and does not suggest that one should tolerate being treated poorly merely because the patient's behavior is being generated from childhood
issues. If the physician does not allow himself or herself to be
manipulated, it is far better for everyone concerned. In some
small way it is sending a message to the patient that integrity
and honesty matter. The physician is also modeling more appropriate behavior. Additionally, the physician is protecting
himself or herself from being abused or manipulated, which
the patient was probably never able to do. In this situation the
physician refused to change the time of surgery, and the patient found a physician who did not feel uncomfortable scheduling surgery based on a psychic's predictions. Another way
to conceptualize controlling behavior is by understanding that
those who need to control others have themselves been controlled. It is a form of the psychological practice of "turning
passive into active." Rather than being a passive recipient of
an uncomfortable event, a person turns it around and becomes
the provocateur.

Example

One patient who was pregnant and suffering from uterine fibroids
made appointments with two gynecologists without informing either of the dual scheduling. When having a problem, she would
call both, resulting in confusion for the doctors and the hospital
staff, possibly compromising her care because of the tumult, in
addition to the bad feelings she was creating in those trying to
help her. Adding even more complications, the patient told one
doctor that she just wanted a hysterectomy, that the pregnancy was
just too much trouble.

Clearly, this patient was markedly ambivalent—about the
pregnancy and about the doctors. We can imagine that she was
raised in a family where feelings toward her were not clearly
loving, perhaps ambivalent. There is the suggestion that she
was not very trusting and honest, which is indicative that she

did not feel confident in her caregivers as a child and that they were probably not forthright with her. Because of her reluctance to seek solace and care from one physician, it is possible that she did not have a consistent and loving parent in her past. Additionally, it is likely that she did not feel particularly valued and cherished as a child. Perhaps she felt herself to be too much trouble. The past has been reenacted in the present.

SUGGESTION. The physician can get some sense of the patient's sense of himself or herself by how he or she treats the physician.

Negative Therapeutic Reaction

Negative therapeutic reaction is a process whereby the patient resists the treatment, denies its potency, and minimizes the effectiveness of the practitioner. Patients who exhibit negative therapeutic reaction make progress in psychotherapy, or in other treatments, but will not acknowledge it or will not make the gains expected.

Example

Mr. Z. was mentioned in an earlier example as being in long-term psychotherapy because of his shyness and social isolation. Despite his resistance to accepting feedback from the therapist he had made several significant gains through the treatment. He was less socially isolated, made more friends, seemed less inhibited, moved ahead in his job, and was able to purchase and furnish a house. He totally resisted the notion that the therapist was important to him or that the therapy had any positive influence on him.

This man, because of his own feelings of inadequacy, was loathe to admit the therapist's potency and thus had to deny any helpfulness. He projected his own lack of effectiveness onto the therapist and berated him just as he berated himself. He derived some sense of potency from thwarting the therapist, even though it was hurting him by destroying the pleasure he could have received from acknowledging his successes in life and in treatment. By denying his therapist potency, he did not have to experience the intense envy that would have developed otherwise. Additionally, his sense of guilt was assuaged by his unhappiness. Patients such as this may have been able to get attention only when they were ill and/or angry, and therefore feel more attached and secure when sick. These individuals were likely to have had a sick and/or depressed mother, and they identify with her and feel the need themselves to remain sick and depressed. The practitioner has a battle on his or her hands to help the patient to transcend the sick role, since the need for security is so great.

Example

Mrs. R. was making constant visits to her internist for mostly minor problems, but continued to complain about problems that made little sense physiologically. The doctor had treated her for a number of years and they had a good working relationship. He was able to see beyond the complaints and asked the patient if something else were bothering her. She poured out her sad story of loneliness and depression. He was able to refer her for mental health treatment and her frequent visits diminished.

The situation above is a rather mild case. Most of those embroiled in a negative therapeutic reaction are quite resistant to health and are frustrating for the physician. Despite their resistance, these individuals do have a healthy side, and an attempt to enlist that healthy side can be beneficial.

SUGGESTION. Negative therapeutic reaction causes patients to fight and deny progress. Typically, the sick role feels safer and more secure. Practitioners should attempt to enlist the patient's healthy desire to get well in order to reinforce the benefits of compliance.

There are many different aspects of negative therapeutic reaction. Falling ill can be conceived by some people as a blow to one's sense of competence. The person may view himself or herself as a failure. It is a blow to one's *narcissism* or self-regard. Consequently, physical illness can be felt as a narcissistic injury, as an insult, and the person can respond angrily, as if he or she is being demeaned. The anger can be externalized and directed at the doctor, and the patient may blame him or her and become noncompliant.

Example

A world-class long distance runner consulted a sports medicine specialist for Achilles tendinitis, a potentially serious disorder for a runner. The physician recommended a reduction in the runner's schedule, frequent icing, and anti-inflammatory medication. The patient took the medication sporadically and, contrary to his doctor's advice, continued training at an intense pace, eventuating in a chronic tendinitis that completely incapacitated him. Throughout the treatment, he was sarcastic and demeaning toward the physician and informed him with barely concealed contempt that he, the patient, probably knew more about running injuries than did the doctor.

The runner reacted angrily to his physician, demeaning him, but this really reflects the feeling that the runner had about himself: that the injury was an insult, a blow to his self-esteem. This anger becomes externalized and directed at the doctor, as if it were his failing, not the patient's. Consequently, the patient blames the doctor and becomes noncompliant, to the patient's detriment. Patients such as this tend to be those who were subjected to their parent's externalizations as children and were unable to satisfy their parent's demands and needs. When these "patients were infants their inborn capacities to elicit needed responses were ineffectual" (Novick & Novick, 1991, p. 313). In other words, their parents were not attuned to them and their needs were not met. These individuals tended toward rageful responses to their neglect, resulting in a kind of negative attention and a sense of omnipotence, since their rage would get the attention of an inattentive parent. This sense of omnipotence is not a realistic sense of efficacy and competence. Rather, it represents a fantasized and magical notion of power. These omnipotent strivings get activated when patients become ill, resulting in angry outbursts and noncompliance. The patient becomes furious at his or her disability (his or her impotence) and may refuse to believe in it seriousness, as if the patent has the power to magically conquer all sickness and disease.

In these cases, the original parental relationship was imbued with hostility and negativity, and this manifests itself in the present-day doctor-patient relationship. If the physician reacts negatively to the patient's attempts to portray him or her as at fault, the working relationship can be destroyed. The illness reminds these patients of their childhood dependent state, where they felt weak, incapable, and ineffectual. This is what gets projected onto the physician. Such a situation can even try the patience of a practitioner of the greatest equanimity. The physician can try to reorient the patient by emphasizing that they are united in working against a common enemy, the disease. The doctor can also empathize with the patient's distress and anger and articulate to how betrayed he or she must feel by his or her own body. In this fashion, the physician helps to maintain a cooperative and nonantagonistic relationship.

SUGGESTION. Maintaining composure in the midst of patients' projections is difficult. Patients may attempt to project their helplessness onto the physician. Helping patients to reorient to the treatment alliance is beneficial.

Oversuspiciousness

In medical practice and in other areas of life, a sense of suspiciousness, mistrust, and hostility has been on the increase. At times, doctors are not viewed as caring professionals operating out of concern for the patient but as adversaries trying to foist some unnecessary treatment onto an unsuspecting victim. Those prone toward this type of attitude will seek out confirmation of their beliefs and might join groups that feed their suspiciousness. Furthermore, realistic fears created by controversies over HMO's desires to minimize costs may fuel suspiciousness and distrust.

Example

> A couple was expecting their first child and had become involved
> in a childbirth support group that emphasized using few interven-
> tions, including no use of medication to stimulate labor. The physi-
> cian spoke with the couple about her concern that they would
> refuse treatment that she might find appropriate. The couple as-
> sured the doctor that they would follow her advice. However, the
> couple did refuse labor-stimulating medication during labor,
> eventuating in the baby developing a serious infection. The rela-
> tionship between doctor and patients became ruptured, and what
> should have been a wonderful experience became one of tension,
> distrust, and unnecessary illness.

The couple's attitude was one of suspiciousness and hostility toward the physician, as if she were trying to hurt them and
their baby. They had accepted the belief that patients need to
be suspicious of doctors lest some disservice be perpetrated
upon them. It is impossible to know what really went on in the
patients' minds. One might speculate that underneath their
veneer of certainty existed a great deal of concern about their
own competence, and this fear of inadequacy was projected
onto the doctor. In other words, it was the doctor, the hospital,
and the medical profession that were dangerous, not the patient and her husband. This kind of attitude is very difficult to
combat, and the best that the physician can do is to maintain
his or her professional manner and recognize that not all patients are going to be able to respond appropriately to the
physician. It is difficult for a caring and competent professional
to be characterized as nefarious.

SUGGESTION. Suspiciousness is all too prevalent in medical
practice. Practitioners need to maintain their confidence and
recognize that pleasing all patients is impossible.

TALKING TO THE PATIENT

Talking to patients about their personal qualities is very
difficult. Most people do what they can to avoid intense interactions, and health care professionals are no different. However,

the nature of medical practice necessitates the discussion of difficult, intense, and painful issues. Noncompliant behaviors are particularly difficult to discuss, since most patients tend to feel defensive because they are afraid of being accused of some wrongdoing. Confronting or challenging patients with non-compliant behavior is only useful if a very strong relationship is in place. Even if that relationship exists, most people do not respond well to extremely forceful interventions.

Mostly it is helpful to broach difficult subjects gently, with a questioning and curious attitude. The physician who encourages the patient to join him or her in a cooperative endeavor to figure out the reasons for noncompliant or unhealthy behavior is going to get better results than one who takes an accusatory and authoritarian stance.

Psychotherapists use *reframing* to help patients understand their behavior. Reframing refers to the process of understanding a patient and the material he or she presents from a different perspective and then communicating that new perspective to the patients. Patients develop certain explanations for their behavior and are often wedded to these explanations, even if they are not rational or are incomplete. For instance, a person may insist that he does not really eat very much and cannot explain weight gain. The truth of this may be suspect but the doctor may choose not to engage the patient in a discussion about calorie intake. Rather, it may be more profitable to reframe the problem into a discussion about the patient's emotional distress in general terms. Reframing helps the patient to think about his or her problems in a new and different way. It is usually done in a nonthreatening and inquiring fashion and tends to enlist the patient's interest and curiosity.

Example

A psychotherapy patient complained of unhappiness but could not identify points of dissatisfaction in his life. He spoke at length about his anger toward his teenage son and the demands that he made upon his father for rides to his various social activities. The therapist knew that the patient's history included significant early family losses and made the interpretation that the patient was really upset and distressed because his son was growing up and leaving him, representing another loss.

The therapist reframed the patient's distress, enabling him to see the problem from a different perspective. This emphasizes a broad perspective and encourages patients to become partners in problem solving.

SUGGESTION. Reframing refers to the process of providing the patient with a different perspective that opens the patient to new ways of considering problem behaviors.

When speaking about problem behaviors it is most helpful to ask open-ended questions and to listen very carefully to what patients say about their difficulties.

Example

Mr. P. had been in psychotherapy for awhile, and the therapist became aware that the patient was coming consistently late to his appointments. The issue was raised with Mr. P., who indicated that he was aware of the problem but did not know why he could not seem to make it on time. The therapist listened to the patient's further associations. He spoke about his difficulty with his wife, who seemed to be very unhappy with him. He seemed to have little influence over her, with her spending money unwisely and being quite uninterested in him. He also described a difficult job situation, in which he was underemployed and subject to the whims of his supervisor. He also spoke about his family, where he also felt belittled. The therapist wondered if the patient felt that he did not have much control in his life and that he was enacting that feeling within the therapy by being late. He could not control the day of the appointment, or the time of the appointment, or the length of the appointment, but he could control when he got there. The patient understood and identified with the therapist's interpretation. This is not to say that his behavior immediately changed. Rather, it opened an avenue of thought for the patient.

Interventions with patients should be as simple and experience-relevant as possible. Small changes that lead toward larger changes are more achievable and mean more to a patient. Suggesting that the preceding patient work harder at being on time will be of little help. He needed a context within which he could consider his noncompliant behavior and possible reasons for it. Through reframing and inviting the patient to consider possible reasons for the behavior, the physician is maintaining a positive working alliance and providing a framework for change.

SUGGESTION. Interventions should be as simple and specific as possible. Open-ended questions and enlisting the patient's curiosity are very important.

CONCLUSION

The nature of the doctor-patient relationship is one of the crucial determinants of the degree of compliance with the medical regimen. Practitioners who are warm and accepting, who show an interest in their patients and in their lives, and who can tolerate the vagaries of humanity are likely to foster compliance. Patients who tend toward noncompliance are those who have been raised in emotionally neglectful families where they were not provided with consistent and nurturing care. They tend to perceive themselves as being weak and ineffective and view their illnesses as narcissistic injuries. They often project their sense of inadequacy onto the physician and consequently devalue the medical treatment prescribed. Physicians can facilitate compliance by providing a framework within which the patient can explore and understand his or her behavior. Some patients are too invested in the sick role and resist the practitioner's efforts. The physician must accept his or her limitations, maintain a professional manner, and not be infected by the patient's negativism.

SUMMARY

1. Noncompliance can be defined as the patient's refusal to follow prescribed treatment recommendations.
2. The relationship between doctor and patient affects compliance.

3. There are a number of physician behaviors that facilitate compliance; becoming better acquainted with the patient, becoming more aware of the patient's lifestyle, providing clear instructions, inquiring about the patient's feelings, being appropriately self-disclosing, and being able to accept negative feelings from the patient.
4. An authoritarian attitude tends to alienate patients and does not facilitate compliance.
5. A warm, accepting, hopeful, and empathic physician promotes compliance.
6. Patients from enmeshed families have difficulty in compliance if it represents separation and loss.
7. Setting small goals and being specific in treatment recommendations is helpful to patients.
8. It is important for the physician to look for and to tolerate negative feelings from the patient.
9. Angry and frustrated feelings are acceptable and inevitable for health care workers as long as they are expressed appropriately.
10. Ego strength, evident in the quality of a patient's interpersonal relationships, will provide an assessment of his or her capability to respond to difficult treatment regimens.
11. Patients resist treatment as a way of avoiding emotional pain. It is important to realize that resistance is ingrained and is usually not conscious.
12. Patients from a background of neglect often feel out of control and may sabotage treatment in order to feel some control. They may also feel more comfortable in the sick role.
13. Negative therapeutic reaction is the attempt to deny the effectiveness of the treatment. Physicians often react angrily to patient's wish to destroy their sense of effectiveness.
14. Reframing refers to providing patients with a new perspective that helps them react to their situation with a new understanding.
15. Interventions should be as specific as possible and should emphasize achievable goals.

4

Psychological Disorders

Probably no other area in the field of medicine causes practitioners as much anguish as do psychological disorders. Practitioners want to tend to patients' physical problems and yet are constantly barraged by the impact of emotional disorders. Either psychological disorders interfere with treatment, or the patient's problems are directly attributable to emotional problems. Medical practitioners tend not to understand emotional and behavioral disorders. This lack of understanding combined with a preference for dealing with physical problems creates tension for the physician and for other health care providers.

Psychological disorders can be viewed from the perspective of several major explanatory models (see Chapter 1). It would be helpful to compare the medical versus the psychodynamic models in terms of psychopathology. The medical model is essentially descriptive, in that psychological disorders are viewed from a symptom orientation. For instance, a diagnosis of an anxiety disorder within the medical model will include a listing of the symptom picture expected, with criteria for the diagnosis. It is not explanatory. Nor does it speak of the personality characteristics expected within each disorder. If personality characteristics are given, they are again provided as a listing, not in a way that describes a living, breathing human being. The foremost example of this medical model is the *Diagnostic and Statistical Manual of Mental Disorders*, or *DSM-IV* (American

Psychiatric Association, 1994). It describes psychological disorders as discrete entities as if they were physical diseases, easily cataloged. The psychodynamic model is also descriptive but is more comprehensive in providing a picture of an individual, not just a disease.

It may seem easier and appealing to an orderly mind to adopt a purely descriptive, statistical way of thinking of psychological disorders, yet that does not do justice to the complexity of people. Psychological problems are not distinct from the individual. Rather, the problem pervades the person, creating consequences in countless ways. A depressed person has psychological problems in many areas of his or her life. It is not a simple matter of providing a "cure" of the depressive affect in order to alleviate the problems of the individual. The emotional disorder is part and parcel of the whole person.

Example

A patient sought out psychotherapy for treatment of depression. As is typical, the psychologist performed an assessment of the patient prior to beginning treatment. He did find her to be depressed, but not seriously so. Rather, he found a perpetually unhappy, anxious, and "lost" person, someone who had gone through the motions in living her life and never felt directed or satisfied with her activities. It was as if she had little sense of self, of ambition, or of desire. Passion in her life was absent. Once treatment began, her depression rapidly lifted and the paucity of her internal life became more apparent and was a major emphasis in the treatment.

The depressive affect and sense of hopelessness were caused by the emptiness of her life, and this sense was pervasive. It is important to note that her life did not really lack substance. She had a family, was well liked, and had many friends and social activities. It was her sense of herself as being detached, isolated, and unfocused that was the real problem. An approach that focuses on "depression" as a disease would miss the boat with this patient and deny her an opportunity to find real satisfaction in her life.

This broad approach applies to all of the disorders discussed in this and subsequent chapters. In this sense, it is hoped that the patient as person will emerge, rather than the disorder or disease as distinct from the individual.

SUGGESTION. An approach that emphasizes the whole person and not just the disorder does justice to the complexity of people and is more meaningful than a purely descriptive, symptom-based perspective.

SYMPTOM CHOICE

While the emphasis should be on the whole person, it is often the symptom that the patient is distressed by and wants treatment for. The helping professions organize difficulties into categories or disorders that have cohesiveness and have meaning. It is reasonable to look at patients based on the symptoms that they present. Intuitively it makes sense to assume that some commonality exists among those with similar conditions.

Why do different people develop different psychological and behavioral disorders? Unquestionably, disorders run in families, either through heredity, learning, or some combination. Heritability is much discussed, but is a source of controversy and is unproven for most psychological disorders. At this juncture, etiology is of secondary concern. It is more important that the disorders be understood phenomenologically. From the psychodynamic perspective, two approaches are salient. One, exemplified by Charles Brenner (1991), an eminent psychoanalyst, suggests that symptom choice should be given little emphasis since what is primarily important is the underlying conflict that gives rise to the symptom. The second, proposed by David Shapiro (1965, 1981), another well-known psychoanalyst, suggests that disorders pervade a given person and that, for instance, a depressed person will have a certain character style that is important to understand and attend to. An approach that gives voice to both orientations is the view that while the underlying conflicts and problems are of basic importance, it is also essential to understand that the symptoms developed by the underlying issues give rise to pervasive, enduring personality characteristics. The relevance to medical practice is that the practitioner needs to give attention to the symptom being presented, while recognizing that underlying feelings, conflicts, and issues are fueling the symptoms and are of primary etiological importance.

SUGGESTION. Symptoms do not exist in isolation. Enduring personality qualities and underlying conflicts and deficits are important in understanding a given individual.

The term "deficits" refers to developmental deficits. Use of this term in describing psychological problems implies that they have arisen out of inadequacies within the patient's background. A patient with an inattentive and distracted parent is going to grow up with deficits in his or her ability to function adequately in the world. In a sense, his or her psychological growth and development have been stunted, and this affects the person's level of functioning. Those suffering from "conflicts" are viewed as people at odds with themselves. They may feel inhibited because of internal prohibitions against certain behaviors and thoughts. There is controversy within the field as to whether conflicts or deficits are the major source of psychological disorders. Like with most things, there is truth in both viewpoints, and most people with emotional difficulties have suffered developmental difficulties and are in conflict with themselves. As medical practitioners, it is important to realize that the symptoms presented in the examining room are only "the tip of the iceberg" and that much remains hidden from the practitioner and from the patient.

The importance of human relationships in the etiology of psychological disorders cannot be overemphasized. Humans are social beings, and difficulties that develop do so within the context of relationships. One's level of psychological health depends greatly on the quality of relationships that one experienced as a child. This is not to ignore constitutional and idiosyncratic variables. Patients' difficulties arise out of the interplay between constitutional qualities, family relationships, external events, and unconscious fantasy elaboration. The variable of family relationships is most important in determining ego strength. Consequently, psychological disorders will manifest themselves within the doctor-patient relationship because relationships are of paramount significance. This further explicates the reasons for the utility of the transference relationship within the psychotherapeutic relationship.

SUGGESTION. Psychopathology is formed within the context of relationships. Consequently, psychological difficulties are likely to become manifest within the doctor-patient relationship.

THE ANXIOUS PATIENT

Anxiety represents a warning signal. It is a sign to the patient that something in the future is going to occur that is going to be problematic. Anxiety is not a disease, it is an artifact of the human condition. Anxiety has adaptive value in the sense that it warns one of impending danger. Unfortunately, anxious responses become irrationally activated, such that the impending danger is not always real or rational.

Basic fears can be categorized. People are afraid of losing a sense of being loved, of being lovable, of being capable and effective, and of being safe, and also are afraid of being overwhelmed, of feeling guilty, and of being punished. The anxious reactions that people experience have at bottom the fear that something terribly unpleasant is going to occur that is outside of their control. Patients are not typically aware of the reasons for their anxiety and only wish for it to be eliminated. Anxiety is so aversive that patients' attempts to avoid it become desperate. Excessive anxiety can result in drug and alcohol abuse, overeating, and difficult and troublesome interpersonal relationships.

Generalized Anxiety

Those who suffer from generalized anxiety tend to respond to many situations with anxious reactions. It is a pervasive personality style whereby the individual generally anticipates the worst and reacts to many situations with anxiety.

The reasons for the anxiety vary greatly from person to person. Some people have been raised in families where anxiety is pervasive, and they have learned to view the world through an anxious lens. Others are not confident of their ability to meet the challenges of life, and each new situation creates fears of failure. Others have had experiences in their lifetime that have been very difficult. They tend to imagine the worst and are greatly afraid of reexperiencing the overwhelming feelings created within the original trauma.

Example

Mrs. J. had experienced a horrific childhood with recurring sexual and physical abuse. She developed a severe anxiety disorder that was incapacitating. She could barely leave the house, was unable to tolerate employment, and assiduously avoided interpersonal relationships. The original traumas had been generalized to the world, such that she felt endangered anywhere outside of her own house. Every person she met became a potential perpetrator and every new experience represented a potential assault.

Mrs. J. had not developed the ego strength necessary to confront the world more effectively. She felt inadequate to the tasks of living in the world as a competent adult.

Visits to physicians are likely to activate anxiety because of the uncertainty of the examination. Even routine exams engender anxiety, producing the well-known increased blood pressure readings at doctors' offices. Patients are uncomfortable undressing and exposing themselves to the doctor. This exposure can represent psychological exposure, in that the patient becomes anxious lest some secret become symbolically uncovered.

Example

A patient became quite anxious upon a visit to his ophthalmologist. He had trouble understanding his anxiety because he was not worried about his vision. He discussed this difficulty with his therapist, who suggested that his anxiety was being generated by his concern that the doctor was seeing something "bad" or "naughty" when peering in his eyes.

In this instance, the ophthalmologist had no idea that the patient was anxious. It was only the patient who was uncomfortable. Since practitioners are so comfortable in doing what they are doing, they sometimes forget the level of anxiety that people routinely experience. Anxiety of this type need not be of great concern to the practitioner since it is not severe or serious and has little impact on the treatment. However, it is helpful to keep in mind that most patients experience some anxiety during examinations. Many patients will calm down considerably if the physician makes an empathic comment if anxiety is noted.

There are some patients, however, whose anxiety is overwhelming and is problematic to them and to the practitioner.

Example

> Mrs. I. visited her internist because of intolerable anxiety. She could not sleep, experienced waves of panic, and felt beside herself with terrible anxiety. She was having marital problems, but the physician had no real sense how that might have created such anxiety. She prescribed tranquilizing medication and referred her for psychotherapy. Before the patient left, the internist lectured her on the dangers of becoming dependent on the medication and suggested that she convey this to the patient's new therapist.

The referral to the therapist was perfectly appropriate and well considered. The lecture on the medication was a bit ill-advised because the patient felt that the doctor disapproved of her and of her condition and was unsympathetic. In this type of situation, a referral to a therapist, a consultation with the therapist, and then a decision on a prescription would have probably worked better. The physician may have felt uncomfortable in prescribing a potentially dangerous medication without a sense of control, and a consultation with the therapist may have alleviated that concern.

It can be seen with this patient that the presenting precipitant (marital difficulties) had some connection with the degree of anxiety being presented. Certainly, marital difficulties are likely to create anxiety, but the patient was incapacitated by feelings of panic. As with most symptoms, the underlying issues were obscure to both patient and doctor. This particular patient had great fears of being alone and of being unlovable. Her marital difficulties triggered old memories of times in which her mother was absent from the home. She interpreted her mother's absence as a rejection, and the feelings of anger and despair were very difficult for the young child to tolerate. These feelings came flooding back and created severe anxiety.

The physician is not in a position to be able to ascertain the underlying problems, and a referral out is necessary and appropriate. With this patient and other anxious ones, anxiety reactions to stress are common, usual, and expected. Anxious people tend to imagine the worst, seem to feel that they have little control over the future, imagine that the future will be disastrous, and are fearful for their well-being. Anxiety reactions are expectations of disaster. The expectations are typically irrational, but the patient is likely to be resistant to reassurance. The anxiety reactions are based on expectations from unconscious sources and are not readily available for conscious alleviation. Regardless, because of the positive transference relationship between the doctor and patient, an anxious patient can feel reassured and calmed by a composed and confident physician. Many anxious patients feel much better after their appointments, provided that they have been given the opportunity to express their concerns. The benign authority of the doctor can be used to advantage to reassure the patient that the reality of the situation may not be as bleak as imagined.

SUGGESTION. Anxious patients are not easily calmed, although reassurance should be attempted and can be helpful. Providing the patient with an opportunity to articulate his or her concerns can be beneficial.

It is important for the practitioner to remember that anxious patients have little or no control over their anxiety. Excessive anxiety is quite noxious and patients would not experience it if they could. Being dismissive or disapproving of anxiety reactions only creates bad feelings and makes the patient feel worse.

Generalized anxiety can be considered "free-floating anxiety" that is waiting for an opportunity to attach itself to an outside event or occurrence. A medical problem provides a venue for the anxiety to be actualized.

Example

Mr. H. was in a panic when he called and requested an appointment with his internist. He was suffering heart palpitations and was convinced that he was seriously ill. He was examined and given a battery of tests, including an electrocardiogram (EKG) and a stress test, and was found to be in good health. The physician knew Mr. H. to be a rather anxious person but had no sense of the precipitant, if any, for the panic reaction. The patient initially was uncomfortable in informing the doctor of his recent extramarital affair, but was able to divulge the secret once asked about any stresses he might be experiencing. The patient was reassured about his physical health, and it was suggested that he address his personal and marital difficulties either with the doctor or with a therapist.

This patient's guilt and anxiety over his misbehavior created a strong anxiety reaction, which manifested itself in a concern about his health. The doctor did not lecture him on the morality of his behavior, which would not have been productive. Instead he was helped to see that he was uncomfortable with his behavior, as evidenced by his panic, and that in order to feel better he needed to resolve his conflicts. The physician was also able to reorient the patient so that he could understand that he was in control of his reactions and that the anxiety was not totally irrational and mysterious. Patients sometimes become panicked about their panic and feel as if their emotions are outside of their control. Identification of the issues stimulating the panic helps put the patient back in charge of his or her life.

SUGGESTION. Anxiety reactions have precipitants, and their identification can lead to relief. Patients may be uncomfortable with facing the responsibility for their reactions, but doing so will help them regain a sense of control.

Many patients come to believe that their anxious or emotional reactions are "crazy" or nonsensical. They become hesitant to remark upon their concerns, fearing that the doctor will think less of them for having such silly concerns. Emotions or thoughts that are not understood are the ones that are labeled as "crazy," and it is quite helpful to encourage patients to articulate their worries even if these ideas seem irrational. Patients tend to have many misconceptions about medical matters, which can exacerbate their anxiety. At times, the practitioner needs to ferret out concerns and anxieties. A certain hesitancy, or perhaps a look of uncertainty, may suggest an unexpressed concern. Questioning the patient at the moment may save the physician from an urgent late night phone call.

Anxious patients tend to have trouble sleeping. Their concerns and worries tend to become stronger when they are not distracted by everyday concerns. Furthermore, nighttime tends to elicit more irrational fears. The childhood preoccupation with the dark revisits the anxious patient. Freud referred to dreams as the "royal road to the unconscious." Thus, many patients are unconsciously afraid of sleep because of the fear that they will have upsetting dreams. One's control is considerably loosened by sleep, resulting in the fantastically varied nature of dreams. Dreams have meanings that are often hidden to the patient. Dream interpretation is an integral part of intensive psychotherapy and can provide considerable information to therapists and patients. Obviously, office practitioners are not engaging in psychotherapy. Regardless, patients with sleep disturbance and with troubling dreams are struggling, and it can be helpful to question patients about life stressors. At the very least, the patient can begin thinking about himself or herself and about what may be troubling, with the idea being planted that the disturbing thoughts and feelings are potentially comprehensible.

Anxiety reactions are so pervasive and can have so many sources that it is often difficult to pinpoint its origin. Those from more intact families can have anxiety reactions that are problematic but are most likely not debilitating. Those who have experienced abuse, neglect, or abandonment can have anxiety that is intense and that can be disabling.

Example

A patient sought out psychotherapy because of panic attacks that prevented her from functioning as a physician. She had worked in a very busy hospital emergency room on varying shifts. The intensity of her work along with its unpredictability felt overwhelming to her, and she was overcome with panic attacks prior to work. The panic became so consuming that she was unable to function and needed to take a leave from her position. Her psychotherapy helped her to see that the intensity of her patients' difficulties and helplessness reminded her of long-suppressed memories of her parents' violent relationship and brought back those original feelings of anxiety, helplessness, and impending doom. In the emergency room she felt like that helpless, overwhelmed child, not the competent physician that she was. Psychotherapy helped her to address those unresolved issues and helped to strengthen her ego so that she was more able to tolerate the difficulties of life.

At first look, this patient seemed perplexing. She was accomplished, always had been, and people were astonished, as was she, at her difficulties. It was only when her life was examined in total did her difficulties become comprehensible.

At times, those with abusive or neglectful backgrounds are quite anxious but have little sense of what may be troubling them in their life.

Example

Ms. X. was an intelligent professional woman who had pervasive problems with anxiety. She had had polio as a child because her parents refused to give her the vaccine. While not physically neglectful in other ways, her parents were uninterested in her, and she grew up mostly alone. She would often become inconsolably upset but could not identify the precipitants of her distress. It was as if there was a gap between the external stimulating events and her distress. Since she had difficulty articulating her difficulties, her physicians were confused as to how they could help. Her psychotherapy was trying to help her increase her self-awareness. For many years she had neglected her physical health, which mirrored her early neglect. Fortunately, she began to address some of her physical problems and eventually was diagnosed with postpolio syndrome. She became enormously distraught, such that her physician wanted her antidepressant medication to be increased. Her therapist suggested that her distress was not out of bounds and that she was experiencing fears and concerns about her present situation but also about the terror that she had felt during the original trauma of having polio. Continued psychotherapy helped her to articulate past and present concerns, and the distress was greatly reduced.

SUGGESTION. Anxiety is a common problem. Its specific precipitants are often obscure. Abused and neglected patients need assistance in making connections between their anxiety, external stressful events, and past difficulties.

Those from backgrounds of neglect and abuse do not have the capability to soothe themselves. As children their parents were not attuned to their discomfort and were not available for comfort. This self-soothing capability was not internalized, and the person can, in the present, become terribly distraught over seemingly minor incidents. It is similar to an inconsolable infant. At times physicians get very impatient with patients who react so extremely to minor events. This represents the reenactment of the patient's childhood experience, wherein their distress was met by irritation and distance. The physician as a positive transference object can be helpful in assisting the patient to calm down by being tuned into their distress and by being available to them, unlike their parents of childhood. The patient can then use the physician as a soothing object to help him or her relax. Some of that soothing quality may be internalized.

Example

An extremely anxious woman was about to embark upon a business trip. She was afraid of flying and of being in strange places. As she became anxious, she found herself visualizing her physician's face and was able to feel more relaxed.

The physician had replaced the parent's negative and anxious parental connection, which allowed the patient to feel calmer and more in control.

Most patients with very problematic backgrounds are very much afraid of being in situations where they might feel overwhelmed. When they were children, they experienced incidents that were far beyond their capability to process. Children have immature egos, and those who have experienced trauma are not capable of integrating the experience. As adults they tend to experience problems as if they are traumas and may again feel overwhelmed. Those whose parents were neglectful also have not developed the ego strength necessary to deal with difficult situations and thus tend to become overwhelmed. The physician's calm and confident manner goes a long way toward helping the patient maintain his or her equilibrium. At times anxious patients become quite provocative by being demanding and acting as if they are the only ones who have ever experienced distress and discomfort. It is important to remember that these patients have lost much of their coping ability and feel panicked by the situation.

Example

Mrs. E. went through what she considered to be a horrible childbirth experience. As far as she was concerned, her pain was excruciating, unbearable, and probably worse than all but a few. She was very difficult throughout her labor, alienating the medical staff with her complaints and demands. She was inconsolable throughout. Soon after the birth, she felt much better and was able to respond appropriately to her husband and to the hospital staff.

In general, Mrs. E. was able to cope with the demands of life. It was only under the extreme stress of childbirth that her coping ability deteriorated. In general everyday situations she had sufficient ego strength to cope. The added pressure from the childbirth was more than she could comfortably handle. In this type of situation, it is best for the hospital staff to remain supportive, even though that is hard to do under provocation.

SUGGESTION. Patients from neglected and abusive backgrounds will feel overwhelmed under stress. Providing supportiveness and understanding will bolster ego strength and coping abilities.

Some patients are so incapacitated by their anxiety that they are not capable of making wise and rational decisions. Physicians and other health care professionals are then required to take a more proactive stance than usual in order to protect the patient.

Example

A patient had always been deathly afraid of being diagnosed with cancer. Her mammogram showed an area that caused the radiologist to request a retake of the mammogram. The patient became so panicky that she was unable to make the appointment, and her doctor had to become quite forceful and insist that an appointment be made. When the patient was still too terrified, the doctor's office staff made the appointment for the patient.

The patient's extreme anxiety was so incapacitating that the doctor and the office staff functioned as an "auxiliary" ego to assist the patient. Patients may need extra assistance in times of great stress until they can regain their equilibrium.

SUGGESTION. In times of extreme stress doctors and staff may need to function as an auxiliary ego by providing extra support and assistance.

Pediatricians are well versed in working with anxiety. Nowhere does anxiety find a more welcome venue than in parents' concerns about their children. Parents feel tremendous responsibility for the welfare of their children. A child's illness can make parents feel like bad parents regardless of the reality of the situation. Most parents feel that it is their responsibility to ensure that their child remains healthy, and many blame themselves if the child falls ill. Additionally, parents often relive their own childhoods through their children and feel the anxiety related to parental responsibility as well as the anxiety that they felt as children. Children, with their immature egos, have trouble understanding that which transpires around them, including their own and others' illnesses. Those parents with a history of childhood illness or those whose family suffered illnesses can become quite anxious when either they or their children become ill.

Example

Mrs. S. was a mother of a young boy who developed asthma. Whenever he experienced symptoms, she rushed him to the hospital in a panic. Her anxiety was transmitted to the child, which exacerbated his symptoms because it created anxious feelings within him. Her intense, demanding, and angry manner alienated the hospital staff, and these asthma episodes became ordeals for all concerned.

This mother was a woman of tremendous guilt who was deathly afraid that punishment for her imagined sins would be visited upon her son. She was also raised within a family that was quite superstitious. Such families have little sense of control over their lives and become superstitious to explain that which they do not understand. The mother grew up with little confidence in the future, always expecting the worst, and felt little trust in health care practitioners because she felt little confidence in her parents' ability to take care of her. Consequently, she was terrified that she could not adequately take care of her child, and this sense of incompetence was projected onto the doctors treating her son. This woman needed reassurance and counsel as to the level of seriousness of her son's asthma. It would be helpful for the health care practitioners to recognize the fearfulness that was hidden behind her angry and demanding behavior instead of reacting angrily to her anger. Her concerns needed to be taken seriously despite the fact that they were exaggerated.

Anxious people tend to want definitive answers. They want to know that their worst fears are not going to be realized. This creates a dilemma for the health care provider since such assurances can rarely be given. It is important not to be seduced into giving false reassurances in an attempt to allay the patients' or parents' anxieties. Helping parents to stay realistic but hopeful is the best course of action.

SUGGESTION. Anxious parents can become demanding and belligerent, which is probably reflective of their concerns about their own adequacy. Realistic reassurance with acceptance of their anxiety is helpful.

Focused Fears

Some patients do not consciously experience generalized anxiety but have focused their concerns onto one organ system. This will be addressed further in Chapter 6, in the section on psychosomatic disorders, but a brief example will be helpful here.

Example

A patient was referred to a psychotherapist because of vaginismus. She would become extremely anxious prior to a gynecological examination, and this anxiety would trigger the involuntary contraction of the muscles surrounding her vagina. She would experience the same problem with intercourse. Her gynecologist was quite patient with her, as was her husband, but the vaginismus continued. Extensive evaluation indicated no obvious history of sexual abuse. The patient indicated that she was frightened of something "foreign" being placed in her vagina, felt that her vagina was too small to accommodate either an erect penis or a speculum and was afraid that her vagina would become damaged by either. She also felt that her vagina, along with menstrual blood, was "dirty," and she really wanted to ignore that whole area of her body. Psychotherapy was successful in helping her to articulate her fears, which resulted in some diminution of her anxiety. However, her closing-off tendency, evidenced by her vaginismus, extended to the rest of her personality such that she was reluctant to let the therapist "in" also.

Although the problem initially seemed to be rather narrow and confined to her sexual functioning, further analysis indicated that the problem was pervasive and was reflective of a personality style. She was extremely private and guarded in general and was afraid of many feelings, not just sexual ones. There was no obvious reason for her difficulties, which was frustrating for the patient and perplexing for those trying to help her. No amount of reassurance seemed to help. She was able to get some relief by having the opportunity to elaborate and to articulate her fears. Her concerns about her body were issues that she was vaguely aware of but had never really put into words. In the patient's mind, she was relatively carefree and unconcerned, other than regarding the issue of her sexual functioning. She had reduced and simplified her concerns into a rather narrow area that she felt more comfortable in dealing with. In reality, her difficulties were not substantially different from others with anxiety disorders.

SUGGESTION. At times anxiety seems more focused and less pervasive. This is usually reflective of an attempt to cope, but there are likely to be still other, broader, psychological difficulties that are less obvious.

DEPRESSED AND DISTRESSED PATIENTS

Depression is a disorder that manifests itself in a variety of ways. At times, depression is not evident to the practitioner or to the patient's friends and family. A person may be quite depressed, yet be able to put on a false front such that those close to him or her are completely surprised to find out the extent of suffering. Additionally, some individuals suffer from depression yet would not label themselves as being depressed. They know that they are unhappy but hesitate to attach the label to themselves. Many will tell themselves that their despair is temporary or transitory and will lift once an external stressor is removed. Unfortunately, some will go their whole lifetime being unhappy without ever seeking out treatment or even completely acknowledging their distress.

Example

A couple was seen for marriage counseling. They described themselves as having a good relationship but were concerned because of frequent bickering and difficulties in communicating. The marital difficulties were resolved very quickly, yet the wife remained unhappy. With further discussion it was determined that she had been terribly distressed for years yet had hardly admitted it to herself. Given the opportunity, she was eager to begin psychotherapy, progressed well, and was able to resolve her underlying difficulties.

This patient was given the opportunity to identify and work on some difficulties that she was only vaguely aware of prior to treatment. It is a common occurrence that patients, while aware of unhappiness, have little conscious sense of the degree or the source of their distress. Marital counseling can be very successful, yet it often highlights for each participant their contributions to the marital difficulties. Individuals hope that the marriage counseling will be the salve but often find that their problems go beyond those found in their marriage.

There are some definitional problems with depression as well, since it describes both an emotion and a disorder. Depressed affect refers to a feeling of sadness, a feeling of being "down in the dumps." A depressive disorder is much broader and includes feelings of despair, lethargy, and hopelessness. Fatigue is often present as is lack of interest in everyday life. Those more seriously depressed have lost the zest for life and see no positives in the future. A depressed person may sleep too much, may eat too little (or too much), and may use alcohol or drugs to self-medicate. Depressed people can be irritable and withdrawn. They tend to lose interest in pleasurable activities and suffer from feelings of inadequacy. Their attention span may appear limited and they seem preoccupied. Some very energetic, "hyper" people are fighting off a depressive process. The depressive category can be very inclusive and as such has lost some of its meaningfulness. Regardless, many people present themselves as depressed, and this disorder or syndrome is often seen in medical practitioners' offices.

Individuals also present themselves to the physician with distressed affects. This describes an emotional state that is not really anxiety or depression. The patient is "upset." They may be tearful without any obvious reason and may feel out of control and overwhelmed. Their relationships may be problematic, with the patients feeling angry and irritable. They feel out of sorts and inconsolable.

Example

> Mrs. L. asked for a referral to a mental health professional for what she described as depression. She met with the therapist, and it was quite clear that she would qualify for a diagnosis of a depressive disorder. She was sad, lacked energy, and felt hopeless. She spent much of her time lying on the couch feeling little energy or desire to do anything. The depressive picture also included strong feelings of emptiness and a longing for peace and comfort. At times she would become unbearably upset without apparent provocation. She often felt overwhelmed by the demands of everyday life.

To label this woman as simply "depressed" is not sufficiently descriptive or explanatory. Certainly her symptoms fit the diagnostic requirements, and she does fall under the general rubric of "depressed," but to label her such without further explorations of her underlying dynamics is simplistic and does her a disservice. She was besieged by feelings of emptiness and a sense of being overwhelmed. The depressive label should be used with caution and with the understanding that it describes a wide range of behaviors and emotions that have complex and varied causes.

SUGGESTION. Depression is not a discrete diagnostic entity. It describes an affect as well as a disorder. The disorder is complex and has various causes.

Depressive disorders run the gamut from mild to severe. In its most serious case, depression can eventuate in incapacitation resulting in hospitalization. Suicide is the ultimate tragedy of depressive disorders. Suicidal behavior will be addressed later in this chapter.

Theorists view depression from a number of different angles. Some emphasize the role of personal loss in depression. Others suggest that it results from punitive feelings over perceived wrongdoings. Still others will look toward neglectful and/or abusive backgrounds for its etiology. Of course, there are many in the mental health field who postulate a biological/ genetic basis for depression. The psychodynamic approach offers a perspective on depression that is experiential—that explains and elucidates the patient's experience of his or her distress and allows it to be understandable and meaningful.

Following the earlier discussion about symptom formation, it is important to remember that many different life experiences will give rise to both depressive affect and to depressive disorders. In a sense, depression is a symptom that indicates that an individual is struggling with unresolved and not-understood issues. For instance, a diagnosis of depression may mean that an individual is having difficulty in coping with feelings from some trauma and that these difficulties express themselves through depressive affect. Nevertheless, there is some commonality amongst those who suffer from a primary depressive disorder. Issues concerning loss, neglect, and anger contribute most significantly to the establishment of depression.

Loss and Anger

The connection between depression and loss was first established by Freud (1917/1955). He suggested that melancholia was very similar to the mourning that people experienced after the death of a loved one. With severe depression, however, the individual is not able to recover from the death and the mourning turns into melancholia. He postulated an underlying ambivalence toward the deceased, with resulting guilt and self-punitiveness. Freud suggested that the patient harbored hostile feelings toward the deceased and that these feelings become internalized and directed back toward the patient, resulting in self-hatred and melancholia. Certainly, in some cases, a person's hostility does result in guilty feelings. It is quite common for people to imagine that their hostile feelings have resulted in a person's downfall. They then become guilty and feel the need to punish themselves via depressive affect. One question to ponder is why such hostility exists in the first case. Hostility and competitiveness are facts within human relationships.

However, not everybody develops psychological disorders. Consequently, it is likely that there were difficulties within the relationship that exacerbated the normal degree of competitiveness and hostility.

Example

A 35-year-old man sought out psychotherapy because of recurrent depression. He was a highly intelligent and sensitive man, yet could not situate himself professionally. His college studies were shaped by a "pre-law" focus, but he never applied to law school. He did not feel that he had the internal fortitude to function in a responsible position. Therapy helped him discover that his normal competitiveness was inhibited by his fears of hurting his rather passive, ineffectual, and depressed father. His fear of losing his father through aggressive competition caused his inhibition. The eventual death of his father exacerbated his depression, and his fear of his own powerfulness caused him to become more passive and ineffectual. Psychotherapy helped him identify these issues, and he was able to use his aggressiveness in productive ways.

This patient's fear of his own aggression and his fear of losing his father resulted in a sense of incompetence and depressed affect. However, this existed within the context of a father who had significant psychological difficulties himself. In this instance, the reaction to the loss of his father coupled with his unresolved and unacknowledged aggression contributed to his depression. Being able to articulate and to understand angry feelings is very important in the treatment of depressive disorders. Many depressed people have anger that is embedded within them to the extent that they feel blocked and inhibited. Their angry feelings seem dangerous and best left unacknowledged, but the suppression of these feelings can increase depressed feelings. Once individuals are able to articulate the reasons for their anger, they often feel much better.

Example

A significantly depressed man had suppressed all awareness of how angry he was toward his wife and daughter. He felt that they took

advantage of him and did not really care for him. His drinking
was related to his wish to get back at them, yet this made him feel
guilty and he punished himself through his depression. Once
aware of this sequence, he was able to talk with his family about
his feelings of being unloved.

Mourning

Individuals in mourning will show themselves in the physician's office. If a personal history is taken, the doctor can become aware of any recent family losses and can help the patient to make a connection between the recent death and the depression. Normal mourning with its attendant sad, guilty, and angry feelings will often persist for some period of time. This will be especially true if the death was unexpected and/or tragic.

Example

A sophomore in college was devastated after the death of her 43-year-old mother. She knew that her mother had had breast cancer but she, the family, and her mother had hoped that the latter would be able to remain in good health. After the death, the daughter's grades plummeted and she had difficulty in functioning in school. There were some difficulties in the family that exacerbated the normal grieving process. Regardless, the young woman needed time to be able to process the death and then to move on with her life, which she was able to do.

In this situation the death was certainly tragic, yet the woman was able to integrate the loss into her life without resorting to severe self-recriminations and attendant punishment.

Example

A 21-year-old young man called a therapist and asked for an appointment because of difficulty coping in college. His father, with a history of heart disease, had recently suffered a fatal heart attack. The son had a great deal of difficulty in articulating his feelings about the tragedy. His relationship with his father was markedly ambivalent, and he felt that he had never really pleased his father. In his treatment he was helped to become aware of his varied feelings toward his father and to experience the normal feelings of grief necessary for him to move beyond the death. He also became aware of how he had thwarted himself in his schooling because of his fears of being competitive with his father. His unresolved aggression made the death all the more unbearable.

This young man would have had difficulty in being successful in life had these issues not been addressed. It was not just the death of his father that caused him difficulty; it was the death in combination with his prior relationship and his level of emotional health.

SUGGESTION. An individual's difficulty in coping with a death is correlated with the person's level of mental health and with the nature of the relationship with the deceased.

There are some deaths that are so difficult and tragic that the survivors never really emerge unscathed. The death of a child, particularly at an early age, is a tragedy that most people never really recover from. The feeling of tragedy will always be with them.

Example

An adolescent girl died in a car crash at age 16. Forty years later, her father, at the age of 86, would become extremely emotional and upset when he thought of her death. He blamed himself for not teaching her to negotiate dirt roads better, imagining that better driving techniques would have saved her life.

The father's difficulty in getting over the death had some connection with his self-recriminations. This self-blaming is quite common when a child dies, since parents' feel it is their ultimate responsibility to ensure the safety of their children. This father felt he had failed his daughter and for some years became alcoholic. Some might consider this patient to have unresolved mourning and that some sort of therapeutic intervention would have been helpful. Without a doubt, psychotherapy would have helped this father, yet there are some tragedies that one can never really recover from. Scarring occurs that will continue to affect the person. It is important for the health care professional to recognize this reality, and not to decide that a reaction is pathological if one has not been able to put it aside.

SUGGESTION. Questioning a patient about losses, both past and present, can provide a clue into the precipitant of a depressive reaction. Some tragedies are not really resolvable.

Another loss that is difficult to resolve is that of suicide. The survivors of suicide are left with a multitude of unanswerable questions. They understandably feel tremendously hurt by the suicide and wonder how the loved one could have left them like that. It feels, and perhaps is, a rejection. Suicide feels embarrassing and shameful. It often is a hostile act, leaving the survivors with questions as to their responsibility. The survivors often blame themselves, feel enormously guilty, and wonder what they could have done differently. This reaction is labeled "survivor's guilt." It is pervasive and difficult to overcome. The survivor imagines that if he or she had done something differently, the suicide would not have occurred. No matter what the quality of the relationship was with the deceased, suicide is an individual decision that indicates individual psychopathology and is not created by another's actions. The physician can help the survivor to articulate his or her feelings and to reassure the person as to his or her lack of responsibility.

Any death is going to create strong feelings, and these feelings may be normal and expectable.

Example

A patient visiting her gynecologist explained that her father had recently died. She stated that she felt that she was coping adequately but that her family physician had wanted to put her on antidepressants. The gynecologist gave her an opportunity to talk about her loss, and the patient left feeling better and decided to see if she could manage without the medication.

The patient's reaction to the death appeared to be appropriate. She was emotional and upset, which is normal and desirable under the circumstances. She did not appear to need medication. Perhaps her family physician was uncomfortable with emotions. Those who have experienced personal losses need to have the opportunity to talk about their loss and should not be judged by some standard as to when they should be finished grieving.

SUGGESTION. Health care practitioners should be willing to allow patients with losses the opportunity to talk about the loss. Grieving is a lengthy process.

Unresolved mourning is seen when the individual becomes incapacitated and cannot come to grips with the loss. They may become negligent in hygiene and seem forgetful, preoccupied, and distracted. They may cry uncontrollably, have trouble eating and sleeping, and seem detached. Those with a preponderance of these symptoms should be referred for evaluation and treatment.

Some patients with difficulty in coping with a death have been too close to and dependent upon the deceased. This usually occurs in families where the parents have encouraged an unhealthy dependency. The patient may have appeared to have functioned well in the world, but the adjustment has been partially due to the dependency on the parents. It is as if the individual has not developed his or her own identity and therefore cannot function effectively once one or both parents dies. This state of affairs is particularly difficult for those attempting to treat such patients since their allegiance remains with the deceased; consequently, they have trouble developing a working alliance with either their physicians or with mental health professionals.

Example

Mrs. A. had been very depressed and despondent since the deaths of her parents, eight and five years ago, respectively. She had been unnaturally close to them and felt absolutely bereft after their deaths. Her husband was not viewed as being supportive, and she could not integrate the insights gained within her therapy. She was overweight but resisted all weight loss programs. She was encouraged to try antidepressant medication but she refused, fearing dependency on the drugs. In reality, she was maintaining her dependency on and allegiance to her deceased parents by not allowing any new relationships to have an effect or influence on her. In this fashion the tie with her parents remained intact.

A physician is not going to have much influence over such a patient since her struggles are so deep-seated and hidden. The physician's only real recourse is to remain supportive and encouraging toward healthy behaviors.

The Physician and Patients Struggling with Loss

Patients who struggle with the loss of significant people are ubiquitous. Oftentimes the health care professional may not be aware of the loss, or the patient's reaction may not impact significantly on treatment. It is most helpful to encourage patients to articulate their feelings and thoughts about the deaths of loved ones. Making oneself available for comfort and reassurance can be very helpful in moving a patient toward a working-through of the loss. Some physicians are uncomfortable with affects and do not delve into the patient's feelings. The patient ends up feeling even more isolated and abandoned. Some physicians attend funerals and memorial services of patients' family members, and this can be very valuable in communicating the doctor's concern for the patient. As a transference object the physician carries great weight, and his or her presence at a funeral can be very reassuring.

Not all losses are interpersonal. People become depressed in reaction to any number of losses. Loss of a job, a marriage, a relationship, or a sense of competence can create depression. In fact, where depression is evident and no loss is apparent, it would be helpful to look beyond the obvious for the precipitant. Often the patient may not be aware that he or she may be reacting to some outside occurrence.

Example

A patient visited his internist, complaining of depression. He seemed to have everything he wanted—a good marriage, successful children, and a recent retirement after a very satisfying career. The internist wondered with the patient if he was having difficulty with the retirement. The patient began to talk about his feeling that he was no longer important and was not contributing to society. He felt useless. Until questioned by the doctor he had no idea that he was troubled by his retirement. The discussion helped him to understand his distress, and he was then able to formulate plans for volunteer activities that would allow him to feel more useful.

The discussion with the physician was extremely helpful in clarifying for the patient the reason for the depression, which led to a corrective course of action.

Certainly job loss or the breakup of a marriage or relationship is likely to result in some depression, although not inevitably a serious one. Much depends on the circumstance of the loss. The health care professional can be helpful by encouraging the patient to articulate his or her feelings about the loss and to provide an opportunity for referral should the patient desire it.

Perhaps the loss most ignored involves the feelings engendered by physical disease and/or decline. It is commonly understood that the elderly suffer depression because of the losses they must endure. They lose friends, spouses, and their ability to function as they once had. They are powerless within this circumstance and often experience depression, sometimes profound. This also happens with younger people, who can become depressed if their physical condition results in a deterioration of their capabilities. The physician should always be alert to the possibility that the loss of physical health is contributing to the patient's depression.

SUGGESTION. Patients can react to job loss, a relationship termination, or a loss of a sense of competence with depression. Loss of physical capability can also result in depressed and hopeless feelings. Making the connection between the depression and the loss can help the patient feel more in control.

Powerlessness, Negativity, and Ambivalence

A hallmark of depression is the feeling of powerlessness. This pessimism may be seen in the doctor's office. A depressed patient who feels hopeless is not going to feel very cooperative with treatment regimens and may frustrate the physician.

Example

A patient was diagnosed with breast cancer. She was markedly overweight and depressed. She felt doomed and saw no real reason to pursue either weight loss programs or psychotherapy.

Those suffering from physical illnesses are somewhat powerless. They have to depend on the doctor, on medication, and on the progress of disease. They can do some things to enhance the probability of success, but much of the course of the disease is out of their control. Some patients are able to mobilize their resources such that they become determined to fight the disease, but those who have felt an inability to control significant others in their lives tend to feel powerless and discouraged when they fall ill. Assisting a patient to feel in control and effective can mitigate a depressive process. To do this the physician needs to keep the patient well informed as to the nature of the disease and treatment and to ensure that the patient realizes that he or she has a say in what transpires. Encouraging the patient to ask questions, to seek alternative sources of information, to join support groups, and to be an active partner in the treatment helps to maintain a sense of control and competence. Furthermore, a realistic yet positive attitude can counteract the expected negativity and pessimism of a depressed patient.

SUGGESTION. Enlisting the patient as partner in the treatment encourages a more active role that guards against a feeling of hopelessness and despair. Realistic encouragement is also helpful in fighting pessimism.

Depressed people have a negative outlook on life. They feel hopeless and pessimistic, and these feelings can interfere with treatment compliance. They may think that treatment is useless since they are not going to get better. Underlying issues may relate to a need for punishment, or they may identify with a parental figure who has died or who was also depressed. Since they are so wrapped up in themselves and take little sustenance or nurturance from others, it is difficult for the caregiver to have a significant impact.

Example

A patient was quite depressed and was put on antidepressant medication. His psychiatrist also suggested increased exercise and relaxation techniques. The patient seemed to be resistant to all interventions. He took the medication, which did not have significant effect (which confirmed his expectations), kept "forgetting" to exercise, and fought hard not to establish a relationship with the therapist. His need to remain in an isolated state was considerable. He had suffered significant interpersonal losses as a child, was determined not to take the chance of being hurt by present-day relationships, and so remained aloof. This created a very lonely and depressed life. The therapist did notice that regardless of how depressed the patient was at the beginning of the session, he would perk up noticeably as the session went on. The patient benefited from the relationship despite himself.

Depressed patients need significant interpersonal contact despite their disavowals. Encouraging a depressed patient to come back for more frequent appointments can be helpful. Their negativism serves to protect them from further hurt and disappointment. It is important for the physician not to allow himself or herself to also get discouraged, as this will only reinforce the patient's pessimism. Depression is not something that a person can get cajoled out of. It is most helpful to be respectful of the patient's distress and to try to listen to the patient in order to help him or her to understand the reasons for the distress.

SUGGESTION. Depressed patients are not trying to be negative and pessimistic. Listening carefully to the patient can communicate a sense of caring and can help the patient to reconnect with the world.

Some depressed patients exhibit marked ambivalence and indecisiveness. Partly this is due to their feelings of hopelessness. It is also due to the internalization of ambivalent feelings toward significant people. This can be vexing to the physician since the patient will not participate in decision making. Taking the decision making out of the patient's hands tends to make him or her feel more ineffective and unimportant and can increase the severity of the depression. It is best for the physician to encourage active participation in the treatment despite the patient's disavowal of interest.

Example

A woman became despondent and then suicidal. Her husband was encouraged to take her car keys away from her and to take all decision making away from her. Tragically, he found her hanging in the garage.

There is no way of knowing exactly what contributed to her suicide, and it is all too easy to condemn others in hindsight. However, taking away her sense of control and effectiveness probably reinforced her sense of hopelessness and made her feel more incompetent. Even severely depressed and poorly functioning patients should be continually encouraged to make decisions and should always be treated respectfully, even if their behavior is exasperating.

The Empty Depressed Patient

A number of patients seen in doctors' offices suffer from depression related to neglectful and abusive backgrounds. These individuals' depression is more severe, embedded, and characterological. They typically have suffered from feelings of emptiness and disconnectedness since childhood. They rarely form good relationships and feel alone and abandoned. These are people who were either left to themselves as children, were woefully misunderstood, were abandoned and neglected, or were physically and/or sexually abused. They have suffered from emotional abuse. The depression that is suffered by abused people is qualitatively different from those whose depression is related to loss. It is more severe, is more resistant to treatment, and exists within the context of a greater degree of general emotional disturbance. Their sense of depression is best described as a feeling of emptiness, and most experience this feeling as so noxious that they will do almost anything to avoid it. Drug and alcohol abuse, overeating, promiscuity, and other maladaptive behaviors are prevalent with such individuals. These behaviors are designed to ward off the terrible feelings of emptiness and depression. Hopelessness, despair, negativism, and ambivalence are also very common. The depression is likely to be secondary to a personality disorder. The most prevalent personality disorder is the borderline personality disorder, which will be addressed more fully in the next chapter.

Treatment of those suffering from this type of depression is difficult. The self-soothing function seen in less disturbed individuals is absent. Therefore, demandingness and dependency needs get expressed toward therapists and medical practitioners. Consequently, these patients tend to alienate their helpers. Since they had been abused as children, they do not view their caregivers as being helpful and concerned. They view them as potentially hurtful. The working alliance is difficult to establish and the transference can become imbued with negativity.

A healthy parent-child relationship enables an individual to grow up and to be able to form new and healthy relationships. Those from backgrounds with severe problems have trouble letting go of the parental relationship, even if that relationship continues to cause them difficulty. Their primary attachment to their mothers has never been resolved, and they feel enormous loyalty to them, despite having been abused. In the patient's mind, "The mother seems to have the exclusive right to provide loving, comforting and soothing, as if she had cornered the love market" (Krystal, 1988, p. 182). They are very reluctant to form a positive transference.

Example

A woman had a particularly bad relationship with both parents and had been moderately depressed throughout her life. She was embittered because of what she had not gotten from her parents, and this feeling permeated other relationships, including those with her doctors. While complaining about not getting what she needed from her caregivers, she became very much like her parents, thus remaining closely identified with them. She would not allow others to intrude upon this identification, resulting in a rather defiant attitude.

This is a difficult situation for the physician, where his or her influence is so limited. This type of depressed person needs psychotherapy in order to help him or her to detach from the parents. In the physician's office they are likely to be quite resistant and defiant because of their need to maintain connection with their parents. Good health may require them to form new attachments, and their fear of being separated from their parents causes them to resist new relationships, including therapeutic ones. In this kind of situation, the practitioner must work very hard at maintaining the alliance and can encourage the patient to do that which is most beneficial to his or her health.

SUGGESTION. Patients with a feeling of emptiness are very difficult to treat. They require enormous patience and sympathy from the physician.

These very disturbed patients are desperately in need of positive, caring relationships, despite their apparent resistance. Establishing a positive transference with someone suffering from such emptiness can be very rewarding.

Suicidal Patients

It is beyond the capability of general medical practitioners to diagnose and treat suicidal patients. However, there will be circumstances where nonpsychiatric physicians come into contact with suicidal patients through routine medical practice.

There will also be times when physicians become intimately involved with suicidal patients. It is an enormously draining and anxiety-arousing experience to work with a suicidal patient. They require extra time and care, and one should not become involved if one is not prepared to commit to the emotional intensity required.

People commit suicide for a variety of reasons. For many, the feeling of despair and hopelessness is overwhelming and the only solution seen is suicide. Suicidal patients are often angry and may use the suicide as a way of punishing and hurting others. Some people feel so bad about themselves that they fantasize that suicide will magically kill the bad part of themselves and that somehow the good side of them will endure. Other people feel so ashamed of their actions that they feel they cannot tolerate the expected embarrassment. Suicide is a violation of the social contract that exists between the patient and others in his or her circle. As such it only occurs out of desperation, when the individual feels he or she has run out of choices. Consequently, it is essential that suicidal patients be provided with control and choices within the context of their life-threatening activity. That is, although suicidal patients should not be allowed to make all the choices normally afforded to competent adults because their thinking is distorted and irrational. They need to be protected from harming themselves; yet they also need to be treated with dignity and respect and given the opportunity for choices, as long as those decisions do not lead to self-destructive actions.

Every suicidal patient should be referred to a mental health professional for treatment. Suicidal patients need proactive treatment, and one should not hesitate to act if suicidality is suspected. Some patients will allude to suicidality without elaborating. It is essential that these hints be followed up by questioning the patient further about his or her intent and whether any means of suicide have been decided upon. Contacting the patient's family, friends, or police is an appropriate and necessary action should the patient indicate suicidal intent, particularly if the means of self-destruction have been decided upon.

SUGGESTION. Suicidal patients should immediately be referred for treatment. Their threats should be taken seriously, and family, friends, or the police should be notified. Helping the patient maintain dignity and control is essential in maintaining the will to live.

Medication

Antidepressant medication is not curative. It can relieve some of the symptoms of depressive disorders. It is not a panacea and should generally be prescribed within the context of psychotherapy. Psychiatrists should be consulted about medication issues since they have the ability to accurately diagnose such disorders and to decide upon appropriate medications. The proliferation of publicity about depression and antidepressant medications has resulted in many patients labeling themselves as depressed when they may be suffering from other disorders.

Example

A patient indicated to her therapist that she was depressed and had some suicidal ideation. The psychologist evaluated the patient and did not believe that she was either seriously depressed or suicidal. He did decide upon a consultation with a psychiatrist to make sure. The psychiatrist agreed with the psychologist's assessment but decided to try the patient on antidepressants to see if they would help, despite the patient not really fitting the protocol. The patient's response to the medication was minimal. The psychiatrist mentioned to the therapist that he saw some mild, psychoticlike symptoms and wondered whether some low dose antipsychotic medication would be helpful. The therapist concurred and the patient was tried on that medication. Her symptoms responded more to the antipsychotic medication. Gradually she was weaned from both.

A nonpsychiatric physician would not have the expertise to have made this differential diagnosis.

Antidepressant medications have been very helpful to some people, somewhat helpful to others, and of little help to still others. Depressive disorders are indications that there are problems in the patient's life, and he or she should be given the opportunity to understand those difficulties in psychotherapy, even if medication is prescribed.

SUGGESTION. Antidepressants are not curative and should be prescribed either in consultation with or by a psychiatrist. Patients should be referred for psychotherapy if their condition is serious enough to warrant antidepressants.

PSYCHOTIC PATIENTS

Psychotic patients are perhaps the category of patients least understood and most feared by medical practitioners. Psychotic patients fall into three categories: schizophrenic patients, bipolar disorders (manic-depressive), and other psychotic disorders, including paranoia.

Psychotic disorders are often treated by the use of medication and all too infrequently by the use of psychotherapy. Medication is not curative of these disorders. It mostly provides symptom relief and is only moderately successful at that. Psychotherapy can assist the patient in trying to understand his or her reactions as well as helping the individual to cope with the disorder and with their thoughts and feelings, which seem so incomprehensible. The notion that psychotic disorders are genetically or biologically caused is short-sighted and seems to consign such patients to the category of hopeless or untreatable.

At times, psychotic patients can be quite frightening. They can be delusional and may hallucinate, and their perceptions of the world may be at odds with those of others. Psychotic patients may be very angry and confused. Personal hygiene may be poor and their personal habits perplexing. It is important to remember that psychotic patients are not nonsensical. Their thoughts and feelings have a logic, even if that logic is irrational or obscure.

Example

A patient was seen in long-term psychotherapy by a therapist who had first had contact with the patient in a state psychiatric hospital. After her release from the hospital, the patient continued with the therapist on an outpatient basis. The patient, prior to her being in outpatient therapy, had been hospitalized on at least 20 different occasions. She had threatened numerous therapists, had been self-mutilating and hallucinatory, and had gotten herself involved in numerous disastrous relationships. The therapy was extraordinarily helpful, and after over 10 years the patient was working full-time, was married, and was functioning at a much higher level. This is not to say that the patient was "normal." She still had numerous problems, would seem to become transiently psychotic, would threaten to cut herself, and could be a very difficult and demanding patient. At times, she would call her physicians in a panic over some real or imagined physical problems. She would become disconsolate and demanding with the physician. If she were particularly angry with the therapist, she would become more difficult with her doctor. Fortunately, the doctor would maintain contact with the therapist, who could reassure the doctor and keep her informed as to what was really transpiring.

This patient had clearly made significant gains but would regress from time to time. It was important for the physician and the therapist to consult frequently. The patient improved in therapy because the therapist took an interpretive stance. That is, she did not assume that the patient was "crazy" and not understandable. She assumed that the patient had reasons for being the way that she was and that these reasons were comprehensible. In fact, this patient had been the victim of horrific child abuse, which had resulted in the eventual psychosis. Helping the patient understand the abuse and its effects greatly lessened the psychotic responses.

Schizophrenia is a disorder whose symptoms may include hallucinations, delusions, incoherence, inappropriate affect, social withdrawal, peculiar behavior, deterioration in usual capabilities, odd beliefs, and a lack of energy. It is an extremely disabling and serious disorder, and immediate referral to a mental health professional is essential. Families often need to be involved and educated as to the characteristics of the disorder. If the patient is psychotic and is a danger to himself or herself, hospitalization is in order and the patient may need to be committed to a psychiatric hospital.

Most schizophrenics are not dangerous. Those suffering from paranoid schizophrenia may be under the delusion that the physician is harming them, and there are tragic circumstances where such patients have reacted violently with physicians and other medical professionals. If one is concerned about the dangerousness of any patient, appropriate action includes informing the family and especially the police. Some patients may not be schizophrenic but are paranoid to a psychotic degree. They are probably able to function at a higher level and do not suffer from the same deterioration as do schizophrenics. Additionally, they tend not to be hallucinatory or to have the same kind of thought disorder as do schizophrenics. Nevertheless, in severe cases, the patient can be dangerous.

In more usual circumstances, schizophrenic and even more mildly paranoid patients are not dangerous. Schizophrenic patients may have great difficulty in following directions since they may be preoccupied with their internal state. Physicians may need to be very concrete and directive, as well as extremely patient. Treating psychotic patients with respect is essential. When psychotic patients become frightened, their psychosis worsens and they tend to act more bizarrely. It is important to explain things to these patients to try to eliminate confusion. Acknowledging and identifying the psychotic patient's fearfulness can be helpful in calming them down. It is always helpful to remain calm in order to help the patient to contain his or her intense emotions.

Manic-depressive or bipolar patients can also be frightening. Symptoms in a manic patient include an elevated and expansive mood with grandiosity. A decreased need for sleep, talkativeness, flight of ideas, increased motor activity, and unrestrained pleasurable activities are other possible symptoms. There is usually a depressive period present, although that may be short-lived. The manic episode may be seen as a defense against a depressive process. The patient may develop grandiosity and expansiveness as an extreme reaction to an underlying sense of incompetence and inadequacy. Most manic-depressive patients are not likely to be violent, although their behavior may be dangerous to themselves or to those who come in incidental contact because of their inability to consider the consequences of their actions. In extreme cases, patients diagnosed with bi-polar conditions have acted in violent ways and caution is always warranted. In the doctor's office, they are going to tend to deny the seriousness of their problems and may imagine that they will be able to conquer problems by will alone. Like schizophrenics, they tend to be self-absorbed and are unlikely, at least when in the throes of their psychosis, to form significant interpersonal relationships. Referral to mental health professionals is essential, and families may have to be involved when patients are particularly unable to listen to reason. A patient who is in a full-fledged manic episode is pretty much untreatable because of denial and hyperactivity. Helping him or her receive the proper treatment and remaining calm and concerned would be most helpful.

Psychotic patients are frightened. They have had to regress into psychosis because of their almost complete inability to deal with the world. Psychosis is the last refuge of the terrified. It is still an attempt to make sense of the world when the world seems incomprehensible. If psychotic patients become violent, it is typically because they feel frightened and at risk. If a psychotic patient is confused or threatening, the physician can try to understand what the patient is frightened of and can question the patient about the presumed fear. Many of these patients have been terribly abused, and many interpersonal encounters feel abusive, even if they are not. Medical procedures can feel life threatening to a psychotic person who may imagine that the procedure is designed to kill him or her. Their thinking is concretistic, to the extent that they may not be able to make the kinds of logical connections and abstractions that nonpsychotic people do. Even if the medical practitioner cannot understand the patient and his or her concerns, the doctor can convey a sense of concern and caring, which can mitigate some of the patient's terror.

Psychotic patients who are purely paranoid are relatively rare. Usually the paranoia is contained within schizophrenia or is not of sufficient severity to be psychotic. Nevertheless, some patients with a psychotic paranoid process will be seen in a medical practice. Obviously, they are going to be very mistrustful. In fact, they are so suspicious that they may not seek medical care for fear of being mistreated. If they do come in, their health may be very poor because of neglect.

The essence of paranoia is the feeling of badness or guilt that must be projected, which is then experienced as being redirected against the patient. The patient fears being attacked and is extremely suspicious of others. It is very difficult for them to admit to shortcomings because of their extreme fear of punishment. Paranoid patients have a need to disavow and disown. Their fear of their own inadequacy may cause them to question the competence of the physician. A medical problem can be experienced as a weakness, and the physician can be experienced as someone preying upon that weakness. Medical problems are likely to be denied or, if acknowledged, may be interpreted as being more serious than they actually are. Paranoid patients will tend to imagine that medical practitioners are not being forthright with them, are taking advantage of them, or are ordering unnecessary procedures. They can become quite provocative by implying misconduct on the part of the physician. It is important for the physician to maintain his or her composure so as to not create the rejection the patient anticipates.

Example

An exceedingly paranoid patient told his therapist that he would leave and never come back if his therapist ever kept him waiting. On his next appointment, the patient neglected to inform the receptionist of his arrival, so that the therapist thought that he was late. The patient left in a huff, never to return, certain he had been wronged.

Some patients are so invested in being victims that they arrange encounters to ensure it.

One aspect of paranoid patients that is quite difficult is that they tend to twist what is heard ever so slightly, leading to confusion and distrust. What they think they hear typically has a negative cast that often just misses the mark. Even more confusing is that paranoid patients have a great deal of difficulty in understanding the nuances of interpersonal relationships. This all translates into a patient who is bound to misinterpret what a physician says. Motives will be suspect and medical regimens may not be followed because of a fear of being hurt. There is no way that the physician can adequately reassure the patient because of the deep-seated nature of the pathology. Nevertheless, being straightforward and calm is the best course of action with such patients. Some patients will not articulate their fears, and physicians should try to be sensitive to any indications of fearfulness and question the patient as to his or her fears. It is also helpful to be very explicit as to the reasons for suggested medical procedures and to emphasize that the patient is in control of the treatment.

SUGGESTION. Psychotic patients have a way of thinking that appears nonsensical but does have a logic. Most psychotic patients are not dangerous. Physicians need to be concerned and respectful and give instructions in very clear and concrete ways. Patient fearfulness will result in an exacerbation of symptoms.

THE ABUSED PATIENT

Patients who have been physically and/or sexually abused create special problems for the medical practitioner. Abuse, particularly when it occurs at an early age, has pervasive and enduring negative effects on the individual. These effects can be categorized as ego weakness and boundary difficulties; anger problems; self-esteem, self-image, and body image difficulties; sexual difficulties; self-direction and competence issues; lack of emotional control and differentiation; lack of affect tolerance; relationship problems and increased anxiety; depression; and distress. Additionally, these patients tend to feel overwhelmed in situations that others may react to with equanimity.

The earlier the age at which the abuse occurs, the greater the degree of psychological problems that it creates. At an early age the victim does not have the emotional maturity to deal with the trauma and overstimulation. The child cannot process the abuse and becomes confused and bewildered. The child's immature ego is overwhelmed by the intensity of the emotions and behavior. The child's intellectual capacity is limited by his or her early age, and therefore he or she cannot understand what is occurring. Children's sense of themselves is very tenuous and an assault interferes with the establishment of a strong sense of identity. Body image is being established in childhood and is also sensitive to disruption. Every developmental stage that follows is impacted, resulting in a cumulative effect.

The damage is far greater if sexual abuse occurs at the hands of a family member. The child's sense of basic trust is violated by abuse by a family member. Sexual abuse by a family member confuses the child as to appropriate boundaries between family members. It destroys the order within the family. Love relationships become distorted and confused. Children function best if relationships within families are structured and consistent, but sexual abuse breaks down the structure. The child becomes unsure of his or her and others' roles within the family. Sexual abuse is too stimulating and overwhelming for children and causes a breakdown in their general capacity to process information. It throws them into an emotional maelstrom. If a father commits incest with his daughter, it disrupts the whole family structure. Mothers can react with great hostility to their daughters, as if the daughters are being blamed for the father's activities and as if the daughters are true competitors. Sexually abused children are frightened, traumatized, and overwhelmed. They often feel alone with their secret and feel ashamed of what happened, as if they are to blame.

Sexual abuse runs the gamut from occasional touching to complete genital, oral, and anal intercourse. Adults' cruelty to children is difficult to comprehend and is horrific in its telling, but a thorough understanding is important in order to help those victimized.

Physical abuse also does great damage to a child's psyche. It creates a feeling within the child of being bad without a real sense of his or her wrongdoing. There is no justification for physically abusing a child. Consequently, the child grows up feeling afraid of asserting himself or herself for fear of being attacked. Physical abuse destroys self-esteem. Love and hate become confused, since the beloved parent is hurting the child so much. Those who physically abuse feel hatred toward the child, which is terribly hurtful and confusing to the child. It teaches the child that those whom they love can be hurtful in incomprehensible ways and for incomprehensible reasons. Those who become hated and abused internalize that feeling and then find others to project it upon others, perpetuating the abuse.

The Abuser

Good parents do not abuse their children, physically, emotionally, or sexually. Most parents do not have the conscious wish and desire to hurt their children. Those that do have come from backgrounds where they themselves have been abused. This does not excuse abuse, but it does provide an explanation.

Physically abusive parents hate themselves. Their children, as a self-representation, are hated as well. The parents cannot tolerate their own feelings of self-hatred and project it onto the child, ridding themselves of their intolerable feelings.

Example

A man was referred for psychotherapy because of losing control and hitting his young son and then throwing him down the stairs, resulting in a broken arm. The child had been crying about wanting a new toy and the father became enraged, resulting in the assault. There were several reasons that the father reacted assaultively. First of all, he could not afford a new toy for his son, which made him feel bad about himself. Even more importantly, his son's tears reminded him of the neglect that he had suffered as a child, and these feelings were painful and had to be silenced.

It is essential to recognize that the father was not actually thinking about his past neglect. Rather, these thoughts and memories were subliminal, since they were so painful. Psychotherapy with people with abusive backgrounds is difficult for many reasons, one of which is that their painful memories and affects feel overwhelming, and the individual will do almost anything to avoid the feelings, including beating his or her children. Additionally, a victim of abuse has learned to express his or her feelings in the same fashion as did the abusive parent, by physically acting out. The individual has not learned how to talk about feelings or frustration and needs to be taught to express angry feelings instead of acting them out. Even more problematic for treatment of abused and abusive patients is the fact that some abuse may have occurred preverbally. Consequently, the assaultive patient does not have the words available to describe the sensations experienced when he or she was abused. Since the assaultive experience was body-bound, distress may be felt bodily and thus is difficult for the person to articulate, reinforcing the need to act out.

SUGGESTION. Abusers are difficult to treat because of their need to avoid painful feelings through acting out.

Abusers of all stripes—emotional, physical, and sexual—are angry and inadequate people who feel enormously powerless and angry. Their anger and powerlessness is expressed toward victims who typically are weaker and more inadequate. Consequently, children and women tend to bear the brunt of abuse. Those men who sexually abuse tend to be hostile toward women in particular and thus express their hostility through sexual assault. Even those men who are pedophiles are expressing hostility toward women by rejecting them as sexual objects, as if saying that the perpetrator can do without women. Their choice of young boys reflects their fear of women.

Medical professionals who are female are going to have to deal with those who have hostility toward and power issues with women. They should take caution and realize that those who sexually assault do not have outward signs to identify them. Women physicians are going to have to deal with both men and women who are angry and inadequate and who may want to symbolically or even actually "put women in their place."

Example

A patient asked a female physician what her first name was. The doctor, astutely realizing that the patient was trying to treat her with disrespect, responded, "Doctor," effectively retaining her professional role and status.

SUGGESTION. Medical practitioners need to be aware that some patients have the dynamics of abusers, and they should be prepared to protect themselves, both literally and figuratively.

Abused patients have some of the similarities of abusers since generally abusers were once victims themselves. Of course, not all victims do physically act out. However, within each victim resides a perpetrator, of sorts. The troublesome relationship tends to get reenacted in some fashion in the present.

Example

> Mrs. E. had been sexually abused as a child. She was married and seemed to have a good relationship. However, she would get involved in extramarital relationships, in effect betraying her husband, abusing him. Essentially, she was now becoming the perpetrator instead of the victim. Of course, she did not view it this way and could not figure out why she was cheating on her husband.

The patient was not conscious of her need to act out the abusive relationship in the present. Psychotherapy aimed to help her recognize the repetition and to assist her in putting it into words, thus enabling her to understand that which transpired and the effect it had and continues to have on her.

Physically Abused Patients

Those that have been physically abused as children carry those scars into adulthood. At times, the effects become manifest within the doctor-patient relationship.

Example

> Mrs. G. had experienced considerable physical abuse as a child. When she visited her physician for an examination, she was overcome with tears and felt terribly distressed. She would become

almost catatonic with fear and her muscles would contract rigidly. The physician was kind and understanding but bewildered. The patient was also at a loss. It was only after she pursued psychotherapy that her experience made sense. In fact, she also experienced some of her psychotherapy visits similarly. If either she or the therapist raised a painful issue, the patient would react fearfully with the same rigidity. She experienced the physician's examination and the psychotherapist's interpretations as assaultive and reacted accordingly. Through her work with the therapist she was able to put her experiences into words and gradually gain mastery over them.

SUGGESTION. Abused patients have difficulty in verbalizing and articulating their feelings. They may react to examinations as if they are assaults.

The physician needs to be extrasensitive with patients with such rigidity and allow them the opportunity to become as comfortable as possible before examinations and treatments. Questioning a patient about what seem to be odd responses to routine exams is appropriate and may open an avenue for discussion of that which the patient has kept secret.

Domestic violence is an unfortunate reality. Medical practitioners must be alert to signs that patients are being abused. Obvious signs are unexplained bruises. Furtiveness, unexplained distress, and a reluctance to talk may point to abuse. Many patients are loathe to discuss domestic violence for a variety of reasons. They are embarrassed and ashamed; they think it is their fault that they were abused. They do not feel that they can be helped since they feel trapped. Economically, they may have little choice as to their living situation and fear that if the abuser is arrested they will be forced to leave and thus to fend for themselves. Many women who are abused have been abused as children or have seen their mothers abused. In a sense, they see nothing strange about it and fully expect to be beaten for wrongdoings, real or imagined. An abused woman marrying an abuser is another example of the repetition compulsion. Again, the person hopes that history will not repeat itself, that she will finally get the love and appreciation she deserves. Unfortunately, she is ultimately bitterly disappointed.

Abused women have been raised to feel that they have little choice in life, that their destiny is to be treated badly. They feel so bad about themselves that they will do almost anything to feel loved, even allowing themselves to be beaten. When these women were children they felt some connection with their abusive fathers through the assaults. Usually such fathers are very uninvolved with their daughters except when they are abusing them. Consequently, the intensity of the abuse represents intensity of connection to the abused woman.

Example

Ms. V. was imprisoned at age 18 after participating in an armed robbery with her boyfriend which resulted in a death. She was sentenced to a life sentence for the murder. She was a somewhat reluctant participant in the crime, but her need to be connected to and loved by her boyfriend propelled her to do something that she would ordinarily not be involved in.

The need for love is so strong that abused women often resist help and treatment. If the practitioner suspects abuse, it should be addressed directly by asking the patient if she has been hurt by someone. Emphasizing each person's right to be safe can be helpful. Victims are often quite reticent and may have to be encouraged to divulge the secret. Physicians and others should have available referral sources that can help and protect victims of domestic violence.

The American College of Obstetricians and Gynecologists (1995), referring to an article in the *Journal of the American Medical Association* (McFarlane, Parker, Soeken, & Bullock, 1992), suggests that physicians routinely include several questions designed to help patients to talk about domestic violence. These questions are the following:

1. Have you been emotionally or physically abused by your partner or someone important to you?
2. Within the last year, or since your pregnancy began, have you been hit, slapped, kicked, or otherwise physically hurt by someone?
3. Within the last year, has anyone forced you to have sexual activities?
4. Are you afraid of your partner or anyone else? (McFarlane, Parker, Soeken, & Bullock, 1992, p. 3177).

SUGGESTION. Domestic violence is an unfortunate reality. Victims often deny being abused, and gentle prodding may be necessary to elicit information about it. Referral sources for battered women should be available.

It is even more heart-breaking to see children who have been abused. They, too, may present themselves in a furtive fashion and may recoil from the touch. They may cry without apparent reason and suffer nightmares and anxiety. Schoolwork is likely to suffer, and they may be excessively aggressive toward other children or toward siblings. Of course, there may also be bruises that point to abuse. Their parents, if they are the perpetrators, are likely to deny that abuse is occurring. It is the practitioner's responsibility to report abuse to the authorities; not to do so gravely endangers children's lives. Children as well as adult victims of abuse are murdered, and some deaths could be prevented. Physical abuse is so abhorrent that many are too horrified to see it. This denial only perpetuates the abuse and reinforces the denial that is already far too prevalent.

Physical abuse does not exist in isolation. A child who is physically abused is a recipient for the parent's frustration. The parent does not have the capability to handle his or her frustrations through reflection or problem solving. Rather, he or she projects it onto the child and acts as if the child were the problem. This psychological process occurs in a more general way. The parent has difficulty in differentiating the child from himself or herself. The child becomes sort of a wastebasket for all of the parent's unwanted and intolerable feelings. This leads to substantial confusion for the child. Consequently, the child will have difficulty in articulating his or her own difficulties and will tend to attribute responsibility for problems to outside sources. Children will not be able to identify, for instance, that their difficulty in school is related to the abuse that they have suffered. Denial of abuse by children should not be taken at face value. It should also be recognized that the abuse is part of a wider problem whereby the child feels constantly misunderstood and is emotionally abused as well.

SUGGESTION. Cases where children have been abused must be reported to the authorities. Practitioners have the common desire to deny painful realities. Physical abuse is part of a wider picture of relating, whereby the child's sense of identity is distorted by the parent's projections.

Some of the nicest patients can turn out to be quite provocative under stress. Those who have been abused may see frustration through the same lens that their parents viewed the world. When their parents were frustrated they would strike out angrily and hurtfully. Patients who are hurt, confused, or frustrated may do the same with their caregivers. If the history of the patient included a neglectful parent who only paid attention when provoked, the professional may find himself or herself being provoked into responding to a patient hurtfully. Patients may also get very angry when they are hurt through medical treatments. Their response is as if they are again being assaulted, this time by the practitioner.

Example

A patient was diagnosed with diabetes. The patient was stunned with the news and became extraordinarily distraught. He also flew into a rage, accusing the doctor of incompetence. This man had often been physically assaulted as a child and experienced the diagnosis as an assault; in effect, he attacked the doctor as if he were the cause of the disease. This is a repetition of his experience with his brutal father, who blamed the child for his own frustrations.

It is very important for the physician not to respond in kind and not to reject the patient. The physician can operate as a container in order to help this patient talk about his frightened feelings instead of acting out. This would be particularly important with a diabetes patient, where compliance is very important. Since patients sometimes lack an ability to reflect on their problems, it is particularly important that physicians help them to learn to be patient and self-reflective. This will assist them in being able to tolerate uncomfortable feelings so that they do not have the need to discharge them through acting out aggressively or through substance abuse.

Some patients use projective identification to rid themselves of unwanted affects, and this can feel assaultive to physicians. Again, this is a repetition for the patient, and a calm and accepting attitude is most helpful for the physician to maintain. Patients who were subject to sadistic beatings tend to try to elicit a type of sadomasochistic relationship. In this way, they feel connected with the doctor, feel more in control, and are able to deal with overwhelming feelings. The practitioner must be careful to resist the pull to respond to the patient angrily even when provoked. Women who have been abused as children and marry abusive men are often embroiled in this kind of sadomasochistic struggle. A kind and sympathetic practitioner may be able to help such an individual find a way out of such a destructive relationship.

SUGGESTION. Victims of physical and sexual abuse may try to engage the medical practitioner in a repetition of a sadomasochistic relationship. Medical procedures can feel like assaults, and gentleness and understanding by the physician are essential.

Sexually Abused Patients

Much of what has been said about physical abuse also applies to sexual abuse. Sexual abuse has effects that are even more problematic than those resulting from physical abuse. Childhood sexual abuse is a violation of the person, of the family, and of society. It seems to penetrate to the core of the victim. It is a violation of the soul.

The present discussion concentrates on females who have been sexually abused since the vast preponderance of victims are women. This is not to suggest that male sexual abuse does not exist or that it does not create enormous problems for a developing boy.

A victim of childhood sexual abuse is confused about family relationships, about her sexuality, and about assertiveness and aggression. Victims have trouble identifying their feelings and are prone toward dissociative reactions wherein their feelings are disavowed and disowned. At times their body does not feel to be their own. Because the abuse often occurred at an early age, they were maturationally incapable of either physically or emotionally handling adult sexual activities and emotions. Consequently, they tend to become overwhelmed emotionally and to feel helpless in many situations. They may have body image difficulties since they did not have the opportunity to comfortably grow into their maturing bodies. Victims of sexual abuse may present themselves with a rather flat affect and may appear quite detached. Similarly, their sexual responsiveness may be limited and they may find it dangerous to become sexually aroused.

Without confirmation from the patient, a diagnosis of sexual abuse is impossible. There are some characteristics that may lead toward that diagnosis, however. Certainly, women who have difficulty in allowing pelvic exams might have a history of sexual abuse. Lack of sexual responsiveness can be indicative of many different issues and is not specific enough to point to a diagnosis, although many who have been abused become unresponsive. Teenagers and some adult women become promiscuous, which is often an indication of a sexual abuse history. The aforementioned flatness of affect can be a significant diagnostic sign. Unfortunately, there are no surefire ways of diagnosing sexual abuse. The practitioner must use sensitivity to the nuances of the patient's responses to questions along with her general demeanor in order to consider the possibility of a sexual abuse history.

Some patients will be able to tell their doctors about their sexual abuse history, and they should be referred for psychotherapeutic treatment. Patients may require considerable encouragement to seek out treatment. They often feel ashamed and at fault and have some intuitive sense that psychotherapy will require them to talk about the abuse and related issues that are very painful. It should be pointed out that the rewards of good treatment will far outweigh the negatives.

SUGGESTION. There are not definitive indicators of sexual abuse. Sensitivity and empathy can be helpful in allowing the patient to feel comfortable enough to divulge the secret. Victims should be referred for psychotherapy.

A physician can expect some typical behavioral characteristics from victims. They tend to have difficulty in dealing with strong emotions and tend to feel overwhelmed. Since they have been victimized when they were helpless children, they often feel helpless and victimized. Consequently, they may not be cooperative with medical regimens, since their diseases may feel like assaults.

Example

Mrs. T. was referred to psychotherapy after becoming distraught on the job. She was reprimanded by a superior, which she felt was unfair. Her distress was so severe that she became incapacitated. She had great difficulty in identifying any contribution that she made toward her work difficulties. She insisted that she was completely a helpless victim. She felt paralyzed and incapable of responding to the allegations. In the therapy, she became aware of having been sexually assaulted as a child. Her reaction to her job problems reflected how she reacted to the original abuse—feeling helpless and victimized.

She needed considerable assistance in being able both to look at her own contribution to her problems and to mount a capable defense.

In the medical office, such patients may again feel as if they are helpless victims and may be reluctant to engage in a cooperative partnership with the doctor. They may insist that the physician take care of them, implying an inability to contribute to their own care. A physician's tendency may be to become impatient in this situation and to accept the patient's protests of incompetence, or the physician may feel very sorry for the patient and reinforce the helplessness. The patient will then act out her feelings about the old relationships, rendering the physician impotent instead. It is important that the patient be encouraged to participate in her own care with the understanding that competence will be rewarding and will build a sense of confidence.

Patients who have been sexually abused as children can become sexually provocative, and male physicians and health care workers need to be quite careful not to allow themselves to be drawn into a sexual relationship. Doctors are in a more powerful position, and a sexual relationship with a patient may very well be a repetition of a previous abusive relationship. Some children who have been overstimulated can become provocative, and some child molesters have claimed that the child initiated the sexual activity. The adult is the responsible party and must never succumb to that kind of provocation. Similarly, health care professionals need to be exceptionally careful to maintain boundaries between doctor and patient. It is the doctor's, not the patient's, ultimate responsibility to maintain a professional relationship. Patients may try to initiate sexual contact as a way of feeling protected and safe. Some who feel out of control in terms of their physical illness or in relation to their life experiences may try to gain some sense of control by seducing their doctor.

Example

A 17-year-old woman was referred to psychotherapy. She described a chaotic family with a seductive father and a neglectful mother. She had been sexually active since age 14 with a succession of partners. The therapist questioned her about any inappropriate sexual activities but she denied any. In her sessions, she exuded sexuality and behaved seductively toward the male therapist. They discussed her seductiveness from a number of angles, and it was clear that she did not know how to relate to a man in any other way than in a sexual fashion. To seduce a man represented power and control to her, which allowed her not to feel overwhelmed and abused. Her relationships never progressed beyond the adolescent heat of sexuality, so she risked little in terms of being hurt emotionally. The therapy was somewhat successful, but the parents terminated the treatment prematurely, ostensibly because of financial reasons. About 10 years later, the therapist received a phone call from the patient indicating that she was again in treatment and that until recently had completely forgotten about the first therapy. She wanted to fill in some gaps in her memory about what she characterized as "that terrible time." She wondered whether she had ever told the therapist about her incestuous relationship with her father.

This young woman was acting out with the first therapist that which she could not bring herself to talk about. The experience was too overwhelming for her to be able to divulge it to the original therapist. It was only years later, when she felt stronger, that was she able to talk about it. The first therapy was probably helpful in maintaining the patient's equilibrium and in showing her that not all relationships with men had to be exploitative.

Many women who have been sexually abused have difficulty within sexual and intimate relationships. As mentioned earlier, those who have been abused tend to internalize the abusive relationship and identify with both sides of the equation. The patient often will play out both sides, both victim and victimizer. Usually those abused have trouble recognizing how they have internalized the victimizer role. They tend to characterize any marital problems as stemming from difficulties originating in their spouses. Internally, some women blame themselves for the sexual abuse and then project blame onto the husband. Physicians rarely are privy to the whole story, and a sympathetic yet neutral attitude is best. Marital difficulties can become quite violent in these situations and a referral to either a marital therapist or to a psychotherapist would be appropriate.

Those who have been sexually abused are often beset with tremendous feelings of self-hate and self-blame. If the abuse occurred when the person was quite young, actual memory of the abuse may be absent or may exist in a fragmentary fashion. The child or even the adult survivor may be beset by frightening and incomprehensible nightmares. The nightmares reflect a child's perspective and distortion over experiences that are beyond the child's ability to process. They may have unconscious fantasies that are also frightening. Some victims develop psychosomatic symptoms as a way of trying to cope with overwhelming feelings. Some people are driven toward suicide as a way of ridding themselves of these feelings and of what they feel are their ''bad'' selves. Any severe psychopathology such as borderline disorders or psychotic disorders can have as their source sexual abuse.

Sexual arousal signals dangerous and forbidden feelings to these patients, and some sexual abuse victims suffer from lack of sexual desire. Others suffer from vaginismus and/or dyspareunia, which is a repetition of the early childhood abuse. Those that sexually abuse often use rationalizations about their sexual assaults being helpful to their victims. This is utter nonsense. Similarly, the notion that a physician is helping a patient who is not responsive by having sexual intercourse with her is misguided, dangerous, and a rationalization. Those who find themselves in such a situation should seek out psychological treatment.

SUGGESTION. Some patients can be sexually provocative. It is the health care professional's responsibility to maintain boundaries.

In recent years, there has been a controversy about the so-called "false memory syndrome," which refers to individuals who "falsely" accuse others of having molested them as children. This occurs when a repressed memory comes to the surface, usually in the context of psychotherapy. The contention is that these repressed memories are false, planted by unscrupulous or incompetent therapists. It is apparent that some small minority of patients reporting memories of sexual abuse are fabricating. This is a tragic situation where innocent people are falsely accused. However, there are many people who have been abused and who have repressed its existence. The reality of repression of painful memories is well established and verifiable. Within medical practice, it is far better to err on the side that believes the patient. It is not the physician's job to determine the truth or falseness of the accusation, and it is better for nonpsychiatric personnel to stay clear of becoming embroiled in this controversy. Medical personnel should remain sympathetic to the patient's plight.

As with physical abuse with children, the health care professional has a legal and moral responsibility to report suspected sexual abuse to the authorities. Sexual and physical abuse affect all social strata, and one should not let preconceived notions blind one to painful realities.

Children who are victims of sexual abuse may produce a variety of symptoms, including nightmares, unexplained tears, fears of strangers, a sense of preoccupation or detachment, touching of the genitals, and clinging behavior. Unfortunately, these symptoms could represent other problems and the physician needs to question the child gently and to encourage divulging of uncomfortable and frightening occurrences.

Physicians and other health care professionals need to maintain awareness that sexual abuse can and does occur and that suspicions should be followed up. Women can be routinely questioned as to a history of sexual abuse using questions similar to those mentioned in the section on physical abuse. Many will not bring it up until asked, and physicians can be very helpful in airing these awful secrets.

SUGGESTION. Medical professionals should be sensitive to the possibility of present or past sexual abuse. Many people would pursue assistance but are often too uncomfortable and ashamed to bring up a history of abuse.

Rape

Sexual assault that occurs when a woman is an adult causes different problems than does childhood sexual assault. At this point, the woman's personality is formed and she is better equipped to deal with trauma. Nevertheless, rape is a horrendous violation of a person's sense of integrity and has long-lasting effects. It is a major trauma and can infiltrate all aspects of a woman's life. Women who are raped often become fearful of being alone and of going out. They may become fearful of men in general and may have difficulty in sexual responsiveness. They are prone toward depression, anxiety, and sleep disorders. Nightmares are frequent, as are horrible flashbacks of the rape. Some women feel guilty, as if they did something to provoke the attack. Marital relationships suffer. Some partners blame themselves, believing that they should have done something to protect the woman. The victim may feel that as well.

Rape is far worse than just being physically assaulted. It is designed to degrade the woman and to make her feel powerless and violated. It is a violation to the core of the woman. A victim will need enormous support and care in order to help her work through the trauma. Rape assistance centers, designed to help victims deal with the many effects of rape, are available throughout the country. These centers offer support and therapy groups, assistance with legal matters, and often shelters for women at risk. Physicians need to be aware of these options in order to refer women, should that become necessary.

Some women who have been raped have kept it a secret because of a sense of shame and because of a wish not to deal with the enormity of the assault. Physicians may be the first or only person to be told about it. Doctors should be kind and understanding with any such victim. Women should not be coerced in any fashion. It certainly would be better for a victim to report an assault since it possibly would remove a dangerous person from society and can empower the victim. Unfortunately, some women are adamant about not reporting the crime and one must respect their wishes, while helping them to explore their options.

SUGGESTION. Victims of rape need understanding and concern. The effects of rape are often pervasive and long-lasting. Referral to a rape assistance center would be helpful. Being available to the victim for support and discussion is important.

PATIENTS WITH MARITAL AND SEXUAL DYSFUNCTION DIFFICULTIES

Marital Difficulties

With the high numbers of divorces occurring, it is not surprising that many patients that consult with physicians are struggling with marital difficulties. Many patients may mention that they are embroiled in a divorce but will prefer not to go into the details. Others will welcome the opportunity to discuss their problems with the doctor, and the physician should provide them with time to talk about their concerns. Still others will not mention marital problems, but their difficulties will manifest themselves through depression, distress, and psychosomatic disorders. Unexplained distress and symptoms point to some difficulty in the patient's life, and gentle questioning would be appropriate. In fact, questions about spouse and family should be a part of a doctor's usual set of questions during examinations. Those with marital difficulties can be referred to a marital therapist for treatment. Unfortunately, people often delay seeking marital treatment until the marriage has irrevocably deteriorated. Some marriages are so bad and the individuals are such a bad match that little can be done to save the marriage.

Example

A couple sought out marriage counseling because of severe marital strife. The therapist immediately thought that they were ill-suited for each other. The wife was highly educated while the husband was a manual laborer. They seemed to have little in common, with the wife being continually critical of the husband for his alcoholic intake and for his lack of ambition. The husband did not share any of the wife's interests and wished that she would be more satisfied with their life. They soon filed for divorce, and the wife continued in treatment to work on several issues related to her self-esteem and the reasons for making a poor choice in marriage. The husband declined further treatment.

Treatment can still be initiated in order to clarify for each the existing problems and to help them through the trauma of the divorce. Almost all divorces are difficult and traumatic for all concerned. The woman described in the preceding example saw her unhappiness in life as partially related to her marriage. She also recognized other psychological problems that needed to be addressed. Others realize that they are unhappy and fasten upon the marriage as the source.

Example

A woman brought her husband to marital treatment, complaining about his lack of communication and his social withdrawal. She was convinced that her problems were due to her husband's difficulties and even warned the husband that he was "going to really need intensive psychotherapy." The therapist was able to help her to see that the situation was much more complex than she imagined and that her problems were also contributing to their difficulties. They were able to work on their individual and joint problems and were able to attain a good relationship.

Some marital problems are indicative of severe emotional problems with one or both individuals.

Example

A couple sought out treatment ostensibly because of the wife's lack of sexual interest. Evaluation indicated relatively severe psychological problems with both. Soon after treatment began, the wife became seriously depressed and was hospitalized. The husband entered intensive psychotherapy to work on his difficulties. The marriage never survived because of their individual difficulties and because they were so ill matched.

Often marriage counseling will lead into individual treatment as psychological problems are addressed within each participant.

Patients will often bring in horror stories about their marriages, and physicians should be appropriately sympathetic without inciting the patient to further outrage. Patients need to be helped to deal with their feelings, and providing a venue to talk and to provide a referral can be very helpful. On the other hand, some patients have trouble recognizing when they are being abused, and it is appropriate for the doctor to point out obvious gaps in the patient's perception.

Example

A woman patient seemed quite distressed to her internist. She was able to say that she had discovered that her husband was having an affair and that he had no intention of terminating it. The patient was confused and bewildered and seemed to feel that she had no options. The physician was able to talk with her and to point out several options, including consulting with an attorney. The patient left feeling more in control.

SUGGESTION. Medical professionals can provide those with marital problems an opportunity to air their difficulties and can steer them to appropriate help. Asking routinely about family and marriage can be helpful, especially with unexplained symptomology.

Sexual Dysfunctions

Sexual dysfunction refers to erectile, ejaculatory, and lack of desire problems for men and vaginismus, dyspareunia, inorgasmia, and lack of desire for women.

Male Sexual Disorders

Men who complain of sexual dysfunctions should be medically evaluated to rule out any organic causes.

There are many men who have transient episodes of erectile difficulty. At times, they may have difficulty having or maintaining an erection because of having consumed too much alcohol. Other reasons include external concerns about job or family, fatigue, lack of sexual interest, performance anxiety, or other psychological problems. Those who have chronic erectile difficulties should be evaluated by a mental health professional once organic causes are eliminated. It is important to remember that organic and psychological disorders can each contribute to creating an erection problem. Additionally, those with an organic problem can develop very strong feelings and beliefs about the disorders and its causes.

Example

A middle-aged man gradually began losing the capability of full erections. He was evaluated by a urologist who ascertained a blood pressure problem. The patient also felt that his erectile difficulties were punishment for masturbation. Psychological treatment did not eliminate totally his erection problems but did mitigate them to some extent.

Erection problems can be due to a number of psychological difficulties. Guilt and anxiety over sexuality in general, angry feelings toward women, and fear of women can all contribute. A husband who is engaged in extramarital sex may have difficulty performing with his lover or with his wife. A man who is angry toward women or toward a particular woman may find it difficult to have an erection as a passive-aggressive way of denying a woman sexual pleasure. Or an angry man may imagine his penis to be a weapon and be fearful of hurting a woman. Some men who are afraid of women and of their vaginas feel endangered should they place their penis within a woman. Men who have had a prior history of erectile problems may find it difficult to be spontaneous because of their tendency to be a spectator of their sexual performance. Men put a high priority on their sexual prowess and are often devastated when they do not perform up to their expectations. Physicians and other medical professionals can be reassuring about transient erectile problems, and this reassurance may be all that is needed. Men need to be encouraged to be more patient with themselves, and the authority of the doctor may help them in this regard. Men are so embarrassed about matters of sexual prowess that a frank discussion with their physician can be very reassuring. Many men are woefully ignorant of human anatomy and physiology, and physicians can provide patients with needed information. Men may have unrealistic expectations for their performance. They may expect themselves to be able to have multiple erections and ejaculations per encounter or to always be capable of erections regardless of circumstance. Similarly, men have expectations about always being able to satisfy women and can become very upset with themselves when that does not happen. Men who are experiencing erectile difficulties should be questioned about external factors that may be contributing to the problem.

Erectile difficulties are treatable, some easily and some with more difficulty. Treatment is often recommended to occur within the marital relationship since relationship issues often contribute to such difficulties. Erection problems can be treated through behavioral techniques along with an exploration of any relationship problems. If this is not successful, more intensive individual psychotherapy is indicated.

Many of the same reasons may underlie ejaculatory problems. Premature ejaculation is the primary ejaculatory problem, and it may be caused by anxiety or by a passive-aggressive wish to deny pleasure to the woman. Again, some men are afraid of women, and ejaculating quickly ends the sexual encounter. Some men have an immature feeling about themselves, which gets manifested in the incompetence of premature ejaculation. Treatment, again, can be behavioral combined with marital counseling or may need to become more intensive. Retarded ejaculation or no ejaculation is suggestive of a general sexual inhibition, of a holding back. Treatment for this type of ejaculatory problem is likely to be intensive individual therapy.

Lack of sexual desire can be due to many psychological factors. Relationship problems are certainly not conducive to arousal. Depression and other psychological concerns can manifest themselves via a lack of sexual interest. The physician can do a great service by opening up discussion with the patient since many men are reluctant to inform their physicians of sexual difficulties. Treatment for lack of sexual interest is either going to be marital or individual.

There are some therapists who specialize in the treatment of sexual difficulties, and they tend to have a behavioral orientation. Other therapists will tend to treat sexual difficulties within the context of the whole person or within the context of the relationship.

SUGGESTION. Sexual dysfunction in men can relate to erectile difficulties, ejaculatory problems, and lack of sexual desire. Frank discussion with the physician can provide a sense of relief and be educational and reassuring to men.

Female Sexual Disorders

As with men, women should be medically evaluated to rule out any physical causes. Sexual disorders with women include vaginismus and dyspareunia, which make intercourse difficult or impossible, as well as difficulties with sexual desire. Some women feel unfulfilled because of being episodically or totally inorgasmic.

Vaginismus and dyspareunia are often related, since pain often will precipitate muscle contraction and muscle contraction will cause painful intercourse. A woman who is complaining about either disorder is likely to be very tense during intercourse. These symptoms suggest that the woman is having difficulty in allowing herself to relax. The physician should certainly ascertain whether there is a history of sexual abuse that could be precipitating the symptoms. Furthermore, an abusive or bad relationship could be causing the difficulty.

Those who complain of vaginismus may be very frightened of intercourse and may have a distorted sense of their vagina. They may be afraid of intercourse, fearing that their vagina is too small to accommodate a large, erect penis. This distorted idea may have its roots in the unconscious fantasy that the patient is still really a child. It is an expression of the reluctance to accept the notion of adulthood. The physician can reassure the woman as to the vagina's physical capability by pointing out that vagina is capable of giving birth to a baby, which is certainly larger than a penis.

Examples

A young woman was referred for psychotherapy because of her concern about her ability to have intercourse. She would not allow her doctor to examine her and dreaded the idea of intercourse. She indicated that the part of her body that she referred to as "down there" seemed dirty and bloody and that she could not imagine that she could accommodate a large and erect penis. She reported a history of parental violence within the family, and, in her mind, she had equated sex with violence, resulting in the belief that sex was a violent act. This is not an uncommon fantasy with those suffering from vaginismus.

Another young woman, recently married, saw a therapist for assistance with vaginismus. She and her husband had not been able to consummate their marriage. She had a history of sexual abuse, and she really had no real interest in being able to achieve intercourse since that whole area of her body brought up memories of the abuse.

It is often difficult for those with a history of abuse or for those currently in an abusive relationship to bring it out into the open. At times, it takes years before some women will feel comfortable enough to divulge an abusive history.

Vaginismus and dyspareunia caused by vaginismus can be treated by behavioral techniques. The therapist would attempt to help the patient relax by teaching relaxation techniques and then use progressive vaginal dilators. Additionally, the treatment would often include the husband or boyfriend in order to take care of any relationship problems and to include the man in the treatment. Physicians can be helpful to those patients with these disorders by reassuring the women that nothing is wrong with them physically. Providing these patients with information about female anatomy and about sexual response would be helpful since they may be ignorant about these subjects. When the pain or involuntary contraction are related to more deep-seated psychological problems, more intensive individual treatment is indicated.

Lack of sexual interest or difficulty in becoming aroused are fairly common difficulties for women. At times, women feel considerable pressure from their partners to be aroused, and some complaints about arousal seem to come more from the partner than from the woman.

Example

A woman was seen by a psychotherapist because of presumed lack of sexual interest. The evaluation showed that the woman was under extreme pressure by her boyfriend to be sexually available at all times. Her lack of response was perfectly understandable considering the pressure she was under. She also indicated that she and her boyfriend battled continuously, and consequently it was quite appropriate for her not to feel interest in sex.

Physicians can be helpful in reassuring women that their presumed lack of interest or lack of arousal may be related to external factors or that pressure is counterproductive to arousal. At times, women have so many pressures on them at home and at work that they are too fatigued to feel much sexual interest.

Other women have difficulty in sexual interest or arousal because of psychological factors. Again, a history of abuse may be behind the difficulty. Women who have been abused may have strong ambivalences about sexual responses, particularly if the abuse occurred when they were children. They may feel that any arousal may be dangerous since it may bring back terrible memories. There are women who feel quite guilty about sexual arousal, and there are also women who greatly fear losing control. Those struggling with relationship problems are likely not to feel particularly aroused. Some women are mad at their partners or at men in general, and these feelings manifest themselves by a lack of sexual interest. Those women with arousal or interest difficulties can be helped by individual or marital treatment.

Women often feel pressured, by themselves and by their partners, to be orgasmic. It is important to ascertain whether the patient or her partner is putting undue pressure on her. If so, educating her or the partner as to the fact that all women are not always orgasmic may remove some of the pressure. As with other sexual complaints, inorgasmia may be related to a prior history of abuse, or to present relationship problems. Also, some women who have trouble achieving orgasm have psychological difficulties that preclude relaxation.

Example

A late middle-aged woman sought out psychotherapy because of being inorgasmic. This issue became an obsession with the woman, with her putting undue pressure on her husband. She incessantly read books on the subject and was frequently masturbating in an attempt to reach orgasm. It was clear to the therapist that something else was troubling the patient that was being manifested through her obsession with orgasms.

Many different psychological problems can have their expression through sexual matters. Differential diagnosis is very difficult for physicians to make and a referral to a psychotherapist is appropriate.

Some women have been taught that being sexually aroused and orgasmic is not appropriate behavior. The physician can be helpful in reassuring the patient that sexual responsiveness and orgasm are natural and desirable. There are some women who are very reluctant to touch or examine themselves and are abhorrent about masturbation. Again, educating the patient can relieve unnecessary guilt. Women who are inorgasmic can more easily achieve orgasm through masturbation than through intercourse. Masturbation can be helpful in teaching the patient about her body and about what she finds pleasing. It also maintains control for the patient if she is worried about control issues. Physicians can be helpful in encouraging an open discussion of these matters.

SUGGESTION. Sexual problems for women can be indicative of a history of abuse, present relationship problems, a lack of information, or psychological problems. Physicians can clear up misconceptions and can give permission for normal sexual behaviors. Some women feel undue pressure from themselves and from their partners, and doctors can provide a more realistic viewpoint.

EATING DISORDERS

Eating disorders endanger millions of people's health. It has been estimated that at least one-third of Americans are significantly overweight. Many who are not overweight are preoccupied with their weight, and many women believe that they are overweight despite not being so according to usual medical standards. There is also an unfortunate group of people, mostly women, who suffer from anorexia and/or bulimia.

Eating disorders are notoriously resistant to treatment since total abstinence, as with alcohol or drugs, is impossible. Medical professionals are intimately involved with eating disorders since these disorders either create medical problems or exacerbate already existing ones.

Example

Ms. M. was morbidly obese and suffered from Crohn's disease, diabetes, and high blood pressure. She was seriously depressed and had difficulty in coping with the pressures of life. Her internist was sympathetic to her and never put pressure on her to do that which seemed impossible to her—to lose weight. He also placed her on antidepressant medication and referred her to a therapist. She was referred to a nutritionist, and her endocrinologist encouraged her to see a nurse-practitioner to help her with lifestyle changes. She was also encouraged to seek out support groups for her medical conditions. Despite this excellent care and support she was completely unsuccessful in modifying her behaviors, which were so seriously affecting her life.

Unfortunately, there are far too many patients like this, whose weight problems compromise their health yet who seem to have little ability to make the changes necessary to improve health. Obesity is certainly the most common eating disorder, although anorexia and bulimia cause significant problems for individuals, primarily women, most often teenagers and young women. Anorexia refers to the propensity of an individual to take insufficient nutrition, sometimes to the point of starvation. Some anorectics exercise excessively, use purgatives, or induce vomiting to maintain an unhealthy weight. Karen Carpenter, the well-known singer, tragically starved herself to death some years ago. Bulimia refers to binge eating with concomitant purging.

Example

Ms. W. was an 18-year-old young woman who was brought to the family doctor after her parents noticed that she had been depressed after a recent breakup with a boyfriend. Her parents noticed that she had lost weight recently and she seemed wan and listless. The physician, in his interview, discovered that the patient was quite concerned with her weight even though she was quite thin. He spoke with her about his concern about her depression and her weight loss, but she assured him that she was not that depressed, that she felt that she was eating sufficiently, and that she felt comfortable with her weight. Her condition did not improve over the ensuing months, and she needed to be hospitalized in a program designed for anorectic patients.

Both obesity and anorexia can be dangerous to the person's health, although the dangers of anorexia seem more dramatic and immediate.

Food is a symbol for love. It is the medium with which the first communication occurs between parent and child. It is necessary to sustain life. It conveys a sense of safety, of nurturance, of security, and of satisfaction. The types of interaction between parent and child are concretely manifested in eating behaviors and are thus readily available for symptom development. Eating becomes a metaphor, a symbol for many feelings about oneself and about others.

SUGGESTION. Eating behaviors become metaphors for a person's sense of self, for safety and security issues, for relationship issues, and for one's sense of his or her place in the world. Eating behavior is readily available for symptom development.

Body Image

Body image refers to one's conception or image of his or her own body. In American society there is significant pressure on women to maintain an ideal body weight that is very thin. A woman's body image may be greatly affected by these societal pressures. Body image is idiosyncratic and provides the individual with an evaluation and assessment of his or her body shape, size, texture, and features. Some people are content with their body, while others feel it to be at great variance with what they desire.

Example

A patient was a frequent visitor to her plastic surgeon. She had had her breasts augmented, her face lifted, her tummy tucked, and her fat liposuctioned. No matter what she did, she was unhappy with the way she looked. The unfortunate result of the surgeries was that she ended up looking artificial and phony. Her sense of self was reflected by her dissatisfaction with her body image. She had been raised by parents who had never seemed pleased with her, and she had unconsciously decided that she would be more acceptable if she looked better.

Often people feel that their physical appearance can expose what they may consider to be defects of character.

Example

> Mr. B. was in intensive psychotherapy for depression and anxiety. He told the therapist that when he looked in the mirror, he thought that he was ugly. When questioned, Mr. B. indicated that he was evil looking, which was reflective of his sins and misdeeds.

This sense of his ugliness was due to his feelings about himself. Those who are continually critical of their looks are most likely self-critical of other aspects.

Body image tends to have two focal points of development. The first would be in infancy, where parents are in intimate physical contact with the child and where the child relates to the world through bodily senses. The child interacts with the world nonverbally, through touch and oral incorporation. A baby who is given frequent affection, is treated gently and confidently, and whose body is treated with respect is likely to develop a positive body image. A child who is roughly treated or ignored is likely not to feel comfortable with himself or herself, and this is reflected in the person's body image. Those children who have the tragic history of sexual and physical abuse can have a distorted body image since their bodies were invaded in such a hurtful and bewildering way. Similarly, those who have had the unfortunate experience of childhood disease with painful medical procedures may also develop a distorted body image. The child usually does not understand the reasons or necessity for medical procedures and tends to experience them as invasions.

The other significant developmental period for the establishment of body image is in puberty. The bodily changes experienced at this time tend to bring forth a number of different feelings that for some children are difficult to integrate. Some children are not emotionally ready to deal with adolescent changes, physical, emotional, and social. Consequently, children may develop eating disorders that affect body shape and size and are thus reflective of the conflict.

SUGGESTION. Body image difficulties may reflect general psychological difficulties or may reflect conflicts that developed in childhood or adolescence.

Obesity

There are a variety of reasons for obesity. Obesity affects the medical practitioner in two ways. One, it is problematic since it is a disorder that causes and exacerbates medical conditions. Two, obesity is associated with certain personality characteristics that can be problematic to physicians.

Slochower (1987) suggests that obesity has its origins in early childhood. She suggests that "the painful, repeated mishandling of the feeding experience itself is likely to result in the development of an eating disorder" (p. 155). She further indicates that separation concerns and issues get expressed in eating issues via food refusal and various food preferences. The parent needs to be able to tolerate the child's rejection of food choices as an expression of independence and separation. "As development continues, early symbolic communication around feeding becomes increasingly laden with additional layers of meaning as the child's psychological world expands" (p. 155). Parental anxieties become expressed in the use of food and the meaning ascribed to food and to eating.

These same issues can become manifest in the doctor's examining room. Patients who have experienced overcontrolling parents may respond to the physician as if the doctor's advice and recommendations are attempts to control. Consequently, the patient may become resistant to following regimens. At times, eating behavior is the one area that a person feels can be used to express a sense of independence.

Example

A young woman was struggling to keep her weight within acceptable limits. Her parents had very high expectations for her and tended to be intrusive in her life. She loved and respected her parents yet felt that she needed to establish her own separateness and identity. Her parents, to make matters worse, were quite thin. The patient developed a respiratory infection that seemed refractory to medication. The physician was not aware that the patient was not taking her medication properly. She was responding to the doctor as if she were her overcontrolling, intrusive parents.

This patient's need to assert herself was endangering her health by being overweight and by her resistance to the medication. The struggle for autonomy was being waged on a number of fronts.

Many overweight patients are resistant. They know that they are overweight and may have tried a number of weight reduction programs with limited success. They are discouraged, yet feel angry about being pressured to lose weight. Physicians can be most helpful by being careful to ensure that the patient feels in control of his or her eating and of any weight control program. An obese patient should not be told that he or she needs to lose weight. Rather, the practitioner needs to question the patient on how he or she feels about being overweight and whether he or she would like some assistance.

SUGGESTION. Many overweight patients have felt overcontrolled and will respond to advice as if it is a threat to their autonomy. Phrasing concern and leaving weight loss decisions in the patient's hands minimizes this reaction.

Some patients' obesity is life threatening, and it may seem irresponsible not to be insistent about weight loss, but being demanding and authoritarian has little utility. However, it is important that patients be fully informed as to the consequences of their obesity.

Food often symbolizes love and nurturance for patients, and those who struggle with concerns about being loved often have difficulty with overeating. The emotional need is so great that it far overweighs any rational explanation of the dangers of obesity. People with these concerns can be helped by psychotherapy to resolve the underlying issues. The weight loss issue needs to be secondary to the insecurity concerns, since those concerns are what are basic and are fueling the overeating.

Some families encourage overeating, and the family has a sense of identity that includes poor nutrition and excess in eating.

Example

Mrs. A., mentioned in the section on "Mourning," in this chapter, was an obese woman with significant heart disease in her family.

It was essential that she lose weight and change her eating habits because both parents died of heart disease. Her internist sent her to a nutritionist, and she joined Weight Watchers. She found the recommendations to be extremely difficult to follow. Losing weight is very difficult if the patient hates the regimen. Fortunately, the patient was in psychotherapy, where it was discovered that her primary allegiance and identification remained with her deceased parents, which meant that she felt she needed to adhere to her parents' poor nutritional habits. This realization allowed her to finally feel comfortable with her weight loss programs and to lose significant weight.

This patient struggled with her therapist, with her doctor, and with her nutritionist for 6 years before she was able to finally attack her problem. Physicians and other medical professionals need to realize that patience is often required in working with seemingly recalcitrant patients.

Health care professionals are often impatient with overweight patients, as they are with all patients whose difficulties are self-imposed. Those without weight problems may not realize how difficult it is for the obese to lose weight. The aforementioned patient had a primary identification with her deceased parents, and losing weight was felt to be disloyal. Furthermore, by accepting a new way of eating and by forming new attachments to her health care practitioners, she felt that she would have to accept the reality of her parents' death, which in her mind was tantamount to killing them. One can see that weight loss is no easy matter considering the difficulties that some patients have in separating and individuating from their families.

Many obese patients have difficulty in differentiating between feelings. As children, their parents had difficulty in helping them to differentiate between hunger and other emotions. For instance, the parent may not have been sufficiently attuned to the child, so that a cry for comfort and to be held may have been misinterpreted as hunger. As the child continues to develop, his or her needs continue to be misinterpreted, such that almost all feelings get experienced as hunger. Additionally, these patients were often not assisted in developing tolerance for dysphoric affects. Consequently, they do not have the capability to be patient when they feel uncomfortable and thus turn to food immediately. Those of different backgrounds have the ability to be reflective when confronted with problematic situations. They may think about the particular problem and consider various solutions. Issues are "held" in the person's mind and reflected upon, instead of acted upon rapidly.

Example

> Ms. M. is the obese patient with Crohn's disease and diabetes mentioned at the beginning of this section. In psychotherapy she reported that she had recently eaten a box of snack cakes. The therapist encouraged her to wonder about what she might have been feeling prior to consuming the cakes. The patient was able to talk about her feelings of being lonely. She and the therapist were then able to make the connection between her feelings and eating the snack cakes. Additionally, the therapist suggested that she try to think about what she is feeling and to try to tolerate the feelings instead of acting upon them. The patient was incredulous about the notion that feelings should be reflected upon and tolerated. Nevertheless, she agreed to try.

The therapist's suggestion that the patient tolerate and think about her feelings is an idea that health care professionals can use with overweight patients and with others who have trouble tolerating affects. In this way, patients can feel more in control of their eating and begin to understand why they tend to overeat.

SUGGESTION. Obese patients have difficulty in identifying, tolerating, and differentiating between feelings. Physicians can be quite helpful by encouraging patients to be self-reflective and to try to tolerate their affects.

A good doctor-patient relationship will allow the doctor to work with the patient with such difficult issues. It is also helpful to refer overweight patients to nutritionists. Despite the plethora of information available on proper nutrition, many people are woefully ignorant of good eating behaviors and nutrition. Some overweight people are so out of touch with their bodies that it is helpful to have a nutritionist available to talk about the importance of exercise and to help the patient focus on and understand the relationship between food and weight gain. Many nutritionists are very supportive and understanding about the difficulty in maintaining a proper weight.

Some obese patients feel so deprived in having any needs met that they turn to food as a source of certain satisfaction. One is not going to be hurt or rejected by food, and gaining satisfaction through food is under the patient's control.

Example

An obese woman would speak about the profound feeling of emptiness that she would experience should she feel any hunger. Consequently, she ate almost constantly to avoid any feelings. She had experienced profound feelings of rejection throughout her early life and had turned to food for solace. Losing weight meant that she would have to tolerate these profound uncomfortable feelings.

This patient would require psychotherapy in order to work through the feelings that she was avoiding through overeating.

Patients who overeat may present certain behavioral characteristics in their dealings with medical personnel. Patients who have difficulty in tolerating and differentiating thoughts and feelings are going to have trouble maintaining medical regimens that require patience and discomfort. Obese patients may eat without really tasting since it is the consumption or the full stomach that is desired as opposed to an appreciation of taste. This may manifest itself with doctors, where information and advice is not taken in or integrated. Rather, it is consumed without being properly "chewed over." Physicians may need to encourage patients to ask questions in order to make sure any information or instructions are properly "digested" instead of swallowed whole.

SUGGESTION. Obese patients may have difficulty in following instructions. Physicians may have to repeat information to ensure that it is properly understood.

Some patients who overeat have never experienced sufficient structure in their lives. Consequently, they are at a loss as
to how to structure their lives in the present, including their
eating. These are people who have typically been neglected as
children and have been forced to fend for themselves. They do
not understand, at a visceral level, how to regulate basic needs
like food and comfort. They do not know how to regulate or
manage their feelings, and turn to food, alcohol, cigarettes, or
drugs to help them maintain a sense of stability.

Example

A patient was beset with a number of addictive behaviors. She had
used drugs and alcohol, tended toward overspending, and was a
compulsive eater. She had managed to get these behaviors under
control and was involved with an eating control program that involved rather rigid requirements. The patient was someone who
was raised without much parental involvement and welcomed such
control and input. However, if placed in an emotionally charged
situation she would feel quite anxious and would feel the desire
to use drugs or to overeat. It was very important for her to feel in
control of herself even though she was in a program that emphasized adherence. Nevertheless, it was her choice, and she felt
calmer in such a program. The program helped "contain" her
emotions.

Patients like this one require significant attention from health
care professionals. Frequent appointments and a referral to
self-help groups may assist the patient in internalizing a sense
of being cared for and provide the patient with the attention
that he or she has lacked in life.

SUGGESTION. Some overweight patients lack structure internally and may require frequent appointments and referral to
outside helping groups.

Anorexia and Bulimia

Both anorexia and bulimia tend to be disorders of young
women, although there are exceptions. Young men sometimes

have struggles with issues about thinness, and some may binge and purge.

As mentioned earlier, both disorders are potentially life threatening, and some young women have tragically starved themselves to death. Anorectic and bulimic individuals should be referred for psychotherapy immediately, although the patient is likely to be resistant. Those struggling with these issues are so preoccupied with food that they have little interest or time for interpersonal relationships. It will be difficult to establish a therapeutic relationship because they will tend to view the helping professional as controlling and because of their relative lack of interest in relationships. The physician may find it frustrating to work with anorectic and bulimic patients because of their superficial conformity and their dismissive attitudes.

Dynamically, those suffering from these disorders have similarities. "These patients are insecure, dependent, and immature. They are extremely attached to the parents, although this attachment may be masked by pseudo independence and hostility. . . . One or both parents are very much involved in the child's life, to the point of intrusiveness and interference with the child's maturation and independence. . . . A great deal of control is exercised by the parents over the life of the child" (Mintz, 1983, p. 87). Anorectic patients are resisting parental control by refusing to eat. Furthermore, they are typically avoiding everyday problems because of their fears about their capabilities. They become very knowledgeable about calories, dieting, exercise, and laxatives, and withdraw from most age-appropriate activities. They tend to have body image distortions, imagining that they are fat even when painfully thin. They are trying to avoid growing up by trying to maintain a prepubescent body shape and by stopping menstrual periods. They are afraid of becoming sexual. By not adequately nourishing themselves they are giving the message that they are incapable of taking necessary care of themselves despite their insistence to the contrary. Their refusal to need food is an attempt to have a sense of self-sufficiency by communicating that they do not even need nourishment. Typically, anorectic patients are very needy and dependent but refuse to admit their need and in fact deny their various "hungers."

The psychological needs that are being denied in such patients are of sufficient intensity to be life threatening. The need for autonomy and fear of losing a sense of identity is of sufficient strength to impel the person to refuse nurturance to the point of starvation. These patients are so afraid of their needs that they will do anything to deny them. Bulimics may take food in, may gorge themselves, but will not allow themselves the experience of adequate digestion. They have a need to incorporate accompanied by a need to reject.

Example

A young woman was referred for psychotherapy after becoming pregnant. She soon thereafter miscarried and then began to lose weight precipitously. She presented herself to the therapist as an extremely thin, frail, and fragile-looking teenager who looked younger than her years. Her posture was rigid and her conversation was stilted and impersonal. She described her family as being rigid, noncommunicative, and controlling. Establishing a therapeutic relationship was extremely difficult. The patient was outwardly compliant but essentially followed her own regimen outside of the advice of her physicians. Treatment was touch and go for quite a while before she was able to "let the therapist in" and look at some psychological issues. Eventually, the therapist was able to help her understand her fears about her emerging sexuality, which terrified her, especially in light of the pregnancy. Although she knew sexual facts, she was not really able to integrate them, as if they did not really apply to her. She had the fantasy of being able to stay immature by maintaining a child's body shape through excessive dieting.

This young woman had several characteristics common to anorectics. She needed to establish a sense of identity and was terribly afraid of sexual feelings. She had felt overcontrolled by her parents and used her dieting as a way of defying them. Most such patients are quite defiant although superficially compliant.

The eating patterns of anorectic and bulimic patients become embodied within personality characteristics. In the office these patients are not going to "take in" that which is offered. Consequently, they may appear as if they are listening to what the physician says but, in reality, are rejecting the advice just as they reject food. The health care worker may feel as if he or she is making an impact on the patient only to later discover that he or she has been rejected. This can be frustrating and hurtful. It is important to maintain the "container" role for the patient and not to react to the patient's provocations. Patients with these eating disorders are dreadfully unhappy and seriously disturbed.

SUGGESTION. Anorectic patients have a strong need to control themselves and their environment because they have felt over-controlled. They deny their needs and are afraid of growing up. Sexuality frightens them and they feel ill equipped to deal with the adult world. Bulimics will acknowledge their needs but then will undo them through purging.

Treatment of anorectics and bulimics can be very difficult and protracted. In their unconscious minds, their eating disorder is a struggle for identity and autonomy. They are so afraid of their own needs, that they must be disowned and rejected.

In physicians' offices, these patients can be very troublesome. They may seem as if they are listening and paying attention but may be totally discounting the physician. Often the doctor is viewed like the parent, controlling and not sympathetic. Medical professionals need to be very patient with these young women and to place special emphasis on relationship building. Trying to persuade a patient to eat more is counterproductive and will result in further defiance. Referral to a competent mental health professional is essential and will allow the medical professional to deal with medical problems resulting from the eating disorder. The patient can then form a different type of relationship with the doctor that is not so centered around the preoccupying eating disorder. In the best of circumstances, the doctor becomes an ally for the patient and, ideally, a new role model with whom she can positively identify. Parents of these patients will try to enlist the doctor on their "side," and it is crucial that the physician maintain primary allegiance to the patient so as not to be viewed as an instrument of the parents.

SUGGESTION. Maintaining a positive relationship with the eating disorder patient is essential. The doctor's allegiance to the patient must be made clear.

SUBSTANCE ABUSE DISORDERS

Substance abuse is pandemic in the United States. Cigarette smoking, illegal drug use, and alcohol abuse cause significant health and social problems. These behaviors negatively affect patients' health and exacerbate existing medical conditions. The prevalence of substance abuse is probably greater than health care professionals are aware, since patients are often less than honest about the degree of their use of harmful substances. An alcoholic patient may only admit to a small fraction of the actual amount of alcohol he or she consumes. Denial is the predominant coping and defensive style of substance abusers. They tend to deny the extent of their use, their capability to stop abusing, and the effects the drugs have on them and on their families. The use of drugs is an attempt to deny their emotional pain and to obliterate their problems. Alcohol and drug abusers exact a terrible toll on themselves, on society, and on their loved ones. The need to block out intolerable thoughts and feelings is considerable.

The propensity to deny will follow abusers into the examining room. Even outside of their drug use, they will deny the impact of external events, attempting to minimize the seriousness of marital, job, or physical problems. They will reassure the physician as to their willingness to follow through on treatment recommendations but will often fall short of accomplishing the goals set out. Typically, patients who abuse drugs are noncompliant. Their primary interest in life is to get intoxicated, and medical problems feel irrelevant. They crave the sense of bliss accompanying drug use. Some will use any means to obtain the drug, including illegal activities. They tend to present themselves as eternal optimists, yet underneath are often seriously depressed. The drug use is an attempt to self-medicate.

Example

A patient was seen in psychotherapy who was quite unhappy in his job and in his marriage. He felt there was no way out of each situation, and he turned to daily marijuana use to help him cope. The more he smoked, the more depressed and isolated he became. He also felt uninterested in pursuing further job training. In order for him to examine the underlying issues for his unhappiness, it was essential for him to curtail his drug use. Marijuana always provided an outlet for his frustrations, so that he did not have to talk about his concerns in therapy. He never told any of his health caregivers of his drug use.

Eventually he was able to curtail his drug use and his concerns about his adequacy emerged. Most substance abusers are highly resistant to treatment. It is often dire circumstances that propel someone into treatment.

SUGGESTION. Substance abusers deny the extent of their use of drugs, are often highly resistant to treatment, and are non-compliant. Their primary priority is to blot out painful feelings.

Those who seriously abuse drugs have lacked stable nurturing figures in their lives and have difficulty in regulating their emotions. The drug provides a sense of nurturance and bliss that mimics what they missed in their early lives. Most likely, their parents were absent or harsh and they were left on their own to face their difficulties. They are typically very lonely people who use drugs to ward off their sense of being dreadfully alone. The alcohol or drug abuser has a friend in their drug or alcohol, and this friend is not one who will hurt or betray them—at least not in the same way they were hurt by loved ones. Because of their preoccupation with substances, they have little interpersonal skills and have trouble with relationships. They tend to not allow people to get too close. Chronic and serious substance abusers plan their lives around the use of such substances and have little time, energy, or interest in other activities, unless alcohol or drugs are predominately involved. In general, substance-abusing patients have not internalized a sense of self-care, with the result being that they may neglect their health and nutrition. Some will get in legal difficulties, suggesting that they have not have developed adequate self-critical faculties.

Example

A couple presented themselves to a marital therapist. They had only been married a few years but were having significant difficulties. The husband described himself as a former drug and alcohol addict who was in recovery. His family background was chaotic, with a drug-addicted mother and an abusive father. He frequently attended Alcoholics Anonymous (AA) meetings, which he found quite helpful. The wife was a former drug and alcohol abuser who had an eating disorder. Additionally, she had trouble being financially responsible. She described a family background that was even worse, with her establishing some semblance of independence at age 15. She was involved in AA and in an eating disorder self-help group. Both had tremendous difficulty in self-regulation of feelings. When external events became difficult, they felt overwhelmed and, in the past, would abuse substances or other people in some fashion. In a sense, it was remarkable that they were able to accomplish what they had. They were still quite lacking in the ability to manage their lives, especially interpersonally. Therapy was designed to help them on a number of fronts. Their lack of interpersonal experience placed considerable strains on their marriage. They had a noticeable absence of empathy for each other. They needed assistance in identifying and in labeling emotions. They had been abused by others and did not understand the desirability of commitment and honesty.

There is absolutely no way that therapy would have had any possibility of success had these individuals still been using substances. Most substance abusers need more support than one practitioner can provide. Referral to self-help or other therapeutic groups is often essential. Their emptiness and inability to maintain their own emotions is too great for them to tolerate infrequent contacts.

SUGGESTION. Substance abusers lack self-regulatory capabilities and have gaps in their interpersonal functioning and in their empathic responses. Group treatment of some sort is often essential.

Many group programs, including AA, are not therapeutic in the sense of helping the patient to understand the underlying issues that promote the substance abuse. Nevertheless, they can be inordinately helpful in maintaining sobriety, which is a substantial accomplishment. Some patients have been so damaged in their early lives that more intensive treatment is not possible. These patients will often continue to be involved in group programs indefinitely, which is perfectly acceptable and appropriate. Others who are more motivated toward self-understanding can be helped through more traditional psychotherapy. There are a myriad of reasons that a person might abuse, and it is often helpful if those reasons can be explicated. At times, a history of sexual, emotional, or physical abuse is at bottom.

The personality difficulties that impel a person to abuse substances will, of course, not disappear once the abuse is terminated. Some patients and families are very disappointed to find out that the substance abuser's objectionable qualities do not disappear, despite sobriety. On the other hand, some families have been astonished to see loved ones flourish once substance abuse is ended.

In the medical office, substance abuse patients are notoriously difficult to treat. Their disorder is self-imposed, which can cause resentment from practitioners. They tend to deny and to be resistant, and can be dismissive and rude. They have difficulties with interpersonal relationships, and consequently the physician may not be able to establish a good working relationship. This is also frustrating to the doctor since he or she is not only dealing with a difficult patient but one with little sense of interpersonal connectness.

Substance abusers make promises that they never keep and seem unconcerned with breaking rules and being discourteous. Of course, not all substance abusers present the same way, and many "closet" alcoholics present themselves as being perfectly polite and cooperative. Nevertheless, they are being deceptive by not disclosing their use of alcohol. The physician needs to be direct and confrontive with substance abusers while maintaining a nonjudgmental attitude. Substance-abusing patients will try to persuade the physician of their intent to stop or will minimize the seriousness of their use. The physician should be skeptical of such promises and should be insistent of the need for treatment. Having treatment options available would be helpful. At times, the office staff or doctor can initiate the first contact with a substance abuse facility, providing the patient gives the necessary permission.

Some physicians have informed patients that they would not continue to treat them should they continue to abuse. This is a drastic action but may be necessary to impart a sense of seriousness to the patient. Furthermore, some doctors feel that they cannot continue to treat someone who is so willfully noncompliant and self-destructive. This is a matter of individual choice and may be necessary to maintain the physician's sense of control and professionalism. Substance-abusing patients need structure, confrontation, and concern, and probably require more directness than most physicians are accustomed to.

SUGGESTION. Substance-abusing patients often require confrontation by medical practitioners. They need considerable structure and care and should be referred to treatment facilities specializing in such disorders. Many substance-abusing patients will benefit from psychotherapy once sober.

PSYCHOTHERAPY

Psychotherapy is a talking cure. It is a very personal encounter between a trained psychotherapist and a patient in emotional pain. In the encounter, each participant puts himself or herself on the line. An aloof and distant psychotherapist is unlikely to be successful. A competent and caring therapist brings his or her personality and humanness to the encounter.

After a referral is made, most therapists will meet with the patient for a brief evaluatory period, typically one to three sessions. During that time, the therapist will assess the patient's difficulties and try, to the best of his or her ability, to understand the nature and cause of the patient's problems. These are gross approximations in most cases because of the complexity of people and of their difficulties. After the evaluation period, the therapist and the patient will decide on a course of action. They will discuss the nature of the problem and the nature of the cure. They will talk about frequency of sessions, costs, duration (if known), and their respective roles.

In psychodynamic therapy, the patient is expected to do most of the talking. He or she provides the data with which they will come to understand the patient's difficulties. Often the patient is encouraged to talk freely, to "say what comes to mind," without censure. At first, patients will talk about the symptom that brings them to the therapist. After awhile, the conversation becomes far ranging, touching on many aspects of the patient's life. The therapist, having accomplished an assessment, is listening to the patient in a particular way. He or she is looking for thoughts and feelings that will provide a different perspective for the patient.

Example

The patient, a man in his 40s, described how much he looked forward to his wife and son being away. He spoke of relishing his privacy and how they intruded on his sense of tranquility. The therapist was puzzled, since the patient seemed to care deeply for his family. The assessment showed a man who was quite disconnected from his feelings, who had suffered significant interpersonal losses as a child and who was quite angry, yet who would typically express these feelings indirectly. There were also indications that he had very strong feelings of guilt over perceived misdeeds. Over time, the therapist hypothesized that the patient probably was angry at the wife and son for some reason and that this was part of the explanation for his wish for solitude. Even more salient was the history of loss. The therapist wondered whether the patient was in some way preparing himself for some inevitable rejection by wishing for his family's absence. It would feel less painful if it occurred out of his own wishes, instead of because of his sense of being bad. The therapist listened to the patient's associations to lend further credence to his hypotheses. When the therapist was about to go on vacation, the patient indicated that he was looking forward to the therapist's absence, again invoking a wish for tranquility. The therapist, who was aware of the patient's reasons for feeling guilty, was able to make a connection between his vacation, the patient's feelings toward his family, his fear of rejection, and his unresolved feelings of loss. The patient was using the transference to work out his difficulties, and the therapist was able to make the connections to provide the clarification. The patient was then able to talk more freely and with greater affect about his concerns about rejection and loss, and this relieved some of his underlying anxiety.

As far as the patient had been concerned, his anxiety was inexplicable, as was his wish to be alone. In reality it was not a *wish* to be alone but a *fear* of being rejected and alone that was the issue, and this concern became manifest within the transference.

Therapy is an ongoing process with the patient and therapist continually learning. The therapist should not take on the omniscient role but should encourage a partnership, a cooperative team. Therapists should strive to be nonjudgmental and should leave most decisions up to the patient. It is usually not the therapist's role to give advice. This can lead to considerable difficulty since some patients expect that the psychotherapist will meet with them briefly and then offer suggestions as to how to solve the problem presented. Most psychological difficulties are quite complex and are not easily resolvable, and it is presumptuous for a therapist to take on the role of the all-knowing seer.

Example

Many patients, either initially or eventually, present a concrete problem that they need help in resolving. Some of these problems involve very serious, life changing kinds of problems such as whether to marry someone, whether to have a baby or to leave a job. Therapists may have opinions about these matters but often need to use restraint in order to help the patient decide for him- or herself. There often is no clear right answer and the patient needs to make these crucial decisions since he or she must live with them.

SUGGESTION. The therapist's role is to help provide a different perspective to the patient and usually not to give advice.

Symptoms are patients' attempt to solve a particular psychic problem. The patient in the preceding example is attempting to protect himself against further despair and rejection by adopting his dismissive attitude toward his wife and son. This solution, although not perfect, makes him feel more secure and less frightened. Nevertheless, it does not work to satisfaction since it still produces anxiety and does not allow him full pleasure in his life. It is a solution developed in childhood and is quite resistant to change because it is motivated by strong fears. Since most people's difficulties are developed in a similar fashion, change is often slow and difficult to achieve. Patient and provider expectation of quick and rapid resolution are not likely to be fulfilled.

Example

A marital couple was referred by their physician for treatment. The husband had precipitously decided that he had wanted them to have children after several years of marriage, although they had agreed at the outset to remain childless. He threatened divorce if his wife did not agree to this change. The therapist met with each partner and ascertained the existence of significant personal and marital difficulties. He suggested that they meet together for a period of time until the marital issues stabilized and recommended individual treatment for each as well. The couple were aghast at the idea that their problems required such extensive treatment. In further discussion, they revealed that the husband had threatened divorce in the past for a different reason and that their individual lives were so busy that they scarcely had time for each other. The therapist suggested that their reluctance to meet regularly for treatment was reflective of their difficulty in spending time with each other and that it would be advisable to explore this further. He also pointed out that the husband's threats were suggestive of serious problems. The couple was adamant and refused treatment, even on a relatively short, 6-month, basis.

Resistance in psychological treatment is a major barrier to success. The recent emphasis by managed care providers on shorter and shorter treatment reinforces patients' fears and resistances and can provide them with an easy rationale not to look at painful issues.

Psychotherapy is a process, an ongoing and changing endeavor with continually evolving insights and direction. Diagnosis is ongoing since both patient and therapist will discover more avenues for exploration as the treatment progresses.

SUGGESTION. Psychotherapy is a process and diagnosis is ongoing. Resistance is a major barrier to success but can never be avoided. Emphasis on short-term solutions reinforces resistance.

In psychotherapy the therapist often uses his or her own feelings as a guide to what the patient may not be able to feel or articulate.

Example

The patient, Mr. Z., mentioned in the section on "Resistance" in Chapter 3, was a young man who was socially isolated and withdrawn. Although successful in his occupation, his social life was almost nonexistent. He was almost completely cut off from his feelings. He would tell the therapist that he had some idea what feelings were but really could not identify or understand them. In therapy he would describe situations that most people would feel sad or angry about yet would insist that he felt nothing. The therapist would often feel sad when listening to the patient. This was a projective identification, since the patient was unable to tolerate the emotion and would project it onto the therapist. The therapist could then use his own feeling to identify that which the patient was incapable of feeling consciously.

This situation is not particularly unusual. There are many patients who disown many of their feelings, and the therapist's job is to help them to identify and accept how they feel. This particular patient was characteristic of many socially withdrawn and isolated patients. They all need very patient therapists since they are reluctant to take a risk by allowing emotions to emerge. These are people whose sense of integrity has been violated and who have retreated from others for protection from intrusion and hurt.

Goals of Therapy

When a patient is referred to a therapist, he or she will often have a particular goal in mind. They may feel depressed or anxious, have a marital or job problem, feel lost and confused, or even suffer from psychosomatic disorders. Generally, individuals do not fully understand the nature of their difficulties and the causes of them. Therapists need to educate and inform patients as to what may be activating the dysphoric affects that they wish to resolve.

Example

Mrs. F. sought out treatment because of depression. She had suffered some significant losses in her life, including some miscarriages. She did seem somewhat depressed to the therapist, and he was able to help her talk about her feelings about her miscarriages. As they talked, however, it became apparent that the patient suffered from much more than depression. She suffered from a pervasive sense of being lost and confused. She had always gone through the motions in life, performing tasks that others would identify for her and not having a sense of self-direction. She did not know herself, and that goal of knowing and understanding herself became the major focus of treatment.

Many people require the kind of treatment described for this patient. There are many individuals who live their lives without a sense of authenticity. They seemingly make choices and decisions but are really only going through the motions. This leads to a sense of falseness and a dissatisfaction with their lives. The anxiety or depression are only the outward manifestations of the underlying problems. More complete resolution of the presenting complaint will require a more thorough treatment. Some people may not have the resources, financial or emotional, to be able to tackle their difficulties fully. Patients can still be helped to identify the precipitants of their distress and helped to identify coping and problem-solving strategies. Short-term treatment can be helpful, but is usually not as helpful as longer term treatment.

Some patients are reluctant to engage themselves in psychotherapy because of concern that it will concentrate on their past while they need assistance in the present. However, it might be said that present-day problems exist within the context of the past with an eye on the future. People exist within a continuum of time, and this must be addressed. Nevertheless, treatment that is most successful will tend to focus on the present with an understanding and awareness that the problems originated in the patient's past. At times, particularly with victims of trauma, it may be necessary to spend considerable time understanding the past. Trauma victims are often fixated by the trauma and must return to it in order to understand its effects, yet a substantial emphasis is still on the present and how the trauma has contributed to the patient's present-day functioning.

SUGGESTION. Goals of therapy often change over time and may be different from those that the patient envisions. The emphasis of therapy is on present-day functioning within the context of the patient's life history.

Choosing a Therapist

As with any field, there are competent as well as incompetent practitioners. It is very difficult for naive patients to be able to choose. The most important factor to be used in picking a therapist is patient comfort. A patient should have a therapist in whom he or she has confidence—someone who has a good sense of what is wrong and who can articulate a way of approaching the problem. A therapist who promises results within a short period of time is suspect. People are complex and certainty of rapid success is questionable.

How does a medical practitioner choose a therapist to whom to refer patients? Asking colleagues for names of therapists whom they refer patients to is probably the most common way. Therapists are often more than willing to meet with physicians and other medical professionals to talk about their services. Patients will often talk about their therapists, both positive and negative, and medical practitioners can get referral sources from that information. The same criteria that the patient uses can be used by the practitioner. Does the therapist impart a feeling of competence and comfort? In consultation, does the therapist seem to have an understanding of the patient? Does he or she come across as being caring and concerned? Does the therapist show respect for the patient? Some therapists (and other professionals) show disdain for their patients, and this is obviously not a positive sign. It is often helpful for physicians and therapists to touch base every so often, particularly with more disturbed patients. Confidentiality is a major concern for those with psychological problems, and neither doctor or therapist should discuss the case with each other unless each has appropriate authorizations to release information.

Example

Mrs. M., mentioned at the beginning of the section on "Eating Disorders," previously had seen a number of therapists, none of whom seemed helpful. Her most recent therapist conveyed a sense of care, concern, and calm to the patient. He was very supportive of her and contacted her physician in order to coordinate care and to discuss medications. The patient felt well cared for and was able to establish a therapeutic relationship for the first time.

Disturbed patients need considerable support and understanding, and therapists who are judgmental or disapproving are not going to be particularly helpful.

The therapist-patient match is crucial for success. At times, personalities conflict and the relationship does not "click." Therapists cannot be effective with every patient. It may take some trials for patients to find the right therapist for them.

Some patients have a poor prognosis regardless of the therapist. In order to be successful, patients need to have an ability to step back and look at themselves. They need to develop what is referred to as an "observing ego." As patients react to life events and particularly to the therapist via the transference, they need to be able to maintain some objectivity in order to learn from the encounter. A patient may have intense emotional reactions to the therapist but still must understand that they are transferential and probably not based upon the therapist's true qualities. Those that cannot establish the necessary distance have difficulty in therapy. Therapy requires that patients think instead of act. Patients who do not have the capability for self-reflection are going to have a difficult time. This can be learned, but some patients do not have sufficient ego strength to endure the deprivations that they experience in psychotherapy.

Examples

One patient made some initial progress in therapy in understanding issues related to her unhappiness. She had been raised by extremely negligent parents and had felt cheated all of her life. This carried over into the therapy, where she experienced the therapist as not giving her enough. She became bitterly angry at her yet could not step back and understand the transferential nature of her anger. There was much more about herself that she needed to explore and understand, but her rage at never being provided with enough precluded any further analysis. Unfortunately, she was becoming the bitter and angry person that she described her parents as being. She quit therapy angrily.

Mr. Z., the socially isolated young man described earlier, was so afraid of criticism that he could not examine anything that the therapist observed. Each observation was felt as an attack, and the patient was continually defensive. Nothing the therapist said was viewed in any other way, including the observation about this occurrence. The patient did make some gains and became somewhat more outgoing, but the essential core of his problems, his sense of isolation and of being odd and different, remained relatively intact.

There are limitations to the ability of therapists to assist patients. Some patients do wonderfully and their life is changed dramatically and substantially. Some are helped moderately, and the minority are not helped much. Tragically, some patients commit suicide despite the best treatment available. Unfortunate results in psychotherapy are no different than those in medicine. They sometimes happen despite quite competent treatment.

Some patients will complain to their doctors about therapists not helping them. This puts the physician in an awkward position since he or she has no way of knowing the true situation. Nevertheless, the patient should be encouraged to speak to the therapist about the dissatisfaction so that the two of them can try to work out the difficulty. Negative transference is not necessarily bad, and a discussion of patient complaints can open avenues for elucidation. Most therapists will be willing to refer patients to other therapists if the patient is truly dissatisfied. Alternatively, the physician may need to refer the patient elsewhere. The physician should be aware that a dissatisfied patient does not necessarily mean that the therapist is incompetent because some patient problems are very difficult to resolve in the manner in which the patient desires.

SUGGESTION. Choosing a competent therapist can be difficult. Therapists who are warm and caring and who show an understanding of and a respect for the patient are likely to be helpful. Recommendations from colleagues and patients can be good sources for reliable referral resources. Not all patients can quickly or easily be helped by psychotherapy.

Does Psychotherapy Work?

Psychotherapy does help a great many people, some substantially and some moderately. Some people are not helped much, and a small minority, treated by incompetent and unethical practitioners, are damaged. Unfortunately, some therapists have abused patients by becoming sexually or personally involved. The number of unethical therapists is small.

Psychotherapy is a very emotionally draining and difficult process. It is irresponsible to assure patients of quick and easy results since success is often hard-fought and time consuming.

Outcome studies of psychotherapy are typically performed from within particular theoretical positions designed to bolster a particular orientation. Success in psychotherapy is difficult to assess because of several difficulties. Adequate assessment is difficult to achieve because there are many different kinds of therapies, many variations in patients and therapists, and external life events that cannot be controlled. Additionally, it is difficult to define just exactly what is a successful treatment. From the patient's perspective, he or she wants to feel better. Intuitively, it can be said that other indicators could be looked at. Generally, a successful treatment will lead to an increase in a person's ability to function in the world. Relationships improve and career and educational ambitions become realized. The presenting symptom is greatly diminished and the person feels a greater zest for life. He or she feels that problems are understood. The individual feels better about himself or herself and feels able to handle pretty much all situations that come his or her way. Therapy is not designed to completely resolve all of a person's difficulties. Rather, it is hoped that the person can use what he or she has learned in the therapy and apply it in the future. The person thus becomes his or her own therapist. At times, a person will terminate therapy and, some years later, feel the need to revisit the therapist to do further work. This is perfectly appropriate.

Consumer Reports published an article titled "Psychotherapy: Does it work?" (1995), which was based on a comprehensive survey compiled by the magazine's staff. The survey, which was well done and scientifically appropriate, provided several interesting results. Perhaps most importantly, a large percentage of the participants felt that psychotherapy was very helpful in resolving their difficulties. "The majority were highly satisfied with the care they received. Most had made strides toward resolving the problems that led to treatment, and almost all said life had become more manageable. This was true for all the conditions we asked about, even among the people who had felt the worst at the beginning" (p. 734). Furthermore, they found that those who stayed in treatment longer showed better outcomes.

They also found that there were no significant differences among therapists within the three disciplines of psychiatry, psychology, or social work. People reported that therapists within each group were easy to talk to, supportive, and insightful. The survey also disclosed that those who were in psychotherapy alone improved as much as did those who also took medication.

The magazine, in discussing the results, questioned the wisdom of the emphasis toward short-term treatment mandated by managed care and insurance companies.

SUGGESTION. Recent research suggests that therapy is helpful to a large majority of participants, that longer term treatment is more effective, and that therapists of the major disciplines are equally helpful.

CONCLUSION

It may be helpful to realize that all people, patients and doctors, have psychological disorders. Fortunately, the psychological disturbance does not always manifest itself in a way that impacts physical health or medical treatment. When dealing with patients, the awareness that we are in the same boat removes some of the defensive distance that is sometimes seen between doctor and patient. The awareness that the patient struggling with anxiety, depression, weight problems, or substance abuse is not that much different from the physician adds more humanness and empathy to the encounter. An empathic response to these various behavioral disorders is effective not only in working with such patients, but also increases the intensity of the encounter with the patient, leading to a more rewarding and enjoyable relationship for the medical practitioner.

Psychological symptoms are attempts to adjust. They are solutions that patients developed in an attempt to deal with situations, feelings, and thoughts that were incomprehensible and overwhelming to the patient. Psychological disorders are not discrete diseases visited upon the individual. They are part and parcel of the person and affect every aspect of his or her being. Psychological disorders often manifest themselves within relationships and consequently are likely to become evident within the doctor-patient relationship. This is inevitable and can be used to advantage by understanding that the re-creation (transference) provides a window into the patient's psyche.

Psychological symptoms differ in their outward manifestations, but a commonality also exists. Underlying conflicts or deficits can give rise to a variety of symptoms. It is important for the medical practitioner to keep in mind that psychological difficulties exist for a reason and have some adaptive value for the patient.

The role of the physician with respect to psychological disorders is generally not that of a primary treater. Physicians can be of great value in helping patients to contain their anxieties and can assist them in identifying that which is troubling them. Referral to the appropriate professional and encouraging psychological treatment can be of great benefit. Understanding of the complexity of psychological disorders and of their various meanings can enable an empathic response by the medical practitioner which can facilitate treatment where the physical and psychological interact. The physician can also assist the patient to deal with troublesome feelings and thoughts that eventuate in behavioral disorders like eating and substance abuse disorders. Some psychological disorders can be life threatening, and physicians may be the first professional to identify a particular disorder, thereby facilitating treatment.

SUMMARY

1. Psychological disorders are best approached from a perspective that emphasizes the whole person.
2. Symptoms do not exist in isolation. Personality conflicts and deficits are important in understanding the patient.
3. Psychological problems exist within relationships and will thus manifest themselves within the doctor-patient relationship.
4. Patients with psychological problems can be assisted in identifying present-day stressors that are exacerbating difficulties.

5. Patients from abused and neglected backgrounds need extra support because of their tendency to feel overwhelmed.
6. Some depressive disorders are related to unresolved mourning. Mourning is a lengthy process.
7. Depressed patients often feel hopeless, negative, and powerless.
8. Suicidal patients should be referred immediately. Police and/or family should be notified if the threat appears to be serious.
9. Abused patients can become abusers, and physicians need to be cautious. Many abused patients have difficulty in articulating their feelings.
10. Physical and sexual abuse needs to be addressed directly. The authorities must be notified if abuse is suspected or evident with children.
11. Victims of sexual and physical abuse should be referred for psychotherapy.
12. Physicians can provide needed factual information on sexual anatomy and physiology to those with sexual dysfunction.
13. Eating behaviors become metaphors for a person's sense of self, for safety and security issues, for relationship concerns, and for one's sense of his or her place in the world.
14. Those with weight difficulties have often felt overcontrolled and may react to the physician as if recommendations are attempts to dominate.
15. Those with weight problems have difficulty in identifying and tolerating feelings.
16. Anorectic patients tend to deny their needs and are afraid of sexuality and of growing up.
17. Substance abusers deny the extent of their use and are often highly resistant to treatment and intervention.
18. Substance abusers lack self-regulatory abilities.
19. Psychotic patients are often frightening to doctors and seem totally irrational. Most are not dangerous, and their thoughts, feelings, and behaviors are potentially understandable.
20. The role of the psychotherapist is to provide different perspectives, not usually to give advice.

21. Goals of therapy change over time and may be different from that which is originally envisioned.
22. Psychotherapy is helpful to a large majority of participants. Longer term therapy is more helpful, and therapists of the major disciplines are equally effective.

5

Borderline Disorders

Borderline personality disorder is a diagnostic category that has been developed within the last 25–30 years and has great utility for describing a group of patients who are vexing for both physicians and psychotherapists. Borderline personality disorders describe individuals who have an enduring personality pattern characterized by a panoply of symptoms that include impulsivity, unstable interpersonal relationships, affect storms, intense and inappropriate anger, feelings of emptiness and fear of abandonment, wildly vacillating senses of themselves and of others, and self-mutilating and suicidal ideation and actions. Patients with borderline personality disorders have a psychic organization with several specific qualities. Primarily, they suffer from ego weakness such that they have difficulty in tolerating dysphoric affects and other states of discomfort; they have difficulty in having integrated concepts of themselves and others; they are not self-reflective and tend to be action oriented; they have breakdowns in reality functioning; and they use more primitive psychological defenses, such as splitting and projective identification.

Example

Ms. M. had a number of physical ailments, which included digestive difficulties, diabetes, and obesity. She was noncompliant with her diabetes regimen since she frequently ate sweets in great abundance. Her job relationships were poor although she performed well on the job. She would become enraged at coworkers for what she felt was their incompetence. Frequently, she would be reduced to tears over the frustration that she felt at her coworkers. She appreciated consistency and order and had difficulty with ambiguity. Often she would feel exhausted and unable to go to work. This was a result of the intense affects that she had to contend with. Her house was described as dirty and disorganized, and she had considerable difficulty organizing herself enough to do basic housekeeping. She suffered from fairly severe depression and antidepressant medication, at her maximum dose, seemed to help. Two incidents were described that indicated her impulsivity and rage. Speaking with a repairman on the phone, she became enamored of his deep voice and suggested seductively that they meet. This came from a woman who had never really dated or had any sexual experience. The man initially agreed to the liaison but never actually showed up. Another time she angrily followed a man who had cut her off in traffic. After about 10 miles, he stopped, and she jumped out of the car, angrily demanding an apology. She had used poor judgment and placed herself in a potentially dangerous situation.

This patient had many of the hallmarks of a borderline disorder. She was impulsive and angry, was subject to intense affects, had wildly fluctuating interpersonal relationships, fought off feelings of emptiness, and had trouble with ambiguity. Those with this disorder tend to see things in extremes, in black-or-white terms. This is reflective of the defense mechanism referred to as splitting. Splitting is a fairly primitive defense whereby ambiguity of affects and thoughts are not tolerated. A patient with a borderline personality disorder does not think of himself or herself in modulated or integrated ways, but rather as all good or all bad, with nothing in between. This splitting also occurs in the way in which the patient sees others. One is either friend or foe.

This disorder describes a level of personality organization and is more reflective of a person's true nature than just that of symptom picture. For example, a person may present himself or herself with anxiety or depression as the primary complaint, yet his or her personality could be organized at the more healthy neurotic level or at the significantly more disturbed personality level.

Example

A patient would become anxious whenever he had a task that he confronted at work. In some ways his anxiety would become self-destructive since he would not be able to get the work done. In other areas of his life he functioned rather well. His marriage was good and he had a number of long-lasting and stable relationships. He could consider actions before acting and was self-reflective. His psychological disorder centered around his conflict over being successful and reflected competitive and angry feelings toward his father.

The preceding two patients reflect two different levels of personality organization. The first, a borderline organization, is much more disturbed and chaotic. The second, a neurotic organization, is healthier and would have a considerably better prognosis in treatment and in life.

SUGGESTION. Borderline personality disorder describes a level of personality organization that has a certain symptom picture. Borderline personality diagnosis describes an enduring organization that has instability as its hallmark.

Borderline personality disorder is one of a whole range of disorders that are contained under the rubric of personality disorders. Nobody welcomes the diagnosis of personality disorder since it carries a strongly negative connotation. It has implied for some mental health professionals a stable yet essentially untreatable condition. People with this diagnosis are seen as being difficult, self-centered, unempathic, and unable to form satisfactory interpersonal relationships. It has a pejorative flavor, as does borderline personality disorder, and is often used to explain away behaviors that make those making the diagnosis feel uncomfortable.

Personality disorders are treatable, yet not easily so. An individual with a personality disorder has a particular kind of personality organization that implies an original disturbance at a relatively early age. Personality disorders tend to suffer from developmental deficits, while more neurotic or healthy patients tend to have more conflictual difficulties. Personality disorder patients have more difficulty in dealing with stress (ego weakness), have problematic interpersonal relationships, and have more psychological symptoms. All people have certain personality characteristics. One has a personality disorder if these traits become rigid, inflexible, and maladaptive. The current lexicon enumerates a number of personality disorders, which include narcissistic, avoidant, paranoid, schizoid, histrionic, antisocial, and, of course, borderline.

Examples

A man was incarcerated for his eighth felony offense. His latest crime had been for bank robbery and attempted murder since he had shot at a police officer while attempting an escape. His only regret was that he had not been successful in escaping and showed absolutely no remorse for the shooting. His relationships had always been noncaring and exploitative, and he had no sense that relationships could have a loving and caring aspect. This man is a prototypical antisocial personality.

A patient was informed that her doctor was not going to be available for her appointment because of a death in the doctor's family. The patient became quite upset with the office staff and had trouble really understanding why the appointment had to be canceled, although she was superficially sympathetic to the physician. She knew how to be socially appropriate but really was mostly concerned with her own needs and had little empathy for and understanding of others. She did not really have close friends and saw relationships as a way of promoting and benefiting herself. She often would discard a relationship if she felt better or worse than the friend. In other words, she would vacillate between demeaning and envying others. This woman would fit the diagnosis of a narcissistic personality disorder.

All of the personality disorders vary in severity, and many people have characteristics of several different disorders. Those with personality disorders tend to have difficulty in coping with stressful situations, which include medical disorders. Furthermore, they tend toward the development of psychosomatic disorders.

Making the diagnosis of a personality disorder is often not necessary or even desirable since it tends to stereotype the individual. Difficult patients are sometimes dismissed with the diagnosis of a personality disorder, as if their complaints and problems are unreasonable and self-imposed. It is helpful to understand that those who have such problems struggle with some very difficult feelings, have had problematic childhoods, and may require special care and treatment. Of the personality disorders, borderline personality disorder is the most serious and the most difficult one. Those with borderline personality disorders are more chaotic, have a number of symptoms, and have more difficulty with reality testing.

SUGGESTION. Personality disorders reflect enduring personality characteristics that are maladaptive. They arise out of developmental difficulties and present difficulties to practitioners. They are treatable. Physicians should not use the diagnosis pejoratively.

THE ORIGINS OF BORDERLINE PERSONALITY DISORDER

Theorists all agree that borderline personality disorders develop in early childhood, probably before the age of three. A number of those individuals with this disorder have undergone severe deprivations, ranging from neglect to abuse. Those who have been victims of incestuous relationships are also prone to develop this disorder. Parents who are severely out of tune and neglectful can help create the development of borderline personalities in their children. Parents who cannot contain their ambivalence toward their children and who communicate their hate also contribute. Those patients whose parents were not able to help them understand and integrate their feelings are prone to develop borderline personalities. Some parents are not able to tolerate their own feelings and consequently are not able to teach their children tolerance of affects. Additionally, those who project or externalize their own difficulties into their children contribute to the development of this disorder.

Borderline personalities develop out of inadequate parent-ing. Consequently, these patients have had an early childhood experience that created personality "deficits" as opposed to conflicts. They are suffering from developmental failures. As these children grow up, they can develop a number of symp-toms. They typically do not do as well as they could in school since their chaotic feelings and sometimes chaotic family life make concentration difficult. Friendships may suffer because of splitting and because of the intense feelings generated. They may become very demanding and dependent within relation-ships, which others may not be willing to tolerate. As they have more and more difficulties, parents are less able to deal with them productively, causing a downward spiral. Eating disorders may develop in adolescence. Drug and alcohol use may appear as a way of trying to get nurturance as well as an attempt to get anesthesia from dysphoric affects.

Example

Mrs. P. was horribly abused as a child. By all accounts, her mother despised her and was terribly abusive, both sexually and physically. The father was essentially ineffective, leaving his daughter to be tortured. The other children were spared from the mother's wrath. It was all directed at the patient. As she grew up, she became more and more troubled. She became socially withdrawn, sexually promiscuous, and prone toward drug abuse. She placed herself in dangerous situations, eventuating in her being raped.

Listening to the life histories of most borderline patients, the development of such a severe and disabling disorder becomes easily understandable.

SUGGESTION. Borderline personalities develop out of neglect, abuse, and inadequate parenting. Most borderline patients have suffered considerably in their lives.

Those with borderline personalities possess a number of different characteristics which can impact on physicians and on other providers.

TRANSFERENCE

Those with borderline personalities have been raised in chaotic families, and it is expected that their internalized sense of relationships will also be chaotic. Consequently, their relationships with physicians and other providers is likely to be difficult.

Example

Mr. M. was an internal medicine patient who never felt that he was getting proper care from his physician. If he got better, he never got better quick enough. If his doctor did not readily diagnose him, he became hypercritical and demeaning. At one point, after experiencing unexplained gastric pain, he became belligerent and threatening with the physician and then deteriorated into tears. He felt in a panic, was convinced he was going to die, and accused the physician of not caring for him. He rushed out of the office, went home, got drunk, and cut himself on his arm with a razor.

This patient could not tolerate his physical distress without feeling extreme panic. He became overwhelmed with emotion and imagined that he was seriously ill. His belief was that since the doctor could not immediately cure him, the doctor did not really care for him. If he did, he would cure him. The notion that he had something seriously wrong got translated into a sense of badness that could only be relieved by self-mutilation. Furthermore, his inability to tolerate his affects caused him to become drunk in an attempt to modify his distress. The physician, meanwhile, was completely at a loss as to what was occurring. He felt that he had been sympathetic and caring and was doing what he could. He was bewildered by the patient's behavior and became angry and unsympathetic.

The notion of transference indicates that the patient is relating to the physician as if he is a figure from his past. In this situation, the patient was raised in a family that was extremely neglectful. Both parents were drug addicts who were barely able to acknowledge the patient's needs, let alone meet them. Consequently, he was at a very real risk of being in grave danger as a child because of his parents' inattention. When he became ill, he did not have the ability to be able to differentiate between mild and serious disorders. As a child, almost any pain was ignored and he never was soothed and nurtured, such that he could not now soothe himself when discomfited. He had very little sense of how his body worked and felt disconnected from it. Many of those who have been neglected and who are intelligent are able to superficially take care of themselves and even appear self-reliant. This is really a pose that collapses quickly under stress. Because of the neglect, they were forced to take care of themselves at an age before they were able to. Defensively, they try to convince themselves that they are really confident and capable. This may become difficult with medical practitioners when the patients adopt a manner of superiority and medical expertise. It is important to remember that those who present themselves as experts are really fending off feelings of inadequacy and fear. This patient, Mr. M., had developed this defensive posture to shore up his failing sense of well-being. Once that collapsed, his infantile self emerged and he behaved like a frightened and overwhelmed child. His using alcohol had two goals. One, it would anesthetize him from his pain, and, two, it made him feel more connected with his substance-abusing parents. He did not feel so alone if he could put himself in the same state of inebriation that he had seen his parents in. The patient's self-mutilation also served multiple purposes. First, it redirected his pain from psychological to physical. Two, it was self-imposed, so that he felt more in control. Third, he had developed the belief that physical distress was equated with moral badness, since his parents would become enraged with him should he complain of physical problems. Cutting himself was punitive and also provided relief because he felt he was letting out some of his "bad blood." Last, it was also representative of his desperation, since the only way his parents would pay him any attention was when he was seriously hurt.

The transference reactions of borderline personality patients are intense, chaotic, and extremely difficult for the practitioner. Because of this intensity and because of the defense of projective identification, countertransference reactions are strong and difficult. There are many different aspects of borderline personalities that need to be elucidated in order for them to be understood. There are also many different perspectives from which they can be viewed. The remainder of this chapter will look at borderline personalities from a number of different angles that relate to the doctor-patient relationship (transference-countertransference).

SUGGESTION. Borderline personalities develop intense transference reactions that are an offshoot of their chaotic early relationships. Countertransference reactions are also intense.

INTERPERSONAL RELATIONSHIPS

Since borderline disorders develop out of relationship failures, it is fully expected that interpersonal difficulties will predominate. As mentioned, transference reactions are often intense and extreme. The patient will also bring into the office issues and concerns about other relationships as well.

Example

Mr. N. worked in a factory assembling parts for automobiles. He was continually beset with physical complaints that seemed vague and elusive. His work history was replete with frequent absences because of his feeling physically unable to work. He felt that he was hated at the plant and that others were out to get him. He worked while listening to a personal stereo to shut out others and their conversation. He was rude and unfriendly yet wondered why others did not seem to like him. He visited his doctor frequently, often wanting excused absences. If his doctor refused, he would storm out angrily, feeling betrayed and unnurtured. His relationships outside of work were similarly disturbed, and he would often create fights over seemingly small slights. He had been married once before but his wife had divorced him because of his erratic moods and discontent. His family background was chaotic, with his father being described as being abusive and his mother as being passive. He had never really felt loved or appreciated and had been overwhelmed by all the powerful emotions acted out within the household. He had struggled with a drinking problem for much of his adult life.

This particular patient was beset by a tremendous number of problems that affected every aspect of his life. Interpersonally, he was very difficult and demanding and tended to alienate many of those with whom he had contact. He would often complain to his physician about his loneliness and about his job problems, yet seemed to have little insight into his own contribution to his woes. As a child he was a victim and, initially at least, did nothing to bring on his problems. As he grew older, he began to identify himself as a troublemaker and began to act that role out within his environment. This provided him with several benefits. He was able to get some attention, albeit negative. He felt more in control of what happened to him since he was the initiator. His self-righteousness provided him some gratification since he could feel misunderstood and maligned. He felt connected with his parents through this negative identification and was, unbeknownst to himself, acting out the perpetrator role. Despite these benefits, he was a miserable man who knew no other way of behaving or thinking. He felt little if any control over himself and really did not have the slightest idea as to how to help himself.

Such a patient presents significant problems to the physician, who might feel angry and frustrated by such a demanding and unpleasant person. The medical practitioner, first and foremost, needs to establish a working alliance with the patient. This is accomplished by maintaining a helpful and empathic attitude and by not being critical and judgmental. This is difficult to do because the patient's behavior is often provocative and may cause the physician to identify with the severe and judgmental aspects of the patient's personality. It is important to remember that a patient with such a background incorporates unintegrated and unmodulated aspects of the images of his or her parents and of himself or herself from childhood. In other words, the severity of the upbringing causes the patient to incorporate within his or her personality aspects of himself or herself identified as either good or bad. If the patient experiences a disappointment, it is felt as an awful failure, without a sense of moderation. In listening to the patient, the physician can start feeling like that punitive side of the patient and become condemning and punitive.

At the beginning of the relationship, establishing a positive connection is of paramount importance. Providing extra time and attention may be necessary. It is often most helpful not to challenge a patient on his or her perceptions, particularly at the beginning of the relationship. Once the relationship is well established, the physician can begin to question the patient as to his or her contribution to the difficulties observed. The positive relationship is established by the physician demonstrating sincere interest and concern for the patient. Focusing on the patient's distress and concern about his or her difficulty in coping is very helpful and communicates a sense of caring to the patient. The patient is unaccustomed to positive and caring relationships and will often respond very positively to the concern. At times, the practitioner may need to make some initial, relatively small concessions in order to reinforce the positive relationship. In the preceding example, the doctor may want to provide the patient with an initial work excuse even if it does not seem absolutely warranted. Being empathic and sensitive does not mean allowing oneself to be manipulated, however. Being overly indulgent is not helpful either, since it creates too many confusing signals for the patient. Oftentimes, such patients' parents have been negligently self-indulgent, which could be overgratifying, resulting in insufficient internal structures in the patient as seen in the following example.

Example

Mr. N.'s parents were not discrete in their sexual relationship, resulting in the patient being overstimulated and confused as to proper sexual boundaries. This resulted in him being inappropriate with women, making ill-advised and out-of-bounds sexual comments to women he would encounter either in the work place or on the street.

If the physician is overindulgent, it brings up old feelings of being confused and overwhelmed for the patient, which can result in even more difficult and problematic behavior. With this patient, continued work excuses would not be helpful or appropriate. Helping the patient to figure out how he can return to work and remain at work effectively would be most beneficial. The physician can listen to the patient's problems, empathize with him, understand how difficult it is for him, and yet still encourage him to continue working. The doctor can emphasize the positive within the patient and communicate how difficult it must be to work in such difficult situations. Providing and encouraging order and structure for the patient can be extraordinarily helpful since the patient desperately needs structure.

SUGGESTION. Borderline patients can be dealt with most effectively if a positive working alliance is established. Being genuinely empathic and concerned is essential. Borderline patients will test boundaries and limits, yet respond best with firm structure.

Many relationships within the life of a borderline patient are troublesome and ill advised.

Example

A professional woman began visiting a prison as part of her church's outreach ministry program. At first, she was relatively neutral about the work, feeling sympathy for the prisoners but maintaining a distance. After awhile, she found herself succumbing to the seductiveness of one of the prisoners. She became hostile to the prison staff and bought into the inmate's declaration of being the injured party without ascertaining the facts of the case. Eventually, her visiting privileges through the church were revoked once she was discovered kissing the prisoner. She continued visiting him on her own and became more and more enamored of him. She was troubled with the involvement, however, and sought out consultation with a therapist. The therapist was able to help her look at her involvement, such that she could eventually extricate herself from a potentially dangerous situation. Interestingly enough, the man was incarcerated for a rape, while the patient had been a victim of childhood sexual abuse. Prior to her being able to terminate the relationship, she had visited her internist because of a host of vague physical complaints.

Several characteristics of disturbed patients are exemplified here. The patient was putting herself in a dangerous situation by involving herself with a man who was incarcerated for a sexual assault. Clearly, her judgment was impaired. By ignoring the reality of the situation and by refusing to find out the facts, she was using denial as a defense. She was simplifying a complex situation and compartmentalizing prisoners and corrections personnel into good and bad categories. One would think that she would find it difficult to be with a sexual offender, having been assaulted herself. One way of coping is to identify with the aggressor, to take his side. Instead of thinking of herself as a victim, she unconsciously identifies with the perpetrator. Also, her whole involvement with a sexual offender is an attempt to come to terms with an extremely troublesome and disturbing trauma in her life. She could find out more about sexual offenders and their motivations but in a relatively safe atmosphere. It was, in a sense, a repetition, but with safeguards built in. She had no awareness that her involvement with this man had such meaning.

If the physician had known of the patient's involvement, she might have felt horrified and might have immediately urged its termination. This would not have been productive since the patient was not in the position to be able to understand her needs that propelled her toward such a problematic relationship. It was only after months of discussion with her therapist that the patient was able to extricate herself comfortably. The most the physician could do would be to express some curiosity about the relationship and to offer the patient an opportunity to air her concerns. This maintains the alliance and may provide space for the patient to become more self-reflective. Being calm and supportive also imparts a soothing quality to the patient, which can be beneficial.

SUGGESTION. Borderline patients often get themselves in predicaments that seem so obviously detrimental that professionals may react with horror and condemnation. Helping the patient to wonder about and to consider his or her behavior is the best approach.

Many borderline patients have relationships that are quite chaotic. They may come to the doctor's office complaining about physical problems but end up talking about their inter-personal difficulties. Time after time, a borderline patient may complain about being abused or misunderstood within a rela-tionship and yet do absolutely nothing to extricate himself or herself from it. Alternatively, the patient may be able to extri-cate himself or herself from the relationship, only to enter into a new one, just as bad or even worse.

Example

Mrs. J. would visit her gynecologist yearly for her examination. The doctor would ask her about her husband and the patient would complain about the abuse, both physical and emotional, that she would be subjected to. The doctor would encourage her to seek out treatment and would provide referral sources for battered women. The patient would promise to do something but never would. Furthermore, the woman's children were struggling in school. The patient seemed forever distracted, and she would be-come extremely upset and almost hysterical during and after the examination. At times she alluded to suicidalness but denied any serious intent upon questioning. She complained of never feeling well and of being continually fatigued.

In this situation, the doctor feels frustrated and impotent, which is certainly an example of projective identification, in that she was experiencing the patient's feelings. The physician can easily get frustrated and overwhelmed by the patient's bushel basket of problems and by her apparent helplessness. The patient does not have the capability to do much about her problems. She mostly lives day to day, putting out small fires before they become major conflagrations. She had no real ex-pectation of her life improving since this quality of living is what she was raised with. Through projective identification, the physician can begin to feel hopeless and despairing. It is important that the medical practitioner not give in to that feel-ing. Sometimes, the doctor is the one person who must hold the hope for the patient. If the doctor gives up and feels hope-less, the patient is likely to give up also. The fact that the patient comes regularly for her appointments does suggest that she is, to some extent, taking care of herself and that she feels comfortable with the doctor. It would be most helpful for the physician to continue to offer support and encouragement and to emphasize small accomplishments when they become apparent. This patient has created a life for herself that she feels is presently beyond her capability of changing. The physician can help her lay the groundwork for later change, perhaps when she feels stronger and when the children are older and less needy.

SUGGESTION. Borderline patients often create chaotic lives that they have great difficulty improving. Patience and support enables the patient to feel "held" and may lay the groundwork for later change.

IMPULSIVITY AND POOR JUDGMENT

One of the hallmarks of borderline patients is their impulsivity and poor judgment. Rather than thinking about the consequences of potential actions or of the wisdom of a certain behavior, the patient acts impulsively. This will often occur within interpersonal relations, where patients may involve themselves in activities that are dangerous.

Example

Ms. K. used amazingly bad judgment in her dealings with men. She would often meet men in bars when drunk and generally accompany them back to their houses or apartments without knowing essentially anything about them. She would then engage in unprotected sex. When questioned about these activities, she would say, "It seemed like the thing to do." It was as if there was little or no thought in her action, and she never considered postponing or delaying sexual activity until she was in a position to protect herself.

This patient really did not have the ability to make proper judgments about herself. She had been neglected by her parents, which resulted in her putting herself in potentially dangerous situations, and her identification with these negligent parents precluded her from taking proper care of herself. This kind of behavior can be viewed from other perspectives as well. In some sense, she had no real understanding of what it meant to take care of herself, as if she did not know what that meant. She had been so deprived of nurturance and comfort in her life that she had no idea how to develop a real relationship that might provide her with warmth and caring. She also could avoid any chance of being hurt emotionally because of the superficiality of the encounter. Hedonistic pleasure is substituted for the deeper satisfactions of an intimate relationship. The primitive self-hatred gets acted out within a rather degrading and potentially dangerous situation.

The physician may very well be at a loss as to how to intervene with this patient. Outrage over such foolhardy behavior might be the first inclination, and this might be appropriate as long as a good relationship has been established. Patients like this one have been beaten and humiliated for misbehaviors, or their dangerous behaviors may have been ignored. Rarely has someone taken the time and energy to confront the patient with the recklessness of her behavior. She has probably been made to feel bad but probably has not been made to feel cared for. Confrontation by the physician may enable the patient to identify with the caring side of the physician and to thus incorporate that within herself.

Confronting the patient does not mean yelling at her and telling her how foolish she has been. Rather, it means being forceful about the physician's belief that the patient is engaging in risky behavior and that it is essential that she curtail these kind of activities. Some patients will try to use their physicians as therapists and will be very reluctant to pursue psychotherapy. Confronting the patient with the denial of the seriousness of her behavior and of her psychopathology can push her to get the type of help she needs. It is important for health care practitioners to recognize the limitations of their expertise and to be forceful in recommending that patients take care of themselves by seeking out therapy when needed.

SUGGESTION. Borderline patients often engage in risky and ill-advised behavior. Confrontation by the physician can communicate caring and can help create internal structures.

"Internal psychic structures" are constructs that have been developed to describe the workings of the mind. Internal structures refer to the individual's capability to use his or her resources to navigate the world, to deal with reality constraints, and to be able to satisfy needs in appropriate ways. They imply a sophistication of thinking, an ability for self-reflection, and an ability to be insightful and introspective. A person can use his or her mind for self-regulation, such that the person is able to receive gratification from a number of sources. Thus, interpersonal relationships can be healthy and enriching. The individual can use his or her mind in a productive way and can find enjoyment through thought and consideration. Internal structures also refer to having a sense of boundary between oneself and others as well as a respect for others.

Borderline patients are not well structured, and impulsivity is one consequence. Impulsivity in borderline patients can be breathtaking in its recklessness. Patients have been known to run off precipitously with strangers, spend enormous amounts of money on ill-conceived purchases, and go on binges of eating, gambling, and substance abuse.

Example

A patient tearfully informs her therapist that she had responded to a phone solicitation a few nights earlier. She had allowed herself to be convinced to purchase a contract for a dating service for $2000, money she could ill afford. Additionally, the service was located about 40 miles away and required visits to the facility at least twice monthly. She also indicated that she really was not interested in dating and really had no idea why she had succumbed. The salesman had kept lowering the price, implying that she was missing out on a great opportunity that would expire that night.

There are many other symptoms and personality characteristics that this woman possesses that lead toward a borderline diagnosis. Impulsivity alone does not make a borderline diagnosis. Internally, this patient did not have the ability to delay her decision making, to consider the potential consequences of her actions, or to evaluate her real wants and needs. She experienced a sense of urgency and discordancy from the salesman, and her only perceived solution was to acquiesce. Her susceptibility to influence is also a characteristic of a relatively undifferentiated personality as is her inability to make decisions for herself.

When the salesman called, she had no particular wish to involve herself either in dating or in a dating service. In general, she suffered from an abiding sense of discontent, the source of which was unknown to her. Consequently, she was always searching for a solution to her unhappiness. Oftentimes she would overeat as a way of trying to make herself feel better. On this occasion, the happenstance of a sales solicitation provided her with an opportunity to fasten upon a solution to her problems, even if it had little to do with her own self-described wishes. Impulsive behavior can also be used by the patient to distract herself, to create some chaos in her life that will preclude her from thinking about something else that may be troubling. This patient was worried about her parents' health, and the worry seemed to be a communication of her imagined inability to cope without them. At the same time, this patient had been neglected by her parents in crucial ways, and this behavior is also a repetition of that neglect.

The physician has to contend with this kind of impulsivity. At times, in the course of consultation, these kinds of lifestyle difficulties become apparent and the patient may look to the physician for solutions. At other times, impulsivity can interfere directly with medical treatment. Patients can abruptly decide to terminate treatments or may insist upon medication or treatment regimen changes without apparent rhyme or reason. Borderline patients also may not show up for appointments; in fact, they may disappear for months or years. Some patients will experience considerable paranoia and may misinterpret mannerisms and gestures from the physician, become enraged, and then terminate the relationship. It is important to remember that borderline patients operate from a terrified position. They are frightened of their own feelings and of the world. There is much that they find incomprehensible, and they deal with this by becoming panicked and by acting seemingly without reason. These are individuals whose family did not provide them with adequate understanding of the world, and they are forced to try to understand and solve problems without the necessary tools to do so.

When a physician is faced with a patient who is operating impulsively and unwisely, several approaches can be used. First, maintaining a calm and confident manner is essential. Becoming overly upset and accusatory will only cause the patient to become more frightened and desperate and will encourage more chaotic behavior. Second, it is useful to try to help the patient to articulate what is behind the impulsive behavior. For instance, is there something else occurring in the patient's life that may be fueling the behavior? If it is a noncompliance issue, is there some problem with the treatment? Or does the patient have feelings about the doctor that need to be explored? If the patient can articulate what is bothering him or her, there is a much greater likelihood of the impulsivity being diminished. Emphasizing the physician's understanding of how frightening the situation may be for the patient can be very helpful. The patient may not have the words available to describe the discomfort, and labeling the fright can be helpful. Many borderline patients' difficulties originated preverbally, so that they are unable to verbalize their feelings. Helping the patient to label what he or she may be feeling can reduce dysphoric affect considerably.

Impulsivity is a result of a lack of a well-structured personality. The patient lacks the ability to process feelings properly and often feels a need to immediately get rid of uncomfortable feelings. Emphasizing to the patient that a particular treatment will require time and patience can help. The patient is not familiar with waiting and with tolerating unpleasant affects, since that was never done when he or she was a child.

Example

A patient was very distressed about an altercation that occurred at work. She became quite angry and distraught and had retaliatory fantasies. In discussing the situation, the patient wondered, with dismay, what else she could do besides acting upon her fantasies. In the past, she had never even entertained the idea of not acting impulsively. In her mind she had no choice but to do something to expel the unpleasant feelings. The therapist suggested that she do nothing with the feelings—that she should feel them, think about them, and try to contain them. The patient was incredulous: "Just *feel* them?" she replied.

This patient was raised in an amazingly abusive family whose members never tolerated emotions. They acted upon them, most often in inappropriate ways that taught the child that feelings cannot be contained and dealt with; they had to be expelled as quickly as possible. The medical practitioner can be quite useful in encouraging patients to stay calm and not to panic. This can be further reinforced by the physician's own calm manner.

Borderline patients often become overwhelmed by upsetting information and have trouble processing and dealing with such information. Since affect tolerance is limited, the potential for impulsive acting out is increased. Furthermore, the patient's ability to apprehend reality is compromised in borderline conditions. Consequently, information may be misheard or misinterpreted, resulting in overreactions and panic. It is imperative that the physician ascertain that medical information is properly understood.

SUGGESTION. Impulsivity is a result of borderline patient's lack of ego structure. Modeling more appropriate behavior is important, as is encouraging patients to contain their emotions. Helping the patient to label and understand feelings can diminish anxiety.

SPLITTING, IDEALIZATION, AND DEVALUATION

There are a number of defense mechanisms that are favored by those with a borderline disorder. Splitting, idealization, and devaluation are quite prevalent and directly affect doctor-patient relationships.

Splitting has already been alluded to and refers to the propensity of those with borderline disorders to compartmentalize their sense of themselves and of others. Rather than having a full, integrated, and modulated sense of self, these patients tend to split their self and other conceptions into polar opposites.

Example

As long as she was healthy, Ms. T. was a happy and cooperative patient. She thought her physician to be wonderful, without peer, and faultless. She would extol his virtues to all who would listen. However, once she fell ill, the physician rapidly fell from his pedestal. Suddenly he was mean, unhelpful, and incompetent, and the patient was enraged about her illness. She attributed malevolent motives to the physician and threatened to sue him for malpractice. The physician was bewildered and distressed. No one likes an angry patient, particularly one threatening lawsuit.

The patient was someone who was raised in a very punitive environment who was harshly punished for any perceived wrongdoing. Consequently, she did not develop an integrated sense of self. When she was happy and things were going well, she felt on top of the world, exaggeratedly so. She denied all of her other difficulties and acted as if she were completely carefree. This might lead her to some difficulties, since she might ignore some real problems that needed attention. On the other hand, if she were unhappy and things in her life were not going well, she felt herself to be horribly defective. She would become depressed with suicidal ideation and would even cut herself. She would engage in dangerous and potentially self-destructive activities. Within her present-day family, she would repeat what had happened when she was a child and treated her children in either an overly indulgent or terrible punitive fashion. This was, of course, confusing to the children, just as it had been to her, and their sense of self became fragmented and unintegrated.

This is exactly the process that occurred with her physician. When she was a child, her parents were overindulgent, without proper boundaries, or, alternatively, were mean and hostile, without a sense of perspective. Her sense of her parents was unintegrated and unmodulated and, transferentially, she viewed her doctor similarly. These are not mild feelings that the patient is struggling with. Her positive feelings about the physician may become imbued with sexual feeling, and she may become sexually seductive and provocative. She may entertain sexual fantasies and imagine her life merged with the wonderful, all-caring, and perfect physician. On the other hand, her feelings of disappointment become rageful and punitive. She may entertain violent fantasies toward the doctor. The recipient of either of these feelings is usually astonished when they become apparent.

Splitting can also refer to other emotions as well. Consequently, the emotion that borderline patients feel is usually of great intensity. When they get upset, they get terribly upset, as if their world is ending. On the other hand, they can become wildly optimistic and positive. At times, nothing is done halfway; everything is done in extremes.

Example

A patient was referred to a nutritionist because of being overweight. His family had significant heart disease and it was deemed imperative for him to lose weight and to exercise more. He described his eating patterns, which were reflective of his proclivities toward extremes. He would not be satisfied with a few cookies; he had to eat the whole box. He would eat enormous quantities of food and would drink prodigious amounts of beer. In fact, he prided himself on his ability to consume such quantities of food and alcohol. It was not just in consummatory behaviors that his extremism was seen. He would fall madly in love with some woman whom he had no real relationship with and then would disparage her mercilessly when he realized that the relationship had no real chance. Everything he did, he did in extremes. He would also become amazingly distraught when disappointed and exuberant when happy. The nutritionist had a great deal of difficulty in helping him since he viewed her attempts to teach him new eating and lifestyle behaviors as being depriving and mean.

Borderline patients have difficulty in understanding that disappointment and discipline are facts of life and are not necessarily being done to punish and hurt. This presents significant difficulties for health care professionals, as procedures may be painful and advice may be viewed as being depriving.

As children, these patients viewed those activities organized by their parents as being extraordinarily hurtful, which they may have been. Some of the abuse and punishment that they endured were handed out in the name of love and concern. Consequently, it is difficult for them to accept the notion that painful and depriving procedures and regimens are truly designed to be helpful. In these situations, the professional can empathize with the patient by indicating that it is understood how difficult the procedures or regimen will be for the patient. Helping the patient to verbalize his or her frustration without insisting on a reality orientation is helpful. That is, in the preceding example, it would not be particularly helpful to point out the reality of the need for proper nutrition. Rather, it would be more helpful to concentrate on the patient's frustration and difficulty in following regimens. Furthermore, understanding and being sensitive to the patient's feeling that he is being injured, deprived, or hurt by the treatment can help make it more palatable. Additionally, the professional needs to understand that the patient is not being resistant just to be obstinate. The medical practitioner should not react as if his or her expertise is being challenged or that he or she is being treated with a lack of respect. The patient is afraid and distrustful of those who are insisting that they are only operating with the patient's well-being in mind.

Example

A patient had recurrent bronchial infections that she never really recovered from. She became extremely frustrated with her doctor and refused to pay her bills. It did not matter that her smoking greatly exacerbated her problems. She was not getting better and felt that the doctor should not be paid, that he should be punished. She felt that the doctor was being cruel to her by not curing her.

One can see in this example what could be characterized as primitive thinking. Many patients feel reluctant to pay bills, especially if they are not getting the help they require. This patient, however, brings unwarranted suspiciousness into the situation by imagining that the doctor is being hostile toward her and by wanting to punish him in retaliation. The patient is reacting far beyond the reality of the situation and is importing feelings and fantasies that have their source in the patient's painful and punitive childhood. She imagines that she is being punished by the physician and responds in kind. At times, the physician or the staff will respond angrily to the patient's provocation, giving further ammunition for her rage and blaming. It is most useful to help the patient to articulate the reasons for her dissatisfaction and to encourage continued treatment. The patient's experience in life has been one of isolation and rejection, particularly once anger has been expressed. She has experienced considerable abandonment and has not learned how to soothe and comfort herself. The doctor and staff may also feel hostile and rejecting, but it would be far more helpful to try to maintain contact with the patient so that her feelings of abandonment and rejection are not reinforced.

SUGGESTION. Borderline patients tend toward seeing themselves and others in absolute and extreme ways. They do not deal with frustration well and often feel that medical regimens are mean and hurtful. Splitting causes them to have self- and other conceptions that are unintegrated and unmodulated, and they often relate to the medical practitioner in terms of good-bad extremes. They tend to attribute hostility where none may exist.

Within interpersonal relationships, borderline personalities tend to go to extremes in their conceptions of others. This often goes beyond having strongly positive or strongly negative feelings. They often get caught up in the idealization-disparagement paradigm, wherein the patient or someone else is either idolized or vilified. This is a result of their experiences as children, where they were reacted to in such an exaggerated fashion that they have not been able to internalize a realistic and integrated sense of self and of others.

Example

A professional man was describing a recent friendship that had soured. He and his friend had become embroiled in an argument over a small money matter. The man in question had become enraged and completely excoriated his former friend. It was as if he had completely lost sight of the past relationship and how much they had meant to each other. He exhibited no sadness or sense of regret and absolutely hated the man whom he felt wronged by.

There are several salient features here. First of all, the man had no perspective on, no sense of relationship with, his former friend. It was as if that friend no longer existed, only to be replaced by this hated individual. Second, the hated man, in some sense, represents a hated part of the first person. In an altercation, such strong feelings of anger and badness get activated that some borderline personalities feel the overwhelming need to get rid of the feelings by projecting them outward. Consequently, the former friend becomes "bad" and hated instead of himself. This is a form of paranoia that relies on hatred and blame. Last, the first man remains blameless. In his own mind, the altercation was due solely to his friend's stubbornness and unreasonableness, and he himself bears no responsibility for the breakup. He is the idealized "good" one, while his friend is the deprecated and disparaged "bad" one. The patient is not projecting the sense of badness solely to maintain a sense of goodness. It is also because the patient can not tolerate the intensity of emotions involved. Black-and-white emotions feel simpler and easier to deal with.

In more healthy relationships, people do get in altercations that can result in termination of a relationship, but there are crucial differences. A higher functioning person would be able to maintain a more realistic sense of himself and of the friend. The extreme hatred would not occur, and the person might very well question his own contribution to the dispute. Additionally, the person would probably feel some sense of sadness and loss over the termination of the relationship.

In the medical office, the practitioner might be subject to this sort of idealization-disparagement paradigm. This could particularly occur when a patient is not feeling better as quickly as he or she expects. Internally, the patient experiences the problem as a fault, begins to blame himself or herself mercilessly and then projects the sense of badness onto the doctor.

Rather than having a cooperative, problem-solving relationship, the doctor and patient have a frustrating and blaming situation. If the physician allows himself or herself to get drawn into such an interaction, a major dispute can result, with each person becoming angry and defensive. Those physicians who are drawn toward omnipotence tend to worsen the situation. They themselves have grandiose self-expectations which they convey to the patient, and the patient comes to expect great, perhaps magical results. When they are not forthcoming, the patient gets angry, feeling betrayed, tricked, and hurt. The physician also feels bad since his or her self-concept depends on great results as well as patient idolization, and a break in the working alliance results.

Practitioners can take several approaches to minimize the activation of the idealization-disparagement situation. It is useful to emphasize with patients that not all treatments work as well as everyone would like, and that it is not their or anyone's fault if desired results do not occur. Tolerating the patient's anger is helpful and not being defensive is essential. It is often helpful to emphasize feelings other than anger. A patient who is not getting the desired result is likely to feel many things, and helping the patient to identify the myriad feelings may mitigate the rage and help the patient toward more depth of emotion. Some borderline patients operate mostly out of rage and blame, and their lives and relationships are limited by their inability to experience a full range of feelings. For instance, in the previous example, helping the individual experience sadness and loss over the relationship would allow him to put it to rest and to not be so tortured by it. As long as he is embroiled in his "paranoid" outrage, he is going to be distressed as well as limited in further relationships. A patient who is not getting the expected relief can be encouraged to speak of his or her fear that he or she may not get well at all or may die, or of any other concern that they may have. A patient who is not getting better *should* feel frustrated, and it is appropriate and healthy to give vent to those feelings. Early on in the relationship, the physician needs to communicate his or her fallibility to guard against grandiosity. If the physician does not know what else can be done, the patient can be told this, albeit in a sensitive and caring way.

Example

> A complaining and hypochondriacal patient was experiencing lightheadedness and dizziness in the morning. She had been examined by her physician, who suggested that she was experiencing an anxiety attack. He told her this, but she did not find this diagnosis reassuring at all. She continued to complain about it, and finally the doctor asked her, "What do you want me to do about it?"

The physician felt bothered and harassed by the patient. He did not know what else he could do for her since he had already referred her for psychological treatment, which she refused. It would have been better for him to have acknowledged her frustration and to have admitted that he had no answers for her, that they had reached the boundary of his expertise. The patient may still rail against him for what she perceives as his inadequacies, but he is not allowing himself to get embroiled in an argument and is maintaining a realistic perspective. Furthermore, taking this kind of stance may help the patient to be more realistic with herself and not be so self-blaming and vilifying. The patient can be helped to expand her feelings about herself and others, to not see each in such a narrow fashion, and to recognize and accept the diversity of possible feelings.

SUGGESTION. Practitioners need to be careful to avoid the idealization-disparagement paradigm. This is not always possible, but the physician should not encourage unrealistic expectations and should emphasize the awareness of other feelings besides anger and blame.

PROJECTIVE IDENTIFICATION

Projective identification is one of the hallmarks of borderline pathology. To review, projective identification is a defense mechanism that is a variant of projection. It occurs when a patient cannot tolerate dysphoric affects and beliefs and projects them into someone else. The projection is such that the recipient experiences the disowned affect.

Examples

> The patient was discussing a situation in which a close friend was diagnosed with a serious cancer. The patient seemed matter-of-fact and without emotion. The doctor listening felt unbearably sad and distraught.

> A patient with gastrointestinal upset phoned the doctor's office in a panic, complaining of his usual symptoms. He communicated them with great urgency, and the receptionist found herself getting mad at the physician for his behavior, which she began to feel was lax. She was accepting the patient's urgency as her own.

> A psychotherapist was listening to his patient complaining about his life and how unfairly he felt he had been treated. The therapist began to feel irritated and impatient. Silently, he wondered what might be going on until he realized that the patient was probably irritated at him—that the patient felt that the therapist was treating him unfairly in some way. The therapist asked the patient and, after some thought, the patient mentioned that he had been quite mad at the therapist the day before.

In all three examples, a patient's feeling gets projected onto someone else and he or she, instead of or along with the patient, experiences the affect. Projective identification is an interpersonal entity and is an attempt to establish and maintain contact with someone else, albeit in a distorted and problematic way.

In a sense, projective identification is an externalization of a feeling state, yet it is a projection *into* another person, creating discomfort for the recipient. It is an attempt to maintain equilibrium in the midst of stormy and overwhelming affects. It is also an attempt to rid oneself of what the person perceives to be "badness." It is a very confusing situation for those caught up in that type of communication, since it is not clear whose affects are being felt and for what reason.

Projective identification reflects difficulty with the sense of boundary between people. It is generally a result of childhood experiences in which the parent was unable to understand the child's feelings and thoughts and impinged his or her own upon the infant. A mild example of this would be when a parent dresses a child warmly because the parent is cold. Unfortunately, a borderline patient has experienced this kind of boundary confusion in extremely painful and traumatic ways. A child who is sexually abused by a parent is having his or her needs misidentified or discarded by the parent. The child is no longer a person in his or her own right, with needs for protection and autonomy. The child becomes a recipient for the parent's power and aggressive needs. This leads to identity confusion for the child that persists throughout adulthood.

Projective identification implies identity confusion, boundary difficulties, disavowal of feelings and thoughts, and a sense of being overwhelmed by affects. The borderline patient often will project what he or she feels to be his or her "bad" self onto those in the environment, including the medical practitioner. The net effect of this is that upset borderline patients can be extremely demanding, insistent, inconsolable, and lacking in consideration for those in his or her orbit.

Example

A patient had been in a relatively good relationship with her obstetrician prior to getting pregnant. She had been rather difficult and demanding but within manageable proportions. The pregnancy seemed to create enormous difficulties for the patient, as evidenced by the way in which she related to her doctor. She would call her in the middle of the night with minor questions and complaints, would continually disparage the doctor by questioning her competence, would seem irritated and dismissive during appointments, would demand appointments at her convenience, and was incredulous when the doctor requested that both she and the office staff needed to be treated with more respect.

How can her behavior be understood? The stress of the pregnancy and the meaning and fantasies attached to it have created a regression and consequent difficulties. The patient has many questions about her own ability to be a good mother. Even beyond that, the patient wonders whether she is capable of maintaining a viable pregnancy. Some patients experience a fetus as a foreign body and have the wish to expel it. They may then project that feeling of "badness" or "foreignness" onto the practitioner in order to maintain a positive sense toward the baby. The pregnancy caused many changes to her body that she did not understand and which panicked her. They were experienced with such urgency that she lost perspective as to the doctor's needs as a person. The imagined and real neediness of the baby also reminded her of her own unmet needs and stimulated her own demandingness. She felt ill equipped to function as a mother since she had never been adequately nurtured by her own mother. This also was expressed toward the physician in the patient's snide, disrespectful, and demeaning attitude. It was as if she is saying, "It is not me that is inadequate, it is the doctor."

Patients who are extraordinarily demanding are those who have both not had crucial needs met and who may have been overly indulged as children. On the one hand, they are hungry for understanding and nurturance because of deprivation. On the other hand, because of deprivation of appropriate needs and because of overindulgence and overstimulation, they have not been able to develop the internal structures that would enable them to take care of themselves. Additionally, these patients have not always been treated with respect for their separateness and individuality, so they do not understand the proper boundaries between themselves and others.

The patient tends to express many of her frustrated feelings by being angry. The office staff and physician tend to find her irritating because of projective identification and because she *is* irritating, and then become rejecting and hostile. The patient feels more unloved and becomes more hostile, panicky, and demanding.

Firm limit setting can be very useful in such situations. Patients need to be appropriately reassured as to what they are experiencing. This is particularly important with borderline patients, who are often fantasy-bound and easily confused. Patients need to be calmly instructed as to when to call and for what reason. It is important that limits be consistent once set, since overindulgence can be too stimulating with some patients. Empathizing with them about their fearfulness and concerns can be helpful. Frequent appointments and phone calls during office hours can short-circuit late night calls. Emphasizing the doctor's availability to talk will be beneficial. It is also important not to respond to the patient's provocativeness. Being defensive when attacked may be the first and usual response but will not be helpful. The practitioner can use his or her feelings to understand the patient's projections. A patient who is disparaging toward his or her physician is likely to be struggling with adequacy issues of his or her own. It would be most helpful to ignore the provocations and simply say to the patient something like "I know that you're worried about your ability to be a good parent" or "I know that this is very frightening for you." When a patient feels understood, anxiety usually diminishes. The physician can empathize with the patient's demandingness but also can point out that the doctor has needs for sleep and privacy, even if it is hard for the patient to recognize that in the midst of a perceived crisis.

SUGGESTION. Borderline patients often use the defense of projective identification. Projective identification implies identity confusion, boundary difficulties, disavowal of feelings and thoughts, and a sense of being overwhelmed by affects.

Borderline patients have a sense of urgency about their problems and do not feel that they have the capability either to figure out solutions or to wait for assistance. They feel like hungry children without a parent to feed them. It is important to encourage patients by pointing out that they are adults and that they are capable and probably more competent than they imagine.

Example

Mr. L. was a chronic substance abuser and had tried every substance abuse treatment program available. He felt he could not tolerate his affects and his loneliness. He continually pressured his physician for medication and for work excuses. He portrayed himself as being helpless. The physician would find himself agreeing to work excuses just to get the patient off his back.

Anyone would experience the patient as an irritant. Of course, the doctor was doing the patient and himself no favor by agreeing to the excuses. The physician needs to help the patient learn to tolerate dysphoric affects, and he can assist in that by demonstrating that he can tolerate the patient. By brushing him off, he is implicitly agreeing with the patient that his pain is too much to tolerate.

The urgency that is experienced gets expressed as demandingness within the doctor-patient relationship. The patient feels overwhelmed by the affects that he or she is experiencing and demands instant alleviation. The patient loses all perspective on what is occurring and behaves as if he or she is in a crisis, even if the situation does not warrant that reaction.

Example

Mr. L. (see preceding example) began to experience recurrent headaches, which his doctor explained were related to his anxiety. Nevertheless, the patient became insistent about the headaches, demanding a better treatment and accusing the doctor of not caring about him. The doctor would patiently explain his diagnostic and treatment rationales but the patient became enraged and belligerent. He became so furious that he knocked over several chairs in the waiting room on his way out.

This patient lost perspective, but also lost what could be referred to as his "observing ego." He was not just embroiled in a transference reaction. It was not "as if" the doctor represented the patient's not caring parent, rather, the doctor became the parent to the patient, and the patient was not able to put distance between his feelings and his behavior.

Example

A patient had to undergo chemotherapy for a lymphoma. She became enraged at the technician providing the chemotherapy, as if the technician was purposely doing something that would ultimately be very harmful. The patient could not remove herself enough from the situation to understand that the technician was only trying to be helpful, not hurtful.

More healthy patients may feel some hostility toward those who hurt them during medical procedures, but they are able to maintain a distance and understand the larger picture. Borderline patients often lose that perspective and act as if the medical practitioner is a real enemy. This can be quite disconcerting and confusing to the practitioner, who is primarily operating out of benevolent motivations.

These borderline patients have been so traumatized and overwhelmed in their lives and so confused by the traumas that they have had difficulty in being able to psychologically distance themselves from painful experiences. They view the practitioner as having evil intent and have trouble understanding that pain is not always the result of hostile intent.

The practitioner is at a decided disadvantage in this situation, since almost anything he or she does that is not gratifying is viewed as an attack. The doctor who cannot immediately cure the pain or disease or who is not immediately available becomes the enemy. Sometimes even benign observations about patients are viewed as criticisms and attacks. When the medical practitioner sees this kind of interaction occurring, he or she can take several approaches. Certainly, it is most helpful not to return the hostility in kind. Instead, it is more helpful to try to absorb or contain the anger and to empathize with the patient. Also, it is useful to help the patient to articulate feelings and to communicate that the doctor understands how much the procedure hurts. Finally, it may be helpful to tell the patient that nobody is trying to hurt him or her, even if it may appear that way.

When a patient acts toward a medical practitioner as if he or she is hurtful or "bad," the patient is really reacting to a projection of his or her own sense of badness. It is important for the doctor not to act out that projection by becoming hostile and retaliatory, which only reinforces the patient's beliefs and fearfulness. Maintaining the therapeutic attitude of concern and helpfulness will help dissipate the projections.

SUGGESTION. Borderline patients experience great urgency about medical problems and tend to view those who are not immediately gratifying as being hostile. It is important for practitioners not to act out the patient's projections; practitioners should not be hostile or rejecting.

SELF-REFLECTION

Borderline patients are often impulsive and seem to act without thinking. They lack an observing ego and struggle with feelings of urgency. They have little patience and will often panic with little provocation. Boundaries between themselves and others are not distinct, and they have difficulty in distinguishing between their feelings and those of others. The consequence of these characteristics is a prevalence of chaotic feelings. Additionally, borderline patients have significant difficulty in affect regulation.

Example

Ms. M., mentioned in Chapter 4, would overindulge in sweets when distressed despite being significantly obese and diabetic. She had little ability to tolerate unpleasant affects and would seek to get rid of the dysphoric feelings as quickly as possible. Her overeating would serve to fill up the sense of emptiness and would make her feel better immediately. She described her mother as being kindly but ineffectual and overwhelmed and indicated that her mother would often send her home after a visit with chocolates and candy despite both of them being diabetic.

Borderline patients have not developed the capability to use their thinking capacity in order to deal more effectively with problems.

The capacity to conceive of the content of one's own, as well as the object's mind, is an important prerequisite for normal object relations. In its absence, the analytic patient, faced with the task of self-reflection, is prone to experiences of meaninglessness, chaos and nameless dread, as his own and others' feelings and intentions can only be represented at a primary (the immediately accessible) level and cannot be reflected upon or thought about. (Fonagy, 1991, pp. 649–650)

This is exactly the situation with many borderline patients. In the examining room, many patients become overwhelmed with the information that the doctor provides and essentially cannot process it or make use of it. This is very frustrating for the physician, who feels that he or she is not being listened to. Although true in a sense, this is not the whole picture. Many borderline patients do not have the capability to reflect upon that which is presented to them. They do not always have the ego strength necessary to reflect rationally upon problematic situations and to work cooperatively with the physician. The physician needs to be aware that disturbed patients will have difficulty taking in the information presented and that it is not willful obstinacy or stupidity that is causing the problem. Patience and understanding are required, of course. The practitioner also needs to communicate information in a number of different ways, sometimes repetitively. Providing patients with both written and oral information can be helpful. Having other office staff present the same information may be useful. Encouraging the patient to ask questions and to call with later inquiries can be beneficial. The medical practitioner can use intuition to ascertain whether information is hitting home. Careful attention to the nuances of the patient's reaction can give a clue as to whether the patient is taking in the information. If it seems as if the information is not getting through, the physician can question the patient as to whether he or she is upset. If the feelings can be articulated, the patient will better be able to listen and to respond appropriately.

Another aspect of borderline's patients' difficulties in self-reflection relates to acting out behaviors. *Acting out* refers to the outward behavioral expression of inner turmoil, often in a maladaptive and destructive way.

Example

A psychotherapy patient was mad at his therapist because he felt the therapist did not pay enough attention to him; the therapist seemed distracted. The patient went home after the session and picked a fight with his wife, eventuating in a physical altercation.

The patient would or could not tell the therapist of his dissatis-faction, and his wife then bore the brunt of his feelings. The patient was not really aware of the motivation for the alterca-tion; he just felt irritated with her. His feelings of rejection were too intense for him to be able to think about. Instead, he acted them out by picking a fight with his wife. When he told the therapist about the fight, they were able to understand how the patient's hurt feelings precipitated the altercation. That awareness helps the patient to broaden his self-awareness and increases the probability that he will be able to talk about, instead of act out, his feelings in the future.

Acting out can occur in medical settings as well. A patient who gets bad news or who is worried about loved ones can find the feelings intolerable and can express his or her discomfort by getting involved in troublesome behavior. The goal in psy-chotherapy is to help patients to be able to verbalize their thoughts and feelings, which will decrease acting out and in-crease understanding and control over behavior. Similarly, helping patients in medical settings to articulate their concerns will reduce maladaptive and unhealthy behaviors and will in-crease compliance. Patients need to be directly encouraged to give thought to their difficulties. Some patients have never allowed themselves to be curious about themselves and about their bodies. The greater the knowledge that patients have about themselves, the more in control they are likely to feel, thereby reducing anxiety and acting out. Borderline patients have not developed space between thought and action. They need to be encouraged to be patient and to take their time before they either make a decision or take an action. This is similar to children's behavior, where they may play one particu-lar game over and over endlessly. They are trying to master the skills involved, and the play is important in that regard. Some borderline patients have not had that opportunity to "play" with ideas and thoughts.

SUGGESTION. Borderline patients need to be encouraged to re-flect instead of acting out. An increase in the ability to consider and think about thoughts and feelings will result in greater patient self-control and in higher degrees of compliance.

BORDERLINE PARENTS

One would expect borderline parents to interact with their children in ways that would likely lead to the establishment of the same disorder. Because of boundary difficulties, parents are likely to be unable to respect the integrity of their children and will likely use them as sources for projections. This can occur through physical and sexual abuse or simply through being too self-absorbed to truly understand and meet the child's needs. Difficulty in reality orientation, ego weaknesses, and inability to cope with external life experiences are likely to create children who feel overwhelmed by life and by their own feelings. The parents are not able to establish a protective barrier for their children against the stresses of life.

The professional who comes into contact with parents who are not meeting their children's needs can become very frustrated and angry and can feel quite helpless. Certainly, the authorities can and should be contacted, but this is barely a real solution, if it is a solution at all. It is beyond the capability of the medical practitioner to solve or to counteract completely these severe societal and psychological problems. The physician or other medical practitioner can offer specific child-raising advice to those parents who are woefully lacking in knowledge and experience. Stern (1985) describes several intervention programs that attempt to help parents who may lack child-rearing skills and attributes. These programs are not concrete, how-to systems but are those which try to help the parent to understand the child and his or her needs on an affective level. They attempt to help the parent to become "attuned" to the child's needs.

Example

Parents consult a pediatrician regarding their child's difficulty in sleeping at nighttime. The doctor asks them to describe the bedtime routine. The parents are at a loss, not understanding exactly what the physician is asking. It turns out that there is no routine. The parents put the child to bed when they are tired, without warning or preparation for the child. He is not given the opportunity to prepare for bed, and the abruptness of the situation causes him distress. The pediatrician spends some time discussing with the parents the importance of bedtime rituals and helps them to bring more order into the somewhat chaotic household.

Borderline parents have considerable ambivalence toward their children but certainly love and are concerned for them. Yet they often do not understand what is necessary for a child to grow up to be healthy, and their pathology may interfere with what knowledge they do have. Significant time and effort needs to be expended to provide support, encouragement, and understanding to parents who have so little affective understanding.

It is often helpful to encourage parents to describe the difficulties that they are having with their child or children in order to ascertain with great specificity where the difficulty resides. The medical practitioner can then intervene in a helpful way. Often this means translating for the parents what their child may be trying to communicate or what he or she may be feeling. By tuning into the parents' concerns, the physician is modeling behavior, and by projective identification he or she may be getting some sense of the child's emotions. Some parents themselves have been either overindulged or sexually abused and may not understand proper boundaries.

Example

A couple described a situation where the family was all sleeping in one room during a recent vacation. It became apparent that the parents were unwittingly providing a highly charged sexual atmosphere by inappropriate touching in front of the children, culminating in intercourse while it was believed that the children were asleep. The next day the children were described as being out of control and upset. There was some likelihood that the children were overstimulated and upset by the sexual atmosphere. The doctor was able to help them understand that their behavior was overstimulating and that it would be wise to use more discretion.

Many parents are very defensive about the notion that they are overstimulating their children sexually. Consequently, it needs to be addressed with great sensitivity, without blame and accusation.

The normal assertiveness and dependency of children may also present a mystery to these parents. Some of them never learned appropriate assertiveness and were encouraged to be either too passive or too aggressive. At times, these parents will encourage, either directly or through modeling, behavior that is maladaptive. Helping parents understand that discipline does not mean beating or even hitting children can often save a child from abuse, although most parents who have been abused have a great need to pass it on to their progeny. Borderline parents need to be told specifically how to discipline children without resorting to physical abuse. Specific suggestions such as time-outs and the use of positive reinforcement can be helpful. Community groups often provide parenting classes that can be useful.

It is recognized that borderline personality disorder is an extremely difficult disorder and that parents in general are resistant to outside suggestion. Nevertheless, any small intervention can be helpful and can sometimes save a child.

SUGGESTION. Borderline parents need considerable help to break the psychopathological cycle. Specific child-rearing advice as well as help in affectively understanding their child can be extremely effective.

HATE AND COUNTERTRANSFERENCE

Borderline patients are infused with hostile feelings since they themselves have been treated so poorly in the past. This hostility becomes manifest in the doctor-patient relationship when the patient reacts with anger toward much that transpires. The use of projective identification charges the relationship with anger and hostility. As exemplars of extremely difficult patients, borderline patients often cause doctors and other health care professionals to dread and resent them. Most practitioners wish to have a positive relationship with their patients and feel even more despair when they experience such extreme negative feelings, even bordering on hatred, toward their patients.

Winnicott (1949) emphasized that all patients have a part of themselves that both they and others can find detestable and that it is unreasonable to expect therapists not to experience hatred toward patients from time to time. This certainly holds true for borderline patients and their medical practitioners. Winnicott suggests that experiencing hatred toward such patients is inevitable and is a necessary component of the treatment since all aspects of the patient need to be explored, felt, and analyzed.

Example

Mr. H. was a difficult man. He was authoritarian within his family and seemed narrow-minded and opinionated. He portrayed his weaknesses as strengths and was loathe to admit to any shortcomings. He was quite self-absorbed and seemed to lack empathy. His therapist found himself feeling quite irritated with the patient and had trouble remaining sympathetic. The therapist found himself silently calling the patient names. This certainly caught the therapist's attention and caused him to wonder about what was transpiring. The patient seemed to evoke within the therapist the feeling that the patient had always had about himself. The therapist was able to recognize that the patient's self-absorption was a defense against his past experiences of being hurt by others. The critical feelings that the therapist experienced were what the patient so often felt about himself. This awareness allowed the therapist to understand the patient in a different way and to communicate to the patient feelings that the patient was only dimly aware of, namely, his self-hatred. This was only accessible through the countertransference. When the patient was a child, he always felt that he needed to be hypervigilant, that he never could be appropriately self-absorbed. His present manner was actually a positive step.

The therapist used his countertransference to help the patient to understand an aspect of himself that was beyond awareness. By allowing himself to experience the dislike fully, the therapist was able to understand it, gain control over it, and help the patient to contain his own self-hatred.

Example

Everything the doctor suggested, the patient resisted. If told to take medication for 10 days, the patient wold take it for 3. If told to come for an appointment at 1 o'clock, she would come at 2 o'clock. She would not listen to the physician and seemed to disregard her advice. Furthermore, she was rude and hostile. She engendered great anger in the physician and in the staff, all of whom dreaded seeing her, and they all looked forward to the day when she would stop coming. For the physician, the reasons for her behavior are probably unimportant. She is not that interested in the patient's personal demons that are causing the behavior. She needs to have a strategy to cope with her own feelings.

The physician and staff are beginning to detest the patient. This, in turn, is upsetting because the office personnel do not want to feel that way toward patients. The staff can take themselves off the hook by understanding that it is inevitable that they would feel this way toward the patient; in fact, it is expected and perhaps, in some way, wanted by the patient. Feeling angry and hostile toward a patient is acceptable. Acting with great hostility and meanness is not. The staff needs to somehow accept and tolerate the behavior without retaliating in kind. Accepting and tolerating the behavior does not mean passively going along with patient acting out. A patient who is considerably late for appointments can be rescheduled. Noncompliant and argumentative patients can, and should, be confronted. Telling the patient that he or she is provocative and causing problems in the office may be necessary and, if handled with finesse, can be beneficial.

Gabbard (1991) speaks at length about the difficulty of patients who are embroiled in self-hatred and provides sound advice.

In my work with Mr. H. I often thought of a piece of advice I had once heard regarding what to do when one encounters an angry grizzly bear in the wilderness. According to wilderness lore, one should neither charge the bear in a counter-attacking posture that is designed to drive him off nor run away from the bear out of fear. If one simply stands one's ground, the bear will usually drop his threat of attack and go elsewhere. While I have so far had the good fortune to avoid any situation in which I would have to test out the soundness of that advice, it seems to me that one can think about the technical problems of handling transference hate in an analogous way. One must yield neither to the temptation to counter-attack nor to the urge to withdraw and retreat into aloof disengagement. Rather, one must be a durable object that holds one's ground and attempts to contain and understand that which is being projected. (p. 631)

SUGGESTION. Feeling strong negative feelings toward border-line patients is inevitable and, at times, necessary. Containing and using the feelings productively is essential.

AFFIRMATION

By now it is quite clear that borderline patients evoke strong feelings in providers. Countertransference reactions are intense, and those in contact with borderline patients often feel critical and hostile. Helpful suggestions sometimes are used as a club to criticize and to control these patients. Killingmo (1989) speaks of the importance of what he calls "affirmative interventions." These interventions are such that the patient feels supported and understood, and they do not emphasize motivation. In other words, they focus more on who the patient *is* than what he or she is attempting to do.

Example

A patient is describing how she cannot stop herself from overeat-ing when nervous. The doctor can take several different ap-proaches. He can lecture her on the need to watch her weight, he can question her about her need to block out painful feelings by overeating, or he can empathize with the difficulty she has in controlling her eating and encourage her to talk more about her feeling overwhelmed. The first two approaches may require more ego strength than the patient has available and are thus not help-ful. The last affirms to the patient that she is understood and provides a venue for her to discuss her feelings of being over-whelmed. Once she is stronger and more capable an elucidation of her motives can be attempted.

Most borderline patients are going to respond better to affirmative interventions. They will feel connected and sup-ported by the medical professional and are more likely to be compliant with regimens. They will be able to use the medical practitioner in a variety of ways. This may consist of asking for advice, discussing troublesome issues, and feeling secure in times of crisis, all of which can facilitate medical care and be rewarding for both doctor and patient.

SUGGESTION. Borderline patients respond better to affirmative interventions that emphasize their present status as opposed to their motivations for their behavior.

CONCLUSION

Borderline patients are a tremendous challenge for medical practitioners. Borderline personality disorder comprises a relatively stable personality configuration that is characterized by chaos. Borderline personalities are characterized by impulsivity, unstable interpersonal relationships, intense affects, fears of abandonment, feelings of emptiness, ego weakness, boundary confusions, and an unintegrated and unmodulated sense of themselves and of others. They can be quite demanding and unpredictable and use splitting and projective identification as major defenses.

The instability of borderline personality disorder is likely to manifest itself within the doctor-patient relationship such that transference relationships are likely to be intense, with a high probability of difficulties being felt in the working alliance. Medical practitioners need to be extraordinarily patient and understanding with borderline patients. A great deal of sensitivity and intuition is essential. Despite their troublesome aspects, those suffering from borderline disorders are psychologically treatable and can be cooperative and pleasant patients. These patients have been so deprived and neglected that they can respond very positively to care and nurturance and can be very rewarding to the physician.

SUMMARY

1. Borderline personality disorder describes an enduring personality organization that has instability as its hallmark. It

is considered the most severe of the various personality disorders.

2. Borderline personalities develop out of developmental failures, and those who suffer from such a disorder have often been subject to abuse.

3. Borderline patients have often been overstimulated and subject to parental neglect and misunderstandings.

4. Transference reactions are often intense and problematic, which matches the patients' childhood experiences with parents.

5. Interpersonal relationships tend to be chaotic, with fluctuating affects.

6. The physician needs to make special efforts to establish and maintain a positive relationship.

7. Borderline patients often place themselves in dangerous situations, and medical practitioners may need to confront patients with self-destructive behaviors.

8. The physician needs to maintain positive and hopeful attitudes despite borderline patients' own sense of hopelessness.

9. Borderline patients lack internal structures, such that problem-solving ability, self-reflection, and self-awareness are often lacking.

10. Borderline patients often vacillate between idealization and devaluation, which can be confusing and distressing to the practitioner. They tend to see themselves and others in absolute and extreme ways.

11. Projective identification can be difficult for the medical practitioner but can be used to understand the patient and to apprehend what he or she is enduring.

12. Patients often feel a great deal of urgency about their difficulties and may try to induce that feeling in practitioners.

13. Borderline parents need extra help in understanding and in responding appropriately to their children.

14. Affirmative interventions that emphasize the patient's experiences are most effective and appreciated by borderline patients.

6

Psychophysiological Disorders

A substantial number of visits to physicians are made by patients who either suffer from a disorder directly attributable to psychological problems or whose physical ailments are impacted and compromised by psychic difficulties. Those suffering from psychophysiological disorders are notoriously difficult to treat because the patient has a significant emotional investment in seeing his or her disorder as being purely physical in nature and is reluctant to acknowledge the impact of the psychological.

Psychophysiological disorders can refer to those patients who imagine that they have a physical disorder but who, in actuality, suffer only from worry and not from any organic pathology (hypochondriasis). It also refers to those whose psychological distress may actually cause or exacerbate physical conditions (headaches, gastric problems, tics, coronary disease, etc.). Furthermore, it refers to the general impact that the psyche can have on those suffering from physical disorders and disease (cancer, immune disorders, other debilitating disorders). This also includes the psychological reactions that patients have when coping with a serious disease.

Examples

Mrs. J. frequently made appointments to see her internist for a variety of ills. She would experience her heartbeat as racing and

235

would be terrified that she was dying of a heart attack. She would feel a bump on her arm and be convinced that she had cancer. A stomach upset would cause certainty that she had an ulcer. Regardless of the reassurance offered by her physician, she continued to imagine that she had terrible diseases and would call his office in a panic. He felt exasperated and impatient and was curt with Mrs. J. resulting in her feeling rejected and misunderstood, which exacerbated her distress.

Every so often newspaper and TV reports highlight a relatively rare but enormously destructive disorder referred to as Munchausen syndrome (or with children, Munchausen syndrome by proxy). This disorder involves the patient inducing or exaggerating symptoms that mimic certain physical disorders and diseases such that medical interventions are performed, including surgeries, all unnecessarily. Tragically, some parents have induced or fabricated symptoms with their children, resulting in unnecessary surgeries and other painful medical procedures.

Mrs. K. was diagnosed with breast cancer, resulting in a lumpectomy, excision of surrounding nodes, and chemotherapy. She became extremely depressed following the procedures and was reluctant to go for checkups as requested. Throughout the treatment, she suffered greatly and seemed to make the worst of a bad situation. The oncologist was disappointed that she did not respond as positively to the treatment as she would have wished.

The preceding examples are just a smattering of possible influences of psychological disorders on physical disease. The first example, of hypochondriasis, is quite common and is often seen in doctor's examining room. The second, Munchausen syndrome, is a very serious disorder reflective of either a borderline or psychotic disorder and is relatively rare. The third touches upon two issues. One is the noncompliance issue. Additionally, it brings to the fore the notion that psychological health can affect actual disease process. In fact, there exists ample evidence to suggest that a patient's level of psychological functioning can have a direct effect on the immune system.

The notion that there exists an interplay between mind and body is well documented. During the 1920s Lewis Terman, a psychologist, followed over 1500 bright California children in order to test his theories about the genetic basis of intelligence. This group of children, self-named the "Termites," have been followed ever since, with considerable demographic data collected (Freidman et al, 1995). There were a number of interesting results that indicated that certain social stressors and individual traits were associated with longevity. "Children of divorced parents faced a one-third greater mortality risk than people whose parents remained married at least until they reached age 21" (p. 71). They also found that those "Termites" who had more than one marriage had a significantly greater mortality rate than those who had been steadily married. The researchers also found that those adults who as children showed traits that indicated social dependability or conscientiousness predicted longevity.

Another recent article (Anderson, Keicolt-Glaser, & Glaser, 1994) indicated that "several recent articles, both qualitative and quantitative have concluded that psychological distress and stressors (i.e., negative life events, both acute and chronic) are reliably associated with changes, that is, down regulation in immunity" (p. 389). The obvious conclusion is that psychological processes affect physical health, sometimes drastically. There are those practitioners who prefer to treat physical disorders solely through medical interventions, yet the research cited suggests that the patient's psychological condition needs to be addressed within many physical diseases, not just with those viewed as traditionally psychosomatic.

Many practitioners in psychophysiology speak of a biopsychological system and maintain that a disruption in any aspect of the system can cause a disruption in any other part. Graeme Taylor, writing in the *International Journal of Psycho-Analysis* (1993) states that "perturbations can arise at any level in the (self-regulating) system, from the cellular or sub-cellular level (as with viral infections, and variations in the expression of genes) to the psychological and social level (as with intrapsychic conflicts, attachment disruptions, affect arousal and loss of self-esteem)" (p. 582). This approach sensibly solves the traditional mind-body issues and postulates the need to view disease from a wide perspective. It also indicates that any given disorder, psychic or physical, can affect any other aspect of the organism.

Example

Mr. H. suffered from constant allergies. In the winter, he complained of dust, and he bought an expensive electronic filtering apparatus for his furnace. In the spring, he suffered from allergies to trees and grasses and in the fall to airborne molds. He also had significant psychological problems, including fairly severe depression based upon rejection and abandonment as a child. His present family situation was poor, with serious marital conflicts. As psychotherapy progressed over a number of years, the problems he presented lessened and he complained less and less about his allergies, although they never completely abated.

It is hard to know if he actually improved based upon a decreased allergic response or if he was more able to handle physical discomfort as he became stronger psychologically. Nevertheless, his allergic reaction improved through an increase in emotional health.

ILLNESS AND THE PATIENT'S PSYCHOLOGICAL RESPONSE

It is certainly expected that patients will have an emotional response to physical illness.

Example

A patient, mentioned in the section on "Negative Therapeutic Reaction" in Chapter 3, had suffered a fairly serious injury while running, which curtailed his athletic endeavors. He became surly, angry, and accusatory toward his doctor, as if blaming him for his own perceived shortcoming. He viewed his injury as a blow to his narcissism and felt bad about himself, which he then projected upon the doctor.

The patient's physical injury caused, or more likely exacerbated, his vulnerability to depression and self-blame. Some type of emotional response to a physical injury or disease is quite common and is to be expected. In fact, a patient who has little or no affective response to a physical ailment is probably denying to himself or herself the reality of the impact of the disease.

SUGGESTION. A helpful perspective with psychophysiological disorders is to think of the organism as not having distinct boundaries between mind and body. Each affects the other, and a disruption in any area within the system can create consequences in any other area.

Many people respond to physical illness and disease with denial, disbelief, and shock. Schell (1996) indicates that most individuals with chronic disease first hope and wish for the disease to have never occurred. Next, the patient wishes for the disease to have little impact upon him or her. Last, the patient begins to accept the reality of the disease and what it will mean for the patient's life and for his or her level of functioning. Schell indicates that the patient must mourn that which has been lost in his or her life in order to move beyond the losses.

Example

A 23-year-old man was diagnosed as being HIV positive. His initial response was anger and disbelief, and he had himself retested several times. Each time the result came back the same, he became depressed and hopeless. After some period of time, he still felt depressed but seemed resigned to the disease. He then imagined that he could still live his life as recklessly as he had before and that he would worry about being HIV positive later, perhaps when he developed symptoms. Gradually, he realized that he was being short-sighted. It became clear that he had a life-threatening and life-shortening disease and that it made most sense for him to live a healthy life in order to maintain his immune system. It was a very difficult time for him as he worked through the reality of how greatly his life would likely be affected by the possibility of developing AIDS. Slowly he became less depressed and was able to mourn the possible loss of some of his life span, and he was able to make plans for the future. It is also possible, although difficult to know with certainty, that his immune system may be helped by the diminution of emotional turmoil.

The reality of the seriousness of disease can be quite depressing for many patients, and a number succumb to feelings of depression, anxiety, and hopelessness. As Schell points out, these patients can be assisted by psychotherapy. Furthermore, the physician can make a substantial positive impact on the patient by giving him or her the opportunity to talk about his or her feelings when faced with serious and debilitating disease. This may require the doctor to actively encourage the patient to articulate feelings and concerns about his or her condition. Not only is the patient going to feel better psychologically, but it may also have a saluatory effect on the patient's physical condition as well.

SUGGESTION. Patients tend to react with disbelief, denial, and anger when faced with serious illness and potential loss of functioning. Physician encouragement of discussion and articulation of the patient's concerns and feelings can have a beneficial effect, physically and psychologically.

Many patients experience physical illness as a narcissistic blow, as an insult to their self-esteem. They react as if they have failed in some fashion, as if they have betrayed themself by falling ill. It is common for people to have a sense of omnipotence and to believe that they will not fall ill because of their inherent goodness or because of their strength of character or strength of will. Consequently, a physical disease can result in a depressive response, based both on a sense of loss and on a sense of failure. It can be very helpful for the physician to bring up these issues with patients who seem to have difficulty in coping with the reality of their disease or disability. Some medical practitioners believe that if a patient is not overtly upset, he or she is coping well with the disease. This may be far from the truth, and silence may mean that the patient is suffering by himself or herself silently or that he or she is denying and not addressing the reality of the situation.

Example

A patient was diagnosed with lymphoma. He seemed quite accepting of the diagnosis and appeared cheerful and upbeat. He cooperated with the treatment regimen without complaint, and everyone was pleased with his "good" attitude. Unfortunately, he was, in actuality, extremely depressed and was actively contemplating suicide, which was not discovered until a nurse got him to talk more about his feelings about his disease. Appropriate referral and treatment was then initiated.

Any serious disease should alert the treater to the potential for emotional upset, and a proactive approach will help ferret out hidden feelings and despair.

It is expected that the individual who is more emotionally healthy is going to be able to deal with physical disease and disability with greater facility than one who has difficulty in coping with life. A physician who knows his or her patients well can predict how a given patient is likely to respond to a distressing diagnosis. If one thinks about the particular patient and his or her ability to cope, one can be better prepared to deal with the emotional response that follows.

Denial of the limitations that a given disease creates can create difficulties for patients. Schell (1996) describes a patient suffering from residuals from cerebral palsy who had difficulty in functioning on the job to the level desired by her supervisor. Neither the patient nor the supervisor were able to acknowledge the real limitations of the patient and instead focused on the supposed need for more training. In this instance, a realistic acknowledgment of the patient's limitations would allow both her and the supervisor to negotiate a more realistic standard.

Schell also suggests that patients create stories within which they define themselves, and that these stories must change via the reality of serious and chronic disease. A new identity must be forged that now includes the disease and/or disability. The physician can greatly assist the patient to forge this new identity by helping the patient to think about the disorder or disease in several different ways. Schell lists six questions to be addressed.

1. What has happened to me?
2. Why has it happened?
3. What is the meaning of my changed life?
4. How is pain understood?

5. How are limitations understood?
6. Do the stories support healthy living with chronic disease?

The creation of a new identity is a lengthy and ongoing process. The patient will need considerable support and understanding as he or she goes through the process of forming an identity that includes the undesired reality of being a person with an enduring and possibly chronic disease. This is not a pleasant reality and is often denied and disowned. Those that are having difficulty in accepting this new identity can be referred for psychotherapy. Additionally, support groups developed around the particular malady can be of great assistance. The patient can feel much less alone and can feel supported by others in the same situation. Support groups can offer concrete suggestions as to ways of coping with disease and disability that may go beyond the scope of traditional medical practice. Those that are afflicted with a given disease often becomes experts on that disease and can be very helpful to those newly diagnosed in running the medical gauntlet.

Example

A patient was diagnosed with multiple sclerosis. She initially became quite distraught by the seriousness of the disease and began feeling rather hopeless. She was referred to a support group that helped her to address some of her concerns about her future and that offered her a venue to talk about her worries. Being with other sufferers helped her not to feel so alone and enabled her to develop new friends who could understand and help her with the situation.

There is often substantial resistance to the formation of a new identity that includes the newly diagnosed disease. Considerable patience and understanding is required to assist the patient to deal with his or her loss of omnipotence.

Example

Mr. S. was an extremely successful business executive whose life seemed to run like a clock. He was supremely well organized and

had smoothly moved up the corporate ladder. He was rather interpersonally aloof, yet always cordial and polite. His wife and children were pleasant and attractive people and gave him no cause
for embarrassment. His diagnosis of prostate cancer put him into
a severe depression. His sense of control and omnipotence were
threatened, and he felt at sea with these profound feelings of fear.
Although his prognosis was relatively positive, it was not certain,
and he needed certainty in his life. Gradually, with assistance from
his physician and with a referral for psychological treatment, he
was able to come to grips with his new status.

This man had arranged his life to give him the appearance or
the illusion of omnipotence and control. There were many
things that he could control in his life. However, there are a
great many things that cannot be controlled, and physical
health may often be one of them. His diagnosis of prostate
cancer threw him for a loop since it smashed his illusion of
omnipotence. He needed assistance to incorporate this new
entity, cancer, into his identity.

It cannot be overstated that integration of a disease into
one's identity is an enormously difficult task and is one that
requires ego strength and support from others. It is always a
difficult process. The reality of aging and death requires all to
face these issues eventually.

SUGGESTION. Chronic and serious disease requires the formation of a new identity. Physicians can assist patients in this
process by helping them to articulate and answer questions that
pertain to the given disorder. Support groups and psychotherapy can be helpful to those who have difficulty in accepting
the disease and in integrating it into a new identity.

Each disorder will result in the patient forming an identity
that is partially based upon the characteristics of the disorder.
A man who suffers a coronary is now a heart patient. He joins
the ranks of those similarly afflicted and now must be more
attentive to diet and exercise. A whole new lexicon enters his
vocabulary based upon his newly acquired cardiac status. He,
and/or his family, become well versed in the intricacies of heart
disease. When he comes upon someone else who has a similar

problem, he feels a sense of affinity, a connection. If so inclined, he might join a support group. More psychologically healthy patients try to become informed about their disorder and attempt to become knowledgeable and cooperative consumers of medical care. Others, unfortunately, are not able to integrate the disorder and can have a variety of maladaptive responses. One group of patients that are particularly problematic are those who become obsessed with their disorders. At times it seems as if the preoccupation takes over the person's personality and his or her identity consists primarily of being a sufferer of the particular disease.

Example

One patient was diagnosed with borderline diabetes and was requested to try to control her glucose level through diet. She became amazingly serious about this endeavor, checked her glucose level several times daily and was driven in her quest to maintain her diet perfectly. Friends and family began to experience her as intolerable since it seemed that all she could talk about was her diabetes. She harangued her doctor with frequent phone calls and often had a laundry list of questions during her appointments. She kept immaculate and complete records of all of her doctor visits and of her various medical test results. She joined diabetes support groups, became active in local and national diabetes organizations, and was consumed by this interest to the point of neglecting her family.

This patient experienced her diabetes in several different ways. In one way, her disease was experienced as a narcissistic blow, and she was stunned by her newfound imagined frailty. She had always thought of herself as being quite competent and unassailable, and the diabetes made her feel weak and vulnerable. It felt crucial for her to regain what control she could by staying on top of the disease. The diabetes threatened her sense of omnipotence, but her continued activities provided the illusion that she was still in control. There is an adaptive quality evident since she was staying compliant and healthy. At the same time, however, she was making herself sick with worry and others sick of her in the process. She had taken a disability and tried to turn it positively to her advantage. The diabetes was so difficult for her that she organized her life around it. This is not substantially different from those who suffer some sort of assault and are unable to move beyond it. For this patient, the diabetes was an assault upon her sense of self, and she felt overwhelmed by it. Physicians can get very frustrated with patients like this who are so single-minded and obsessed. The doctor may very well feel impatient and irritated that so much time is being taken by ground already gone over, seemingly endlessly. If the physician is curt and unsympathetic, the patient is likely to feel hurt and rejected and to redouble efforts to gain mastery over the disease. The best approach is to be sympathetic and to encourage the patient to talk about how upsetting it must be to have the particular disorder. However, it will be important for time limits to be placed on the encounter. The practitioner can gently inform the patient that he or she has only a certain amount of time available and that the appointment will need to end at a specified time. This helps structure the patient and his or her anxiety and may actually help contain it. Certainly, many patients may still experience a time limit as being hurtful, but most will be able to accept it.

SUGGESTION. Some patients experience their diseases as narcissistic affronts and as confirmation of impotence and imperfection. Encouraging discussion of feelings can be helpful. It may become necessary to explicitly control appointment lengths in order to help contain the patient's anxiety and to maintain the doctor's equanimity.

While some patients seem obsessed and upset with their disease or disorder, others seem positively pleased. They seem to relish the sick role and to play it up and exaggerate it. Some patients who find life to be boring and empty find some meaning in their disease. It tends to operate as an organizing quality in people who find little order in their life. Others who are perpetually anxious and unhappy have a concrete reality upon which they can rest their dissatisfaction. Some who do not have a firmly established sense of self can take solace in their new identity. Lonely and isolated people can use disorders as ways to become more involved with others via support groups. Sick people can get considerable care and attention that they may feel that they would not get otherwise. At times, patients are said to receive "secondary gain" from disorders, and this term emphasizes the pleasure or benefit received by patients for being ill. It is important to remember that these patients are not consciously aware of being manipulative. Any pleasure received is not easy to admit, either to the patient or to anyone else. Physicians are usually devoted to fighting disease and may find abhorrent those who seem to relish cavorting with the enemy. It is important for the physician to remember that those who react like this are lonely and isolated people whose preoccupation with their disorder is more sad than anything else.

Example

A psychotherapy patient, Ms. A., suffered from a variety of symptoms, the primary one being depression. The depression did not seem to be consistent, though. When events in her life became chaotic and seemingly overwhelming, she seemed energized and alive. When events were progressing smoothly, she felt empty and bored. At one point in the treatment she became quite bored and depressed, and it was decided to refer her for medication evaluation. The psychiatrist felt that she would benefit from antidepressant medication and a prescription was given. Prior to her filling the prescription, her father was diagnosed with prostate cancer. Almost immediately her depression lifted and she became energized and happy, and never filled the prescription.

There are several reasons for the patient's improvement in functioning. With a crisis she felt involved and enlivened. Her family, who had serious conflicts, came together more cooperatively than usual. In some fashion, she was more connected to negativity than to positive events and would become excited by crises. Of course, any hostile feelings toward her father, of which there was an abundance, were getting actualized. Most importantly, this patient suffered from profound feelings of emptiness that were abated by medical crises.

Many practitioners become critical of patients such as this one, believing that they are cruel and uncaring. Although there is some truth in that conception, it is not the whole story. It is their emptiness and their desire to avoid that terrible feeling that motivates the behavior.

SUGGESTION. Patients accept the sick role and gain some satisfaction from it as a way of warding of feelings of emptiness and despair.

In the past, some diseases would engender shame and embarrassment in the afflicted and his or her family. Cancer was certainly viewed that way by a number of people and probably still is by a small minority. Of course, AIDS and sexually transmitted diseases create strong feelings in those that have the disease and in those that do not. Some view these illnesses as punishment for sinful behavior. There are patients who feel that way about other diseases as well. The guilt-prone can find anything to imagine as punishment for what they perceive as their "badness." This kind of attitude may be difficult to discern, patients are not likely to be forthcoming with this information since they feel so ashamed. Those that feel this way can become very noncompliant. It can be helpful for the physician to question the patient about any feelings of shame or embarrassment, especially with disorders like AIDS and sexually transmitted disorders.

THE PATIENT AND THE FORMATION OF PSYCHOSOMATIC DISORDERS

Many physical disorders seem more related to psychological problems than to an underlying biological substrate. As mentioned, some medical practitioners find this fact to be upsetting since their training and mind-set are more oriented toward biological treatments. Nevertheless, a large proportion of patients seen in examining rooms suffer from disorders that have a significant psychological foundation.

An explication of the reasons for the formation of psychosomatic and hypochondriacal disorders can help the practitioner to better understand how to confront these patients with such intractable disorders.

Joyce McDougall (1989) suggests that psychosomatic patients have two characteristic qualities. The first is the propensity toward "operatory thinking." This describes an affectless way of relating to others.

Example

A patient was describing to his doctor a situation in which he fell seriously ill with a bacterial infection. His treating physicians were concerned that he might succumb and his recovery was in doubt for several days. The current physician indicated that the experience must have been frightening. The patient replied, "No, all my affairs were in order."

A situation where intense emotion would be expected was instead replaced by a matter-of-fact and irrelevant comment. In some sense, this represents a denial of the affect because of its overwhelming and intense nature. However, McDougall also suggests that patients such as these do not have the capability to express affects via thoughts and words.

Example

A psychotherapy patient was describing an incident where, as a child, he was tormented by peers on the bus. The therapist asked him what he might have felt in that situation. The patient responded that he knew intellectually what "feelings" meant but really could not describe or understand them.

This was a patient who was so removed from his emotions that he had no words for them. In fact, often he was not even aware of feeling anything, even if his facial expressions gave evidence to the contrary. The term "alexithymia" has been coined to describe those individuals who have no ability to describe their feelings. These patients are not "repressing" feelings because they are painful. Rather, in McDougall's (1989) word, they are "pulverizing" feelings (p. 24). Emotions get destroyed prior to being made available for cognition. Thus, the patient does not have words to describe what he or she may be feeling. Asking such a patient what he or she may be feeling is, at some level, experienced by the patient as being both confusing and absurd. It is not a language with which they have any familiarity.

Such patients have sensations and emotions that are not "mentalized." As children, their affects were overly intense and overwhelming and their parents were not available to help them to interpret and to label emotions. The person's bodily sensations did not lead toward verbal description of them. The young child was not able to gain mastery and understanding of his or her body by the use of language. The early childhood nonverbal, bodily expression of affects remained predominant.

Example

Mrs. M. had a long history of gastrointestinal (GI) problems. When she became upset, it would manifest itself through GI symptomology via excessive gas and diarrhea. She could not really articulate what was bothering her during these episodes, yet had a sense of being vaguely distressed. She had been raised in a family where the parents were rather depressed and were consequently not able to help her to learn to identify and label her feelings. She was forced to turn toward her body functions as a way of ridding herself of uncomfortable and unacceptable feelings. This enabled her to remain positively connected with her parents, since they were more able to deal with bodily discomfort than with emotional discomfort.

This is a fairly typical case where a patient is forced, by her inability to process feelings mentally, to split off into her body. This protects her from overwhelming and confusing affects. Additionally, GI upsets commanded attention from her parents, and they were able to rouse themselves from their depression and attend to their daughter. Psychosomatic patients can be very emotional and demanding, yet in certain crucial areas experience a sense of "deadness" or emptiness. The psychosomatic disorders serves to activate bodily sensations that combat that sense of deadness.

McDougall (1989) speaks of psychosomatic patients arising out of a fantasy of "one body for two" (p. 36). She suggests that psychosomatic patients do not develop ownership of their own bodies. They are seen as having had parents who did not encourage separateness and individuality; who retained owner-ship of the child far beyond necessary periods. This results in the child being unable to regulate his or her own bodily re-sponses, resulting in the formation of psychosomatic disorders.

Example

> Mrs. P. was raised in a family where the parents were forever in-volved in her and her siblings' affairs. Her parents did not seem to recognize her as the competent and effective adult that she was. They were always giving her advice about how to relate to her husband and to raise her children, and about almost everything that the patient did. Mrs. P. was frustrated by this but seemed not to object really strongly. She herself seemed to have difficulty in separating and often sought out her parents' approval. She suf-fered from a host of psychosomatic disorders, including dermatitis and headaches. She frequently imagined that she had contracted some dread disease.

This patient had not separated from her parents and was tied to them in a destructive way that manifested itself through the formation of psychosomatic disorders. Her family was overin-vested in physical illness and had not encouraged a sense of privacy and self-care for the patient. Consequently, she had not developed sufficient ability toward self-regulation and could not process emotional upset via cognition and problem solving.

SUGGESTION. Psychosomatic patients have had difficulty in sep-arating from their parents and in developing the ability to self-regulate emotions and bodily sensations.

PSYCHOSOMATIC DISORDERS

Psychosomatic disorders involve a physiological change that can be discerned in the patient. This differentiates them from hypochondriacal disorders, where the patient imagines illness where none exists. Psychosomatic patients have a mea-surable physiological response that appears to be at least partly related to psychological difficulties. As mentioned, almost any disorder will impact patients psychologically, and one's degree of psychological health will affect his or her ability to cope with the disease. Additionally, any disease course can be greatly influenced by psychological factors.

There are a number of disorders that are seen as being greatly influenced by psychological issues. These disorders would include myocardial infarcts, gastrointestinal disorders (particularly irritable bowel syndrome), asthma, headaches, dermatological disorders, premenstrual syndrome, and temporomandibular disorders. Causation factors are not always known, but there may be significant contributions from genetics and/or constitutional qualities. For instance, predisposition toward heart disease is likely to be inherited but personality factors can greatly influence morbidity and mortality. The well known studies on "Type A" personalities are relevant here. Similarly, many dermatological and gastrointestinal disorders seem to run in families.

Since causation issues are so murky, it seems most prudent to assume that psychological and physical factors each make contributions toward the development and maintenance of these disorders. Consequently, to adequately treat them, emphasis must be given to each causative factor.

Example

> Mr. E. suffered a heart attack while eating breakfast. He was taken to the hospital, where his recovery was satisfactory. He was placed on a rehabilitation program that emphasized nutrition, exercise, and stress management. He followed his program to the letter, perhaps even to the extreme. He became obsessed with following the regimen and would get very upset if he deviated from his diet or if he was not able to get proper exercise. He approached stress reduction with a vengeance, being determined to be completely stress free.

Mr. E. was ostensibly following the rehabilitation program, yet his manner of following it was likely to minimize any gains. His driven personality caused him to become obsessed with his recovery, putting unnecessary and unwise pressure on himself.

Eventually, his physician was able to talk to him about his approach and the patient was able to relax a bit. It is too superficial just to chalk up this patient's response solely to his supposed "Type A" personality. Certainly, he had many of those qualities. Additionally, his heart attack terrified him, and he was going to be diligent in doing whatever he could to forestall a repetition. It would be helpful for the physician to approach the patient from the positive side. The patient's determined and energetic qualities are commendable, and he should be congratulated for them while also counseled on the advisability of being less consumed by his regimen.

In this instance, the physician is addressing as many causative factors as possible. He is helping the patient to identify risk factors and to eliminate them as much as possible, while also trying to help the patient to deal with personality factors that can impact on his health.

Example

> Mrs. G. had three children, all of whom suffered from asthma. They all, at various times in their young lives, became sufficiently ill to warrant brief hospitalizations. Needless to say, the parents were extremely worried and concerned about their children's health and tried to maintain an atmosphere at home that was as free from allergens as possible. They were more reluctant, however, to address the emotional problems within the parents that might also have been contributing to the prevalence of the asthma attacks. The parents had a number of marital difficulties that caused them to argue loudly, which frightened the children. Additionally, the mother was very volatile and emotional, resulting in the children fairly often feeling overwhelmed. The parents' emotionality would also seem to stimulate asthma attacks.

The parents were aware of the emotional difficulties and were also aware that they may have had a deleterious impact on the children, but they were not able to see that the problems may have contributed to the frequency of the asthma attacks. It was necessary for the physician to inquire about the emotional situation at home and then to make a proper referral for them to get the psychological help that they needed. Parents will often be more accepting of the need for psychological help if they are aware of a negative impact on their children. They may still need to be convinced of the hurtful influence of emotional conflicts since they will most often want to see the asthma as being solely related to physical and/or environmental issues. To help the parents with seeing a broader picture, the medical practitioner can question the parents as to what was occurring when the child or children suffered an attack. At times the parent can directly identify an emotional trigger if given the opportunity. It is always more helpful for the parent or for the patient to identify the psychological difficulty since it feels more palatable that way. It is most helpful to encourage the parents to wonder about what may be triggering the asthma since they are likely to feel less defensive. The physician should always emphasize the multiplicity of factors present so as to not put too much pressure on the parents. If parents believe that they are at fault for their children's asthma, they are likely to feel quite guilty and that may propel them to deny any culpability. Consequently, tact and sensitivity is especially important to maintain a positive working relationship.

SUGGESTION. Medical practitioners can be most effective in the treatment of psychosomatic disorders by emphasizing a wide range of causative factors. Treatment can then be prescribed that will impact the various causes.

Dermatological disorders, gastrointestinal disorders, headaches, and temporomandibular disorders are all known to have strong psychological components (Gatchel & Blanchard, 1993). Estimate of the presence of psychiatric comorbidity runs in the 40-50% range, which may actually be low.

Example

Mrs. N. was a woman who frequently sought out treatment from her dermatologist because of outbreaks of psoriasis. Both she and the physician were quite aware that she would suffer when emotionally stressed. Neither ever thought that some sort of psychological intervention would be helpful. She was told to try to avoid stressful situations.

Mr. C. visited his dentist because of recurrent jaw and tooth pain. His dentist diagnosed temporomandibular joint disorder caused by clenching and grinding. The dentist took impressions for a bite splint. The patient and the dentist did discuss his level of anger, which was considerable, and tried to come up with ways in which he could dissipate his anger less self-destructively.

Ms. B. had recurrent bouts of irritable bowel syndrome for which she could find little relief. She was a dreadfully unhappy woman who had never really been able to establish a life independent of her parents. Through psychotherapy, she was eventually able to move out and become more self-confident. Her gastrointestinal problems gradually abated, although she was subject to occasional flare-ups.

Both health care practitioners and physicians may be resistant to acknowledging the impact of psychological factors on the etiology and maintenance of these disorders. Patients who suffer from psychosomatic disorders prefer for their problems to be the result of physiological malfunction. Even if the physician is accepting of the influence of psychological factors, the patient is likely to be quite resistant and sometimes hostile to that notion. Physicians have great difficulty in convincing patients that their psychological disposition is a major contributing factor.

Psychosomatic patients are not consciously denying psychological difficulties. In their minds, they often believe that their physical disorders are related to physical causes, not to the contribution of any emotional difficulties. Even when they are able to acknowledge some contribution, it is usually at a more intellectualized level.

Example

Mrs. N., the patient with psoriasis mentioned earlier, had no difficulty recognizing that she was a very tense person and was aware that her psoriasis flared up when she was upset. Unfortunately, she really had no idea as to what was really troubling her and had great difficulty in articulating her feelings in general. Her marriage was very troubled and she was very aware that her family background was dysfunctional. Yet there was no connection in her mind between these events and her skin problems.

Like many such patients, her feelings seemed to bypass her mind and go directly to her body via her symptoms. In a sense, she obliterated any thoughts and ideas about herself and could not really talk about herself in a meaningful, affectively genuine way. She had significant difficulty in psychotherapy since she lacked the words to give voice to her affects. Mrs. N. had also been seriously neglected as a child. The consequences of this is that she did not internalize the self-soothing function that healthier patients develop out of nurturant parenting. Patients who have been neglected as children often develop psychosomatic disorders. Those who have not had the experience of loving touches may develop dermatological disorders.

Other patients are considerably more resistant to the awareness of distressing psychological difficulties. These are patients who are insistent that their disorders are solely the result of physical problems and who become angry and upset when suggestions are made to the contrary.

Example

Mr. W. was diagnosed with irritable bowel syndrome. He was an unusually tense man who had suffered from anxiety and insomnia for much of his adult life. Nevertheless, he always attributed his distress and his physical problems to external reasons. He would indicate to his physician that once his job stress cleared up or once his son got better grades that his difficulties would clear up. He was certain that emotional difficulties had nothing to do with his gastrointestinal problems. In fact, he insisted that he was "perfectly normal."

This stance is not an unusual one. Some doctors are so familiar with the denial and resistance of psychosomatic patients that they do not even attempt to address psychological contributions. Others prefer to treat such disorders solely through medical treatments.

To counter the resistance of psychosomatic patients, Wickramasekera (1989) suggests using psychological tests and psychophysiological measures (electromyogram, electrocardiogram, galvanic skin response, etc.) to show patients that upsetting events in their lives can create physiological changes. He suggests having psychologists directly involved with the physicians treating the patient, which communicates a psychophysiological approach for a psychophysiological disorder. This is an intriguing approach that may offer a method to present patients with information about psychological causation in a palatable way.

Many patients, however, regardless of the method used, hear the physician telling them that their disorder is "all in their heads" or that they are "crazy" or mentally ill. Considerable tact must be used in order for patients to be able to consider all possibilities of causation. It is very difficult for many psychosomatic patients to be able to reflect on the causes of their psychophysiological problems. Their emotions tend to be frightening and overwhelming, and they are not sure what to make of the idea that their emotions are contributing to their symptoms.

Cardiologists and other cardiovascular specialists have made substantial progress in helping patients to see the connection between lifestyle issues, stress, and cardiovascular disease. Although personality variables are still not given great emphasis, these doctors' successes give clues as to the direction that other health practitioners can follow. These programs all offer an integrated approach whereby the physicians and the adjunctive professionals work together and are able to consult and interact. This enables the patient to feel that his or her program is a comprehensive approach. One major problem in referring psychosomatic patients to psychotherapists is that the patient tends to feel abandoned by the physician. This can be very hurtful and can represent a narcissistic blow. Neglected patients, in particular, are liable to respond negatively to a referral since they will experience it as another rejection. The patient is already extraordinarily sensitive about his or her difficulties, and a physician who does not reassure the patient that continued contact will be maintained risks noncompliance. It is also helpful for the medical practitioner to emphasize the medical realities of the disorder and to reinforce the notion that it is recognized that the patient is truly sick and not malingering.

The physician with a good and positive relationship with the patient is most likely to be successful in helping the patient to look at a wide range of factors that may be contributing to his or her disorder.

Example

The patient, a 50-year-old married man, had a number of complaints for which his physician could find no physical cause. The doctor and patient had a long history of a positive relationship and the patient trusted the doctor implicitly. When the physician suggested a mental health referral, the patient was reluctant but agreeable. He knew that the doctor had his best interests in mind, but was still wary. Nevertheless, he began psychotherapy and made progress despite his difficulty in being able to describe or even to acknowledge his feelings.

The patient's confidence in his doctor enabled him to take the frightening step of trying to confront areas of his life that he had deeply buried years ago.

Doctors can collude with patients in the denial of the psychological contribution to psychosomatic disorders. It is not their field of expertise, and most physicians are most comfortable when they are operating within their area of competence. They may then insist on solely treating the patient medically, even when adjunctive treatment is advisable. Some medical practitioners are very possessive of their patients and do not like to refer them out anywhere. It is important for these practitioners to realize that most patients will still wish to maintain contact with the referring physician. There are also those doctors who believe that they should be able to handle any disorder that crosses their threshold. This is, of course, unrealistic and places far too much pressure on the physician.

SUGGESTION. Both patients and medical practitioners can be resistant about acknowledging the psychological aspect of psychosomatic disorders. Both may fear abandonment. A positive relationship between doctor and patient will mitigate that fear for both.

HYPOCHONDRIASIS

Hypochondriasis is a condition that both practitioners and patients find very frustrating. Patients seem to be searching for a disease, while doctors become impatient with their time being wasted chasing symptoms that have no basis in a physical disease.

Example

Mrs. D.'s mother was diagnosed with colon cancer. Suddenly Mrs. D. became terrified that she was going to contract the same dread disease, although she had no real symptoms to speak of. She panicked, became extremely distraught, and insisted on having an appointment with her mother's doctor. Her family's concern over her exacerbated the distress that was already being experienced over the mother's very real life-threatening disease.

Both the physician and the patient's family felt exasperated with her. They knew that she was prone toward imagining physical ills, but thought that this behavior was completely out of bounds. They felt that she was being manipulative and that she was only attempting to draw attention to herself. In a sense this was true, but it was not the complete story. Mrs. D. had been unusually close to her mother and could not bear the thought of losing her. By identifying with her illness, Mrs. D. felt more connected and less frightened of being abandoned, while still being terrified that she was going to die. In essence, she was afraid that she could not survive without her mother on whom she felt utterly dependent. The patient's overly close relationship with her mother caused her to feel like she and her mother shared everything, including bodily reactions. The level of distress displayed via her concern about her own physical well-being reflected her intense upset over her mother's condition.

None of these concerns were apparent to Mrs. D. She knew that she was upset about her mother but not to the extent of her distress. She did not really understand the pathology of her relationship with her mother. She only felt that they had a close relationship. If her family were to talk to her about being manipulative, she would become defensive, angry, and perplexed. She really was worried about her own health. In this and in most instances of hypochondriasis, the patient is having concerns in other areas of his or her life that are becoming manifest in health-related worries. The medical practitioner can address the patient's concern by helping her to talk about her worries about her mother's health. This is likely to relieve the immediate distress, although she is likely to have difficulty throughout the ordeal of her mother's illness. The other aspects of the patient's psychopathology are beyond the scope of the medical practitioner and are unlikely to be addressed in that venue. By continuing to focus on the obvious; that is, the patient's concern about her mother, the physician can defuse the emotions in a very commonsensical and straightforward manner. Families and medical personnel can get quite caught up in the confusion and machinations of patients and lose sight of the obvious. This is partly by design. The patient manages to distract herself and others from the painful reality of her mother's very serious illness.

Hypochondriasis is a condition whereby the patient cannot articulate that which is bothering him or her. It is a persistent belief that the patient has something wrong and that it is usually dreadful. It is an attempt to concretize and to make physical that which is psychological. The patient does truly experience a sense of something being wrong and imagines that it is a medical problem. There is certainly something wrong, but it reflects a sense of emotional vulnerability and despair.

Hypochondriasis is usually characterological, which means that it is an enduring way of solving psychic problems. Its presence waxes and wanes depending on the patient's psychological state. The physician should always look for external precipitating events that may be stimulating the hypochondriacal belief.

Example

Mrs. F. felt a tightening in her chest which she was convinced indicated a heart attack. Her physician put her through a battery of tests and found nothing. In conversation, the patient told the doctor that she had suffered the breakup of a long-term relationship. The physician asked her about how she was adjusting to the breakup, and the patient collapsed in tears. She was able to talk about her distress and was later surprised to discover that her chest pain had disappeared.

The patient certainly knew that she was upset about the breakup but had no idea that her distress was being somaticized. If the doctor had told her that she was causing her symptoms via her emotions, she would have been put off and distressed. Providing her with the opportunity to talk about that which is bothering her in her life provided relief. There are many, many patients who need an impartial and sympathetic ear and who, temporarily at least, gain great solace from an empathic physician. Expertise in psychotherapy is not necessarily needed or expected from physicians. Astute and careful listening can be highly palliative.

SUGGESTION. Hypochondriacal patients experience exacerbations of their complaints when they are having trouble coping with upsetting events and feelings. Providing an opportunity to identify the distressing precipitants and to talk about the distress will often minimize physical complaints.

Unfortunately, this approach does not always work, since most patients are insistent that they have something physically wrong with them. The extreme example of this is Munchausen syndrome, where medical practitioners become convinced, through willful deception by the patient, that a physical disease is present.

Physicians sometimes become caught in the trap of trying to cure all patients of what ails them. It seems to become a matter of pride and, at times, practitioners may ignore their own knowledge and expertise because of their desire to be helpful. Physicians and other practitioners may need to emphasize to their patients and to themselves that they do not always have all the answers and that some disorders have causes that are either elusive or have psychological causes. It is most helpful for doctors not to dismiss their hypochondriacal patients out of hand. They have real distress and are in need of assistance, even if their particular medical practitioner is unable to find the solution. Telling them it is "all in their head" is, of course, never helpful. Communicating to them the physician's concern for them and the belief that it is understood that they are in real pain can be very beneficial. Continued availability and sympathy may be the best that the physician can offer. The patient may still want more and may need to be referred to a mental health practitioner.

Some very lonely patients who suffer from profound feelings of emptiness imagine that they have medical problems. Imagining that they are ill can focus some of their distress and can distract them from their psychic despair. Contact with office personnel can ward off feelings of loneliness. If patients such as this become troublesome for the office, it may be necessary to politely and gently suggest a limitation on calls and visits while also helping the patient to address the loneliness that he or she may be struggling with. It is not easy to bring up these issues but the results may be surprising. Patients often keep these feelings to themselves and imagine that nobody has "caught on" to their unhappiness. They may be greatly relieved to be able to unburden themselves.

SUGGESTION. Hypochondriacal patients can be very demanding and insistent. Maintaining sympathy while emphasizing the physician's limitations is most realistic and may relieve pressure on the doctor.

CONCLUSION

Those suffering from psychophysiological disorders create problems for the medical practitioner because of their resistance to acknowledging the contribution of psychological processes to their difficulties. Many of these patients do not have the capability of verbalizing their conflicts, concerns, and feelings, and this inability produces a maladaptive biological response. Physicians who feel angry because of what they may perceive to be malingering are not seeing the whole picture.

It is often most descriptively accurate to think of the development of psychophysiological disorders as relating to a disturbance within the entire self-regulating system of the organism. This holistic approach encourages a focus on the biopsychological system and gives equal status to all aspects of the person.

Patients who have physical illnesses need to develop a new identity that encompasses the disorder. Participation in support groups can be very helpful to some patients. For others, disease can be felt to be shameful, and this may cause them to shun treatment. Still others may experience disease and disability as an organizing function. These individuals are typically lost and lonely people who have not developed a strong sense of self.

SUMMARY

1. A substantial number of patients visiting physicians suffer from a disorder that has psychological underpinnings.
2. Ample research evidence exists that supports the notion that psychological distress and stressful life events have a negative effect on the immune system.
3. A view of the organism as a biopsychological system is sensible and accurate.
4. Patients will have a psychological response to disease. Some become depressed, others become angry, and some experience shame. Patients suffering from emptiness and despair may find disease to be organizing.
5. Patients need to develop a new identity when suffering from illness or disability.
6. Psychosomatic patients have a propensity toward "operatory thinking." They also have little or no ability to describe feelings.
7. Psychosomatic patients often do not feel ownership of their bodies and have had difficulty in separating from their parents.
8. Practitioners can be most effective by emphasizing a wide range of causative factors.

9. A positive doctor-patient relationship is most helpful in assisting the patient to look at the many possible contributions toward the development and maintenance of disorders.
10. Hypochondriasis is a characteriological reaction and waxes and wanes depending on the stresses that the patient is experiencing.
11. Hypochondriasis reflects a patient's sense of vulnerability.

7

Medical Specialities

Within each medical speciality, patients will bring different problems and will have different expectations. Each organ system and medical specialty have both real and symbolic significance, which create particular problems and issues. For example, an internist is likely to have to deal with a wide range of problems and should expect a patient to look at him or her as the first option when the patient is confronted with difficulties, both medical and psychological. Obviously, an obstetrician-gynecologist will be working with issues that are germane to women, and these will run the gamut from reproduction to relationships. Pediatricians have split allegiances: to their patient—the child—and to the parents. Oncologists need to be adept in dealing with death and dying and with the soon-to-be and already bereaved. This chapter will concentrate on four specialties—internal medicine, obstetrics/gynecology, pediatrics, and hospice medicine, including a discussion on death and dying. This chapter is not designed to be a comprehensive explication of the difficulties that doctors in each discipline encounter. That would be beyond the scope of this book. It is hoped that the major points are touched upon and that a general sense of the particular problems are described.

INTERNAL MEDICINE

Internal medicine physicians are generalists. They are expected to be conversant and capable with a wide range of medical difficulties. Many internists will develop enduring relationships with their patients, and often each will become quite attached to the other. The doctor and the patient will age together and will view each other progressing through a number of the stages of life.

Example

Mr. S. had moved to town to take a new job when he was in his late 20s. In looking for a regular physician, he was referred to a young internist, about the same age, who was just beginning a new practice. They seemed to take to each other, feeling a kinship and an understanding. The patient was basically healthy and only saw the doctor for bacterial infections, minor backaches, and a regular difficulty with allergy. After the patient married, he started to have marital difficulties and turned to his doctor for a referral. The patient always felt that he could confide in his physician and would keep him abreast of his life events. As he aged, he struggled with many of the typical problems of living, which included some relatively minor problems with his children, continuing aches and pains associated with aging, and job problems that sometimes became intense. At one point the doctor needed to intervene and get him some time off when he felt the job pressure to be unbearable. Throughout their relationship the doctor was helpful and the patient was appreciative. At age 65, the physician decided to take a part-time administrative position at the hospital as a way of easing into retirement. He arranged for the transfer of his patient to a younger colleague. It was a bittersweet time for both Mr. S. and for the doctor.

This story could exemplify the experiences that many doctors and patients have. It was satisfying and meaningful for both participants. Unfortunately, not all doctor-patient relationships go so smoothly.

Example

Mr. K. was also an internal medicine patient who had also started with his doctor when both were relatively young. Mr. K. was a far more disturbed individual who was not particularly pleasant to work with. He was demanding, complaining, and noncompliant. He felt attached to his physician but the attachment, like his other relationships, was infused with negativity and anger. He seemed to have some sense of not being a very pleasant person but always felt justified for his bitterness. He often wanted something from the doctor, but it was never quite clear to either one exactly what he was looking for. The doctor barely tolerated the patient but was able to keep his frustration from leaking out and becoming evident to the patient. When the doctor retired, he certainly had no regrets about not working with Mr. K. any more.

There are several reasons that the doctor found Mr. K. to be so difficult. He was an unpleasant person and was often angry and obnoxious. He seemed to feel like he was entitled to something, like he had been cheated in some way. Most importantly, however, was the fact that the doctor felt that too much was being expected of him. The patient was suffering and expected the physician to cure him of what ailed him, even if it was outside of the doctor's area of expertise. He had financial problems that he complained about in a way that seemed designed to make the physician feel bad for having the ability to make a comfortable living. The doctor forever felt that he was not satisfying the patient, that the patient's expectations were being unmet.

Expectations

Internists labor under intense expectations generated from patients and from themselves. There is strong pressure on internists to diagnose a wide range of disorders and to provide appropriate and meaningful treatment. Numerous decisions need to be made: what is wrong, how to treat, whether and to whom to refer. Internists often experience these self-generated expectations as being stressful, especially when confronted with a difficult case. Some patients present with vague and ill-defined complaints, and diagnostic testing may give little useful information.

Example

A patient visited her internist and, in passing, mentioned that she was extremely fatigued and had, in fact, fallen asleep at the wheel on the way to work. She had even gotten in a car accident that was, fortunately, a minor one. The doctor was quite concerned about her and investigated several possibilities, including a contribution from her diabetes. The patient was on antidepressant medication at her maximum dose, and the fatigue was not obviously related to external stressful events. In fact, although quite emotionally disturbed, the patient felt better than she had felt in years. This she attributed to her work with a new therapist. The physician referred her to a sleep disorders clinic for evaluation, and they could find nothing amiss. She returned to her internist for consultation, and he was unable to provide any definitive answers. She was quite overweight, and a diet and exercise program was recommended, as was careful monitoring of her glucose levels. Both patient and doctor were frustrated. After some period of time, the sleepiness abated.

The patient had ample reasons, both psychological and physical, that possibly could explain her symptoms. Unfortunately, neither physician or therapist could definitively account for her symptoms. The patient became quite upset with both of the practitioners since she expected them to have the answers. She felt frightened because of the unexplained symptoms. Since she suffered from a borderline disorder, she had trouble integrating the notion that her caregivers were fallible. In her mind, either they were perfect or they were incompetent. Her therapist was able to help her articulate her frustration, which gave her some relief. He was also able to speak of her unrealistic expectations for her doctors and to acknowledge his own imperfections. She realized that she had idealized her doctors, and the therapist's acknowledgment of his fallibility also allowed her, via identification, to be less self-critical.

It seems that younger doctors are more prone toward having unrealistic expectations of being able to cure all patients. More battle-tested (and battle-wearied) physicians seem to become more humble and realistic about their ability to solve all of their patient problems.

Some patients become very insistent and frustrated with doctors when their problems are not solved. Patients have the strong desire to be returned to perfect health and become upset with the realization that they may have to live with their disorders. Internists will see many patients who have to adjust to chronic and debilitating diseases for which there may be no absolute cure. In fact, adjustment to disease is a task that internists spend considerable time and energy on. It is important for internists to come to grips with their limitations quite quickly. Otherwise, they will become prone toward self-doubts and depression or will become angry and dismissive toward patients.

SUGGESTION. Internists are the first line of defense for patients. As such, much is expected of them, and this expectation can become burdensome.

Patients often have expectations of physicians that do not always coincide with the nature in which either medicine or hospitals function. For instance, an anxious patient wants results of his or her blood tests immediately and has trouble understanding why the results are not available instantaneously. Some patients become enraged and insistent, as if the doctor has some control over the laboratory. Explaining to the patient the reality of the situation may be helpful. However, anxiety is likely to override rationality. In this situation, it is best to empathize with the patient, to acknowledge his or her concern, and to provide reassurance that the results will be conveyed as soon as they are received. Of course, the practitioner should make every effort to do this. Medical matters are so commonplace to physicians that they may sometimes forget how frightened and ignorant patients are about their medical condition. It is always useful to keep this in mind and to communicate this understanding to patients by returning phone calls in a timely way and by ensuring that results are provided expeditiously.

Patients have the expectation that they will receive the "best" medical treatment available. They want to think that their doctor or hospital is the finest, without peer. Some patients become panicked with physical problems, such that even minor problems cause them to feel that they should be referred to world-renowned specialists.

Example

A patient had suffered a parental death at a very early age. Consequently, he became very anxious whenever he had to have a medical procedure performed. Because of gastrointestinal problems of
unknown origin, he was scheduled to have a colonoscopy. He first
insisted that his internist send him to the "best" gastroenterologist. The internist reassured him that the doctor was very competent. This was not good enough. He wanted the "best," and
became quite angry and upset. Eventually, he calmed down and
agreed to the procedure. He confronted the gastroenterologist,
again wanting to know if he was the "best." The doctor felt a bit
put out but did try to reassure the patient. The patient was quite
upset and remained so until the doctor began to question him on
his anxiety and the patient told him about his parent's death. This
seemed to relieve the patient, and the procedure proceeded
smoothly.

This kind of interaction can give an insecure physician
ample opportunity to become defensive and angry. A patient
who challenges the doctor's competence is usually frightened,
and an elucidation of that fear will often diminish the underlying anxiety that is fueling the obnoxious behavior. If a positive
transference becomes established, the patient comes to feel
that his or her doctor will make sure that any other physician
is competent.

Some patients are very diligent consumers of medical care.
They read the latest medical news available and become experts
in their diseases. In many cases this is desirable, since the patient can become an active participant in his or her care. At
other times, such patients become quite obnoxious, continually
second-guessing their physicians. This attitude is usually generated by anxiety, and the physician can work with this by helping
the patient to identify his or her fearfulness and encouraging
its expression. Some physicians, as well as other practitioners,
may respond to patient probing with irritation. This is generated by insecurity as well, and the doctor needs to understand
the source of his or her reactions.

It is very difficult for competent and caring physicians to
be confronted by patients who are suspicious of doctors and of
the treatment that they recommend. Part of the suspiciousness

is an artifact of the nature of our society, where distrust and hostility is rampant. Some of it represents personality styles of patients who are suspicious of everyone. Unfortunately, some distrust is generated by newspaper and TV stories on unscrupulous health care providers. There is really no way to persuade a person of one's trustworthiness. When confronted with a suspicious patient, the doctor can only suggest that the patient give him or her a chance and encourage a second opinion, if desired. Over time a patient will either grow to trust the doctor or will take his or her business elsewhere.

SUGGESTION. Patients who are frightened can become insistent about getting the "best" treatment and can alienate their doctors. Patients who challenge doctors' competence are usually frightened and feel inadequate. Suspiciousness can have several sources, and the physician can only earn the patient's trust over time.

If the positive transference or working alliance is not well established, referrals to specialists can be problematic. Patients often want their doctors to take care of all their problems and react negatively to a referral. Some patients become frightened with a referral, believing that it means that they are seriously ill. Others have a sense of rejection, feeling as if their internist is trying to get rid of them. Still others will become anxious, fearing that the new doctor will not be helpful or sympathetic. In these situations, it would be helpful for the internist to spend some time encouraging the patient to talk about his or her concerns and offering realistic encouragement.

Patients who are quite anxious often pester doctors with unnecessary phone calls and may expect quick responses. At times, it becomes necessary and extremely helpful to educate patients as to what are appropriate reasons for phone calls. Some offices may find it helpful to print up information on phone call procedures. Others may find it better to have the nurse or doctor discuss it with the patient face to face. Many patients will respond well if provided with the parameters of the office. Of course, some will be hurt and resentful, but that cannot be avoided. It is best to be as explicit as possible, while emphasizing that calls should be made if the patient feels his or her condition to be urgent.

Patients often expect, understandably, that they will receive the most complete treatment available. Some patients use up a considerable amount of resources, in terms of both physician time and energy and general medical resources because of their sense of *entitlement*.

Example

A chronic alcoholic was admitted to the medicine service with an exacerbation of his cirrhosis of the liver. He was a pleasant enough man, but the medical staff knew that any treatment delivered was only delaying the inevitable. Both the patient and his wife were demanding that everything possible be done for the patient, even though recovery was impossible. The medical staff felt uncomfortable with the patient's demandingness.

This case is complicated by the fact that the patient's problems were the result of his own self-destructive behavior. Medical personnel often have trouble with self-imposed disorders, as if the patient deserves less sympathy and care. Resentment can become palpable, making everyone uncomfortable. This is a situation where the medical staff needs to discuss the situation among themselves, creating a sense of support and a place to express the resentment. Furthermore, it is not the physicians' place to make such judgments. Remembering one's own inadequacies and occasional lapses in healthy behavior may increase empathy. Those who tend toward judgmentalness and moral disapproval are those who themselves struggle with integrating and accepting aspects of themselves that they view negatively. The patient then comes to represent the disliked part of the physician, and the internalized criticalness becomes externalized and directed toward the patient. The patient probably feels guilty enough already and does not need further reinforcement of his or her culpability. It should be emphasized, though, that physician resentment is not inappropriate. It only becomes problematic if it spills over and becomes evident to the patient.

There are cases where the futility of treatment becomes obvious to everyone except to the patient and family. The desire to be restored to health is intense and patients are often reluctant to accept the inevitable. Communicating painful information to patients is very difficult and should be done with directness and yet with sensitivity. Not communicating the inevitable is eventually more hurtful and difficult for all concerned.

At times, family members can have more unrealistic expectations and may place more demands on the medical staff than does the patient.

Example

Mr. J. was dying of bone cancer. It was a long, grueling, and painful treatment and the patient was ready to let go. The family, however, was insistent that treatment should continue, despite being told that there was no possibility of recovery and that Mr. J. was in enormous discomfort. The family consisted of the man's three adult children, none of whom had been particularly attentive to the patient for many years. Their guilty feelings over their neglect caused them to overcompensate and to insist on prolonged treatment. Ironically, this insistence was again causing more pain to their father, just as did their neglect.

This kind of situation may put the doctor in the middle. The physician realizes the futility of further treatment and recognizes how much pain the patient is enduring. If he tries to persuade the children of this, he is risking invoking their rage and the projection of responsibility for their father's predicament onto himself. The best approach would be for the physician to act as an intermediary between the patient and his family by assisting the patient in communicating his wishes as to the treatment. Additionally, helping the children to articulate their own guilty feelings as well as their feelings of loss will help reduce the tension for all. This may help open lines of communication that have not existed before and may help all participants to make peace with themselves and each other prior to the patient's death.

SUGGESTION. Being explicit about what is realistic to expect from physicians can help minimize unrealistic expectations, facilitate communication, and assist patients and families come to grips with their particular difficult situation.

Angry and guilty patients are very difficult for internists since they are often noncompliant and demanding.

Example

A 50-year-old woman was admitted to the medicine service with a pleural effusion. Diagnostic tests indicated lung cancer that was inoperable. She was a chain smoker. In her anger, she told the staff that she had had five family members who had died of cancer and that she had recently taken care of her husband who had eventually died of cancer. She continually wanted the fluid drained since she was having difficulty breathing. She was enraged and demanding, and alienated the staff. She was aware of the reality of her impending death and was furious with the raw deal that she was getting.

The patient was so obnoxious that nobody in the hospital wanted to deal with her. The staff tried to reason with her, but she would explode in a rage. The best approach would be to try to take an empathic approach and to help her talk about her rage and guilt and her feeling of being cheated out of life. It must be recognized that some patients will remain bitter and angry until the end and that there is little that the physician can do about this, other than listen. This negativity can take a toll on the internist. Patients usually visit internists because of problems, and it is hard to be confronted with problems day in and day out. In times of discouragement, it is important for the internist to remember and to keep in his or her mind that most people improve through his or her efforts.

At times medical practitioners put tremendous time and energy into the care of a patient and end up feeling resentful because the patient seems to feel little or no gratitude. Everyone expects to receive some acknowledgment and appreciation for hard work, and physicians are no different. It is perplexing and frustrating when parents seem to treat their health care providers with such cavalier lack of interest.

Example

A patient was hospitalized with a serious bacterial infection. His physician was quite concerned for him and put considerable time and energy into his care. After recovery and upon discharge, the patient said to the doctor, "Well, I'd thank you but you were just doing your job." The doctor felt hurt and confused.

There are a number of possible explanations for patients' lack of expression of appreciation. Some patients are very uncomfortable with outward displays of emotion and try to minimize the extent of their feelings. Others want to deny the seriousness of what occurred in order to deny how frightened they were. Still others have trouble recognizing needs other than their own and do not even think of their physicians as being individuals who need to be appreciated. Regardless of the possible reasons, it is a bitter situation for physicians. Fortunately, most patients are able to express their gratitude and to convey their appreciation.

The concept of negative therapeutic reaction can also explain a lack of patient appreciation. Patients may feel envious of their doctor's capabilities or are guilty over perceived wrongs, and these feelings may preclude expressions of appreciation. The patient's envy would be increased if he or she acknowledges the doctor's competence. Any guilt would be activated if the patient feels undeserving of getting better.

Another group of patients who tend to be irritating and difficult are those who seem to use the medical system in a manipulative and dishonest fashion.

Example

A 40-year-old man showed up at the hospital emergency room complaining of chest pains. He recounted a history of heart disease and, in fact, showed evidence of having suffered a mild heart attack. It was not deemed debilitating, yet the patient insisted that he was unable to work and demanded to be placed on disability. The physicians took great pains to explain why the patient did not qualify for disability. The patient was not deterred, however, and became more and more insistent. Eventually, he became threatening, and security was called. The physician felt very concerned that his life was in danger. Eventually, the physician insisted that the patient seek medical care elsewhere.

Some patients believe that they have been shortchanged in life and feel that they should be compensated. Physicians have often worked very hard to get where they are and find such attitudes difficult to accept. There are limits to what can be accomplished with some patients, and it might be necessary to terminate care, as long as the patient is not abandoned. At some point, all the explaining in the world is not going to convince a patient who feels that he or she is entitled to some special treatment that it is not going to happen. The medical professional may need to withdraw and to concentrate efforts on those who can be more reasonable. One unfortunate side effect of this kind of encounter is to increase cynicism and possibly even to cause unnecessary suspiciousness with other patients. Medical professionals need to be careful not to let a few bad experiences determine their manner with the majority of patients, who are honest and forthright.

Since internists are on the front line of medical care, they must be careful to protect themselves. There are psychotic and violent patients, and one should take threats seriously and call the authorities when threatened. A physician should also not work under veiled threats, either. It is best to confront such threats directly, which can actually defuse some of the tension.

Example

A patient was frustrated since he did not seem to feel better after treatment for an ulcer. He made some allusions to his frustration and talked pointedly about his gun collection. His doctor asked him if he was threatening him, and the patient became flustered and reassured the physician. The patient became more cooperative and less demanding.

It is best to handle these situations directly, but caution is always advised. The physician should not ignore feelings of being threatened.

Emotional Disorders

Internists are often the professionals who first become aware of emotional and family difficulties. This can occur from direct communication from patients who request help and/or a referral or may need to be inferred by patient manner and characteristics.

Example

Mrs. M. requested a consultation with her internist because of fatigue and listlessness. She was certain that something was wrong with her, perhaps that she was suffering from anemia. The doctor ordered a blood test after an examination and set up a return visit. The results of the blood test were normal, and the physician spent some time with the patient discussing the patient's life and any difficulties she might be experiencing. In this discussion, the patient indicated a number of family problems, including her son's drug problem. It was quite clear to the physician that the patient's emotional state was the cause of what appeared to be her depressive symptoms.

Some patients are quite unaware of their own psychic distress and may require assistance from the physician in identifying the precipitants of their despair. In this instance, the patient was denying to herself the degree of upset engendered by the family conflicts. This is a common situation, where patients prefer to have a physical disorder as opposed to a psychological one. Additionally, many patients really hope that the physician will question them about their emotional difficulties, since they find it difficult to bring it up themselves. Many people are embarrassed by their difficulties and are afraid that others, including physicians, will think poorly of them. After patients bring up their difficulties, it is very usual for them to become upset, and tears are common. It is essential that the internist become comfortable with tears and emotional distress. After speaking with the doctor and being responded to with concern and empathy, many patients will feel considerably better. If the doctor does not aggressively pursue the patient's emotional and family difficulties though, the patient may not bring it up and the opportunity to help the patient is lost.

Some physicians are reluctant to question patients about any possible emotional and/or family problems. Most often it is a result of the doctors being uncomfortable with their own emotions. They prefer to talk about physical problems. They may rationalize their lack of interest by insisting that they do not have the time or the expertise to deal with emotional problems. Physicians are often under a time crunch, some of which is generated by practice pressures. Some doctors set up their practices such that they do not schedule sufficient time to deal with patients' psychological problems, and this is purposeful. Such health care professionals are uncomfortable with patient emotions as well as with their own. Furthermore, doctors communicate their willingness, or lack thereof, to discuss such problems through their manners. Since such a large proportion of patient problems are related to psychological and family difficulties, it is really in physicians' best interests that they become comfortable and conversant with emotional problems.

Reluctance to discuss emotional difficulties is not only seen in physicians. Patients are often reluctant to discuss such problems and, as mentioned, prefer to have a physical problem as opposed to a psychological one. Many doctors have been frustrated in their attempts to help patients to understand and to accept the underlying psychological etiology of their difficulties.

Example

Mr. L. made regular visits to his internist, complaining of stomach problems and an ill-defined sense of malaise. The doctor thoroughly investigated each complaint yet could never find any organic pathology. He came to the conclusion that the patient was experiencing a previously undiagnosed psychological disorder. The patient was extremely reluctant to accept the diagnosis and became angry at the doctor. The doctor tried to reassure the patient that a psychological problem did not indicate that he was "crazy" or "bad." The patient was still unhappy, and it was suggested that he think about the situation. He was rescheduled for a follow-up appointment in a month. It took several such appointments before the patient was willing to consider a referral to a mental health professional.

Physicians need to have patience in working with patients who they feel are suffering from psychogenic disorders. As the preceding example attests, it may require considerable time and effort before a patient is ready to accept a referral.

Some physicians prefer to handle many patient problems by themselves. This is commendable and may be workable if the doctor has sufficient training and understanding. Because of the positive transference that is established, patients listen very carefully and seriously to what their doctor says, and the doctor can have a strong impact on patients' lives. This can be both positive and negative, depending on what the physician says and how he or she communicates it.

Example

Mrs. D. had a long and satisfying relationship with her internist. He was unfailingly supportive and sympathetic to her while she traversed life's difficulties. As she approached the age of 50 she started to become depressed and unhappy. The doctor tried to be helpful and suggested that she concentrate more on the positive aspects of her life and be less negative. She tried this, but she remained depressed. He then suggested antidepressant medication, speculating that she may have a chemical imbalance that would be addressed by the medication. She showed some improvement in mood from the medication and decided that she would just have to live with her chronic feelings of dissatisfaction. When asked, she told her internist that she was fine.

Without doubt, this physician was trying to be helpful and was, within the limits of his expertise. Understanding the true nature of psychological distress requires considerable training and sophistication, which is often beyond the training of most internists. A patient with recurrent complaints of depression or of other psychological symptomology should be referred to a mental health professional for evaluation and diagnosis. Depressive affect can be concomitant with a number of different disorders, and an intensive evaluation is necessary to make an accurate differential diagnosis.

Example

The doctor in the preceding example had known the patient for a number of years but had never been told of the patient's history of sexual abuse. For years, Mrs. D. had been preoccupied with present-day family concerns, which allowed her to push her uncomfortable feelings and memories to the background. Now that her children were grown, she felt directionless and unhappy. Without a referral to a mental health professional, Mrs. D. would never have the opportunity to examine her life and to come to grips with her past traumatic experiences. She would have to be consigned to living the rest of her life in a chronic state of anxiety and dissatisfaction.

Despite the current ethos, psychotropic medication should primarily be prescribed by psychiatrists or, at the very least, in consultation with a mental health professional.

Many problems that patients face have no easy or readily identifiable solutions. It is unreasonable to expect internists to be able to have answers for many of the difficulties that patients struggle with. Family and marital problems are very complex and are not readily resolvable. Listening to patients and being sympathetic and understanding is often very beneficial and may be all that a doctor can accomplish. Providing referrals to competent adjunctive professionals is a very important component of medical practice.

SUGGESTION. Psychological difficulties are commonly seen in internal medicine practice. Internists need to be prepared to confront such difficulties and to make appropriate referrals. Psychological and family difficulties are very complex and require intervention by a mental health professional.

Residents

Medical residents have a number of constituents. They are beholden to the patient, to the medical attending staff, to the medical specialists, and to the hospital administration. At times, they may find themselves in the middle of these conflicting groups.

Example

A patient was admitted to the medicine service because of her blood being too anticoagulated. Her cardiologist admitted her to ascertain the reasons. She had no internal medicine doctor, so she was admitted to the resident service. The cardiologist did not seem to want to take care of her, mostly, it seemed, because she was a needy and demanding patient. The patient was angry because the cardiologist "dumped" her and would not come to see her. The resident physicians were upset because they felt that a difficult patient was "dumped" upon them.

The resident physicians and the patient were in similar positions. Both were being treated poorly by the cardiologist. In some ways, this is a problem that needs to be solved at a level above that of the residents. However, the residents can try to gain some satisfaction from the situation by, if possible, forming a relationship with the patient and trying to help her and learn from her. It would be unfortunate if the residents were to replicate the cardiologist's behavior with the patient by withdrawing.

Some patients are very uncomfortable with residents and only want attending staff to examine or treat them. Patients may be unaware of the practice of teaching hospitals and may need education regarding their nature and function. Others are adamant that they do not want residents or, even worse, medical students anywhere near them. It would be hard not to feel somewhat put off and insulted by this attitude. Fortunately, such patients are in the minority, and residents will need to get their satisfaction elsewhere. It is difficult for young physicians who are already unsure of themselves to be rejected. It is important for residents to form attachments with each other in order to offer support and encouragement.

Residents are also required to deal with patients who may have a multiplicity of problems and to take care of them quickly, without really getting to know them very well. This can be somewhat unsatisfying, since it is often the human relationship that makes the profession most rewarding. It is in the doctor's and the patient's best interest to try to form some sort of relationship, however brief. This can be accomplished by taking a genuine interest in the patient and by letting the patient see the doctor's sincere interest. Resident satisfactions can be limited and should be gained wherever possible.

SUGGESTION. Medical residents are often placed in the unenviable position of trying to please a number of constituents. Angry reactions to being mistreated are understandable but must be addressed appropriately and not acted out upon patients. Good relationships with other residents can help reduce pressure.

Conclusion

Internists must be prepared to deal with a number of different patient problems—medical, psychological, and societal. This requires internists to be well versed in a variety of disciplines. Expectations of internists are high and are sometimes unrealistic. The nature of internal medicine often places the physician in the middle, trying to treat and please many. Internists often gain significant satisfaction from the long-term relationships they form with their patients.

Summary

1. Internists are expected to be conversant and capable with a wide variety of difficulties.
2. Internists often appreciate being involved with the totality of patient's lives.
3. Internists labor under intense expectations.
4. Internists may need to educate patients on many fronts.
5. Patients can challenge internists' competence, which can be, at the least, upsetting and, at the most, threatening to physicians.

6. Internists may react negatively to those patients who feel entitled to treatment, especially if their problems arise from self-imposed behaviors.
7. Psychological problems often manifest themselves via physical discomfort.
8. Physicians need to be comfortable with and adept at dealing with psychological difficulties.
9. Most psychological problems require referral to a mental health professional.
10. Patients do not always express appreciation toward internists, which can be frustrating for the doctor.
11. Physicians need to protect themselves from patients who are threatening.
12. Medical residents have multiple constituents, which can be very trying.
13. Being direct both with patients and with other medical staff will often achieve the best results.

PEDIATRICS

In a certain sense pediatricians also have more than one constituent. It is often impossible to think about the treatment of children without a consideration of their parents. In fact, many difficulties in treating children relate to the demands and expectations of parents.

Pediatricians have a responsibility that other physicians do not have. Their primary responsibility is the care of those who are not fully able to care for themselves. Pediatricians have a moral and legal responsibility to ensure that the rights of children are addressed. Their patients often do not have a voice to protest abuse or neglect, and the physicians must act as protectors and intermediaries. At times this may put them at odds with the parents, who may have other agendas. It must be quite clear both to pediatricians and to parents that the primary allegiance is to the child. This responsibility is considerable and may feel burdensome and difficult for some doctors.

Pediatricians and Parents

Children represent many different things to parents. From a healthy perspective, children represent a biological need to propagate. They also represent the culmination of a loving relationship—the desire to form a family in order to increase and enhance loving relationships. The desire to be a successful parent and to see one's children move beyond oneself can also be a healthy motivator. On the other hand, there can be a number of unhealthy desires that get expressed through children.

At times, parents view their children as possessions with whom they have the right to exercise complete control. This means that they feel they can completely dictate all that occurs with their children. They may become demanding and obstinate with medical personnel and can even refuse treatment that is necessary and medically advisable. There are, of course, parents who refuse treatment for religious reasons, and these situations need to be handled with great sensitivity and tact. Consultation with hospital legal professionals is a necessity. Some physicians and other medical personnel become quite angry with those patients whose religious beliefs endanger their children. This is nonproductive and can alienate parents who may reconsider if given proper support. The best approach is an even-tempered one that encourages the parents to articulate their beliefs and concerns. Giving them an opportunity to talk about their feelings and to be given noncondemnatory information may assist them in getting the proper treatment for their children. Some of those with these beliefs are primed toward having a confrontation and many become defensive and provocative. It is essential that the physician maintain his or her professional manner.

Other parents may also resist medical treatment, but for different reasons.

Example

A 4-year-old child was brought to a pediatrician complaining of a sore throat and fever. The doctor took a throat culture and prescribed an antibiotic since it appeared that the child had a strep throat. The father made it quite clear that he was not going to allow his child to take the medication until it was absolutely verified that the child truly had strep. However, the father never filled the prescription, even when the infection was verified. The child became very ill and was taken to the hospital emergency room by his mother, who agreed to the administration of antibiotics.

This father is, de facto, abusive by denying his child necessary medical treatment. It is counterproductive to confront the parent with his poor parenting. This will only result in defensiveness, anger, and further resistance. A parent with these personality dynamics is demonstrating a tremendous degree of insecurity and a need for absolute control. Most likely he is greatly threatened by the doctor's knowledge and expertise and feels inadequate because of his ignorance and inability to make his son better. His self-absorption and need to address his own needs are of sufficient intensity to completely override his son's need for medical attention. This is a man who is likely to be unable to be attuned to either his wife's or his son's needs. Appealing to his rational side is likely to be ineffective because of his consuming need to be in charge. A possibly effective technique would be for the physician to take a very cooperative stance with the man, enlisting his advice and counsel. This will allow the father to feel more involved and less threatened if he is treated with careful consideration. The physician accomplishes this by speaking directly to the father, explaining everything fully and encouraging him to fully consider the information. The doctor also needs to impart a sense of confidence in the parents' ability to make good decisions. Showing respect for their opinions despite disagreeing with them imparts in the parents a sense of being taken seriously and tends to reduce defensiveness. It is always important to remember that more may be going on with parents than may be apparent. For instance, the father may have reasons unknown to the physician for his reluctance.

Example

A mother was very resistant to giving her child any medication for the fevers that he would develop. She seemed quite concerned about her son but was adamant about not giving him any acetaminophen. Upon questioning it was discovered that she had a sister whose son had developed Reye's syndrome, perhaps after taking aspirin. The mother was ignorant of the distinction between the two medications and was then able to take proper steps, once she was reassured.

SUGGESTION. Resistant and controlling parents are often insecure and need to be treated with great care and respect. Involving them in the treatment decisions helps to minimize needs for dominance and control.

Another group of overly possessive parents who cause difficulty to physicians are those who see their children as extensions of themselves. These are parents who do not allow their children to form separate identities and who are overly involved in their lives.

Example

A mother would bring her daughter to the doctor's office for visits and would never let the child answer any of the doctor's questions. She would respond first, essentially cutting the daughter off and effectively interfering with the establishment of a relationship between the doctor and the child. Furthermore, the doctor could never be quite sure that she was getting accurate information since it was always filtered through the mother. The doctor was very gentle in firmly insisting that the daughter be allowed to answer her questions. Gradually the mother became accustomed to letting her child be the focus.

There can be a number of reasons for this kind of behavior. Such parents themselves were treated as extensions of their parents and have not developed their own secure sense of identity. They do not understand the nature of separateness and boundaries. The physician can be helpful to the child by helping her to establish boundaries between her and the mother. This can be very difficult to achieve because of the parent's profound overinvestment in the child. Such parents are so overidentified with their child that they experience severe psychic and even physical pain when their child is sick. They can become quite panicky over even minor illnesses. They have not learned to self-regulate, and this kind of behavior can impart the same difficulty to the child. Consequently, early intervention can be very useful. Any change in the parent's behavior is going to be achieved very slowly and over time. They need considerable reassurance about their own abilities to take care of their children. Such parents also have a great difficulty in not being the center of attention and have trouble ceding center stage to their child. The physician needs to be careful to give considerable attention to the parent so he or she does not feel neglected.

Parents who are overinvolved with their children can cause difficulty throughout the child's life. Since the pediatrician is likely to be involved with the parents and the child for a number of years, a good relationship with the parents is essential in order to do the best for the child. In the heat of the emotions that are sometimes generated in working with families, the physician can get very upset with parents. It is important for the medical professional to always keep focused on the primary goal of the encounter—the welfare of the child. This means that maintaining a working relationship with the parents is crucial, despite extreme provocation. At times, the pediatrician, like all caregivers, must "park his or her ego" in order to nurture the relationship with the parent and thereby protect the child.

Parents often do not understand that the doctor's primary allegiance is to the child. They may imagine that the doctor is working at the behest of the parent, especially since the parent is paying the bill. However, this attitude is based on issues beyond the financial. Some parents feel that they "own" the child and that the child has minimal rights. Of course, children do have substantial rights, based on law and by virtue of basic human rights. It may be necessary to point out the individuality of the child and to encourage an attitude that does not include the notion that a child is the property of the parent. This can partly be accomplished by the physician taking great care to treat the child as an individual and to show him or her the respect necessary. Physicians should take great pains to not speak about the child as if he or she is not there.

SUGGESTION. Children whose parents do not treat them as individuals need assistance in developing secure boundaries between their parents and themselves. The physician can foster this by developing an independent relationship with the child and by ensuring that his or her needs are being met.

Parental Hostility

In previous chapters (see especially Chapter 4) physical and sexual abuse issues have been addressed. It is quite clear that children need to be protected and that it is the medical professional's legal and moral responsibility to report suspected and actual abuse. It is important, however, that this be accomplished in as productive a manner as possible. It is not the physician's job to be judge and jury. The parents who are abusive are emotionally disturbed and have almost certainly been abused themselves. This is not to excuse such behavior. The child in question needs to be protected and the parents assisted in getting the help they require. Most physicians and medical personnel become angry when they become aware of abuse. It is important that these feelings be put aside in order to effectively protect the child and to enhance the probability that the parent-child relationship will improve in the future. A parent-child relationship exists for a lifetime, and the individuals will be dealing with each other for many years to come. The medical professional needs to take this long-term perspective by recognizing that improving the parent-child relationship is crucial in determining the welfare of the child.

Example

A child complaining of pain was brought to the hospital emergency room (ER), with his parents indicating that he fell down the stairs. The physician who examined the child noted other bruises and began to be concerned that the child's injuries were due to parental abuse. The physician spoke with the parents and told them that she was concerned about the child and about the bruises. The parents indicated that the child was "accident prone." Nevertheless, the physician remained suspicious because of the nature of the injuries and because of the child's furtiveness. The ER social worker was contacted, as were Protective Services. Neither the doctor nor the social worker accused the parents of anything and remained concerned and sympathetic throughout. Their orientation was not condemnatory or accusing and was helpful to the family in their crisis. This perspective helped the ER personnel to maintain their treatment function and left legal matters to the authorities. Oftentimes, a team approach is helpful providing the parents and the child with opportunities to connect with mental health professionals.

SUGGESTION. Medical professionals' primary responsibility is to protect the child. This is often facilitated by maintaining a treatment alliance with the entire family, including parents suspected of abuse.

Parents may have considerable hostility toward their children that is not necessarily expressed in obvious ways.

Example

Throughout the visits with the pediatrician, the mother was continually correcting and fussing over her son. Many of the things he was doing were perfectly normal and age appropriate. Nevertheless, the mother seemed uncommonly critical. The doctor commented upon it, and the mother went into a diatribe about her son that stunned the doctor with its vehemence. It seemed to the physician that the mother hated her son.

This situation is difficult for the pediatrician. He wants to help the child but does not want to alienate the mother. The stance he took was to wonder with the mother whether she felt pressured in dealing with all the pressures in her life, including the care of a child. This approach validates the mother's distress without reinforcing her scapegoating of the child. This opens the door for the mother to speak about her distress and for the doctor to be able to point her in the direction where she can receive the help she needs. The mother did speak about her martial difficulties, which worsened after the birth of the son. In some sense she blamed him for the problems. Speaking with the doctor helped her to identify the real issues, which will enable her to seek out assistance.

There are other parents whose hostility toward their children is masked by oversolicitousness.

Example

The mother prided herself on being an excellent mother. She was meticulous in caring for her daughter, never letting her watch TV, which she viewed as being intellectually stultifying. She did not feel the neighborhood children were sufficiently intelligent or gentle enough for her to daughter to associate with. She fed her only nutritious food that she made herself. She hovered over her daughter, ready to protect her from any untoward eventuality. The child was clearly desperately unhappy. The pediatrician could see that the child felt suffocated and overwhelmed by her intrusive and overprotective mother. In point of fact, this mother enormously resented her child, which was being acted out in the guise of great concern.

This is an extremely delicate situation, since any suggestion that the mother is not doing the best for the child will be met by anger and resistance. The mother has an enormous need to deny her hostility and cannot bear to admit its presence. Of course, hostility is not the only emotion felt toward the child. The mother also loved and cared about her, but could not integrate opposing feelings comfortably. She felt that any hostility indicated that she was a bad mother, and she could not tolerate any such notion. The pediatrician again needs to maintain a positive and sympathetic attitude, while pointing out that the child needs more freedom. A positive relationship with the doctor will provide a venue for the mother to be able to express some of her difficulties. The mother does not want to feel such hostility toward her child and needs assistance in understanding its origin. If possible, referral to a mental health professional would be warranted. This should only be attempted once the physician is certain of the therapeutic relationship with the mother, to ensure cooperativeness and not hostility. Unless the mother raises the issue, it would not be helpful for the medical practitioner to speak about the mother's disguised hostility. Instead, an emphasis on the degree of the mother's distress will be more productive.

Helping professionals often have a bias that can result in children not getting the assistance that they need. Parents who are most like the medical professionals, that is, intelligent, well dressed, and financially well off, are often viewed through rose-colored glasses, and some signals of abuse are ignored. Similarly, those who are poorer or perhaps are people of color are judged as being more likely not to provide adequate care to their children. This is an unfortunate bias that has the potential to be very detrimental to some children. Medical professionals need to be careful not to make such unwarranted assumptions, which are prejudicial and short-sighted.

Family Problems

Pediatricians are often the professionals who first become aware of family difficulties. Such difficulties are often identified through a child's behavioral difficulties. Children are extraordinarily sensitive to family distress and often react via behavioral signals. In fact, any psychological or behavioral disturbance should alert the treating professional to the possibility of family problems.

Example

The 10-year-old boy was brought to the pediatrician's office by his parents since he seemed listless and fatigued. The parents were concerned about the child and wondered if he suffered from some unknown ailment. The child seemed depressed to the doctor, and she asked to speak to him alone. He verified that his parents had been arguing lately and that he was worried about them getting divorced. This enabled the doctor to raise the issue with the parents and to offer herself as a resource if the parents wished a referral for marital difficulties.

Parents may ignore their own needs and may thus be resistant toward treatment for their psychological difficulties, but awareness that their child is suffering may impel them to action. In this instance, the parents reluctantly admitted their difficulties and agreed to accept a referral to a marriage counselor.

It is impossible to view a child in isolation. Any problem that he or she is encountering cannot be separated from the family system within which the child is operating. In fact, psychological treatment with a child often includes some sort of treatment for the parents since it is recognized that a child's difficulties are usually indicative of family difficulties. To diagnose a child as "depressed" or "ADHD" without examining the family situation does a disservice to both child and family.

Parents may expect that the pediatrician has ready solutions available for what are very complex and difficult problems. Situations where the child is not living up to parental expectations in school are common complaints. A child who is not studying or is not handing in assignments is difficult for all concerned. Parents are often furious with their children when they do not seem to take their schoolwork seriously. It is often viewed as a "slap in the face," which may be the truth, in part. Children who are not performing up to their capabilities are unhappy children who are likely to be struggling with a psychological problem. At times the difficulty seems to dissipate by itself. Other times psychological treatment is in order. The pediatrician can be of assistance by helping the parents to maintain the most productive attitude while the problem is being ironed out.

Example

The 13-year-old boy was brought to the pediatrician for his checkup prior to entering high school. He felt a good rapport with his doctor and was able to talk with her about his school problems. He seemed to have little interest in his schoolwork and, surprisingly, would do his homework and would not hand it in. The doctor was very sympathetic to the child and questioned him about family difficulties. He could not identify any and seemed to have a decent, although somewhat contentious, relationship with his parents. He was as perplexed as his parents about his "forgetting" to hand in his assignments. The pediatrician spoke to the parents, and they could not provide any explanation for the difficulties. Their relationship was stable. It did seem, though, that the parents were overcontrolling and demanding with the boy. As the doctor investigated the family dynamic further, it became clearer that he was most likely reacting against their overcontrol. Additionally, the parents were enraged with the child and were very active in considering punishment for his "misbehavior."

Refusal to hand in homework is a fairly common problem and probably represents a passive resistance to parental pressure. The more that the parent pressures the child, the more he or she feels the need to resist. Since these patterns can be very subtle, and the nature of the difficulty may not be clear, a referral for psychological evaluation is an option. Meanwhile, it is important to counsel the parents to try to maintain their relationship with the child since it is clear that he is struggling as well. He is not consciously trying to be difficult. Punishment will not result in the child being more conscientious. Motivation to study is not something that can be forced. In addition, this child may very well be reacting against what he perceives as parental overcontrol, and further attempts to control him may exacerbate the problem. It would be helpful for the parents to distance themselves from the difficulty and to reinforce the child's positive qualities. The parents would be well advised to enhance their relationship with the child while they all work toward figuring out a solution for the problem.

SUGGESTION. Some parents expect pediatricians to have all the answers. Others expect them to be their agent and to lecture the child on misbehavior. A punitive approach is counterproductive.

Some parents need quite a bit of help in parenting. There are, of course, those with obvious difficulties who are grossly ignorant and are poorly equipped to raise children. Families such as these will benefit from an approach that emphasizes a variety of health professionals. Mental health professionals, financial and social assistance, and programs designed to teach appropriate child-raising techniques will be beneficial.

Discipline

There are many other parents who are not grossly deficient but who do have difficulties in some areas. Parents often have trouble understanding the nature of discipline and are either too lax or too strict. It needs to be emphasized to all parents that spanking and other kinds of physical punishment are not helpful or appropriate. Undesirable behavior is only temporarily suppressed and physical punishment sends the message that problems can only be solved by hurting someone. Furthermore, it is confusing to the child, creates strong negative self-image feelings, and increases the child's degree of anger. Children are usually taught that it is not appropriate to hit another yet are being hit by their beloved parent. This inconsistency is confusing and hurtful.

Children who act out aggressively and who do not listen to their parents have not been treated with respect and consistency. Parents sometimes act as if their child's behavior is completely alien to them while in actuality it is probably a reflection of how the parents react. Parents can and should be counseled on appropriate discipline techniques. Affirmation of the child's positive qualities will be far more successful in developing the behavior that the parent desires. Furthermore, those children who are treated with kindness and respect are likely to treat others that way. This is a very sensitive issue that requires considerable tact and patience by the physician. To address this situation requires the pediatrician to tell the parents that they are doing something wrong in the way in which they are raising their children. It is important that this is approached by emphasizing the positive things that the parents are doing while making some suggestions that may be helpful. It is far easier to do this if the parents acknowledge that their child is out of control. It is much more difficult for the doctor to have to identify for the parents that their child is not behaving appropriately, which may be exemplified by the child's behavior in the office. Forming a positive and lasting relationship with the parents will enhance the likelihood that they will respond positively to the pediatrician's intervention in these behavioral issues. Some parents, because of their own difficulties, are truly ignorant as to appropriate discipline techniques. They may be loath to admit it but will welcome assistance if the doctor can identify this problem.

Feeding Problems

Parents often visit pediatricians with feeding problems. Pediatricians need to use great sensitivity and tact in dealing with an issue with such emotional weight. The first area of potential conflict with the child centers around when to give up the bottle. Errol Soskolne (1996, personal communication) suggests that it is important that the parents help the child give up the bottle at about 9-10 months. By 15-16 months, the desire for the bottle is well entrenched and a battle could ensue. In fact, food and eating behaviors are areas that are rife with battles over control. Parents do not feel comfortable in allowing the infant's natural appetite to govern eating. Instead, they often try to force children to eat, particularly at age 10-12 months, when appetite typically slows. This can result in children being out of tune with their own hunger, laying the groundwork for more serious eating disorders. At times, parents can act out their family's eating dynamics with the doctor. He or she tries to give advice regarding appropriate feeding practice and the parent can be very resistant, like a picky eater. The physician can become frustrated and angry, and an unsatisfying encounter ensues. Parents need to be encouraged to relax with their children and to develop consistent mealtimes, with snacking kept to a minimum. It is expected that disorganized families will have dysfunctional eating patterns.

Example

A family had developed what seemed to be a rather unusual eating pattern. In essence, there was no pattern. Each member of the family could eat whatever he or she wanted, whenever and wherever. There were no set mealtimes and no family dinner. The family seemed to have little sense of cohesion, and several of the members were overweight. Furthermore, their diets were nutritionally poor. Intervention by the doctor had some success, although changes were difficult to initiate because the family had firmly established a habitual pattern. Psychologically, it seemed to represent the parents' reluctance to accept their adult role.

Food has great symbolic value and many a battle is fought over eating. Battles often represent control issues, and pediatricians can be helpful in identifying the difficulty and by helping the family to extricate themselves from these conflicts. It must be recognized that these issues are very complex and involve many deep-seated psychological issues (see Chapter 4).

SUGGESTION. Feeding problems are commonly seen in pediatrician's offices. Helping to calm parents and to develop consistent patterns is beneficial. Eating problems are usually part of a larger picture of psychological disturbance.

The recent emphasis on the Attention-Deficit Hyperactivity Disorder (ADHD) has created problems for pediatricians since some parents insist upon that diagnosis even if their child does not fit the criteria. There are many family issues that can create behavior that the ADHD diagnosis describes, and it is essential that these difficulties be addressed for the long-term benefit of the child.

Our society places a great premium on success. Parents want their children to be the best and the brightest and often put undue pressure on their children. Frequently this is a result of the parent being dissatisfied with his or her own level of success. Pediatricians often encounter parents who are convinced that their child is a genius or has other abilities that are superior to other children. This can become a problem when the parents either put undue pressure on the child or when they request a statement from the pediatrician regarding the child's brilliance. The doctor must use great tact and sensitivity in emphasizing the child's positive qualities while encouraging the parents to adopt a more realistic and less pressured expectation.

A problem that is also quite resistant to intervention is when parents allow their children into the marital bed. It is best to emphasize that children need to learn to soothe themselves and to be by themselves under most circumstances. Once a child becomes accustomed to the parent's bed, it is extremely difficult to remove him or her. This situation can be overstimulating to the child and can certainly wreak havoc with the parent's relationship. Although tact is helpful, directness is necessary to ensure that this situation is dealt with as soon as it arises, which is usually in infancy.

Parents may also need to be informed as to appropriate sexual boundaries. Some parents have intercourse when their child is in the same room, assuming that the child is asleep. Children wake up during the night and often find the sight of parents having intercourse confusing and frightening. Furthermore, parents should be encouraged to maintain appropriate dress with opposite-gendered children once the child approaches 3 years old. Parents often take umbrage at these suggestions, implying that the doctor has a "dirty mind." It can be emphasized that children can get easily overstimulated and overwhelmed.

SUGGESTION. Considerable tact is required of pediatricians in dealing with behavioral issues. Parents can be very defensive about their child-rearing abilities.

Adolescents

The potential for behavioral difficulties increases as children reach adolescence. At the same time, parents begin to lose the degree of control that they were able to exercise when their children were younger. Adolescents provide special challenges to many who work with them, and this certainly includes pediatricians.

Teenagers tend to be quite self-absorbed and have little awareness of the impact that their behavior has on people, including their parents and their doctor. Consequently, they may seem very sullen and noncommunicative with the pediatrician, but this pose often drops if the doctor is able to create a comfortable atmosphere. Adolescents require tremendous patience, and the doctor must be prepared to expend considerable time and energy on relationship building.

Example

> It was quite clear to the pediatrician that something was troubling his young patient, but the 13-year-old continued to speak about relatively meaningless activities. The physician suggested that the girl schedule another appointment in 2 weeks' time. The patient was agreeable to this and was then able to speak to the doctor about her recent involvement with drugs.

Physicians may want to take a very relaxed approach with those patients who seem reluctant to talk. Most crucial, however, is to allow sufficient time for the child to feel comfortable and not rushed. Most pediatricians are very busy and do not routinely schedule time for extended appointments. Adolescents will not respond well to being put off. Their concerns need to be addressed at the time that they raise the problem. Some pediatricians routinely try to schedule adolescents toward the end of the day. At times it may be necessary to request the young patient to come back another day or even later in the day. It is helpful to train the receptionists and nurses to look for subtle clues that suggest that the child needs more than just a medical evaluation. Vague and unusual complaints may signal that the teenager may have some pressing issues on his or her mind. Teenagers are often very concerned about the confidentiality of the information that they divulge. The doctor may want to reassure them ahead of time that the doctor's primary allegiance is to the teenager and that information will not be divulged without the patient's permission. This is a very difficult position to be in but is necessary, with some exceptions. Any health care professional aware of an abusive situation involving a child must report it to the authorities. Furthermore, any life-threatening behavior, be it suicidal or homicidal, requires action by the medical professional to ensure the safety of anyone in danger.

The doctor's patient is the teenager, not the parents. If the doctor violates the pact, the treatment relationship will be ruined. Throughout the difficulty, the doctor must remain on the child's side. This often means that the doctor encourages the child to tell the parents about the particular problem he or she might be struggling with. Pregnant teenagers obviously cannot hide that fact for long, but it is still best for the teenager to tell the parents on her own terms. The doctor should offer himself or herself to be available to meet with the family, should the patient desire that assistance. The same holds true for drug or alcohol use or for eating disorders. The pediatrician may need to meet several times with the adolescent before he or she feels comfortable in telling the parents. Most will eventually inform the parents once they have taken the step of confiding in the doctor.

SUGGESTION. Adolescents require considerable time and patience from pediatricians. Relationship-building is crucial. The doctor's primary allegiance is to the adolescent. Sullenness is often a pose that falls away once the adolescent feels comfortable.

Dying Children

It is hard to think of a greater tragedy than that of the ending of a young life. It is heartbreaking for all involved. Doctors and other medical professionals are not immune from feeling devastated by the death of a young patient. It is a part of the practice that one comes to expect but that one never really gets accustomed to. Some pediatricians dissociate themselves from the death and dying of their patients. It is probably related to a feeling of wanting to avoid the pain of the situation as well as a concern that they will be blamed for the child's death, by themselves or by the family. By avoiding this situation, the physicians are ignoring an important part of their job and are not allowing themselves to deal with their own feelings of sadness and grief over the loss of the child. It is more useful for all concerned for the pediatrician to stay involved in the treatment of a seriously ill child and not to back away. Attending the funeral is often helpful, especially since the parents often

feel ostracized by the nature of the tragedy. If the doctor realizes that by maintaining the helping role, he or she is enormously helpful to the family, this helpfulness in turn will help
the physician deal with his or her own emotional distress.

One pediatrician (E. Soskolne, 1996, personal communication) suggests that children seem more able to accept their
deaths than are adults. Parents and other adults are often reluctant to accept the impending death, and children often need
to lead the way to help their family accept the unfortunate
reality. Pediatricians can be very helpful in being available to
the families during the period of deterioration.

SUGGESTION. It is important for pediatricians to maintain their
availability to both the child with terminal illness and the family. Such availability will also enhance the doctor's ability to
deal with the child's death.

Conclusion

Pediatricians have a special responsibility in that they must
protect their patients, who are not able to be advocates for
themselves. This may put the doctors at odds with some parents
who may feel that their needs override those of their children.
The physician needs to maintain his or her primary allegiance
to the child. Additionally, the physician needs to maintain the
alliance with the parents despite provocation. Adolescents can
be particularly trying and require exceptional patience and
considerable understanding. Pediatricians are fortunate in being able to participate in the growth and development of children and families. Most pediatricians find it enormously
gratifying to be an important part of this process, and many
become quite attached to the children and families that they
treat. Pediatricians often find the long-term relationship with
children and their parents to be extremely fulfilling.

Summary

1. Pediatricians must often act as intermediaries for their patients.

2. Parents have both healthy and unhealthy perceptions of children.
3. Some parents are overcontrolling, as if they "own" their children.
4. Resistant and overcontrolling parents are insecure and need reassurance.
5. It is important for the pediatrician to establish independent relationships with both the parents and the child.
6. The treatment alliance needs to be nurtured with both the child and the parents.
7. The pediatrician is often the first professional to become aware of family difficulties. He or she is in a unique position to make a positive impact on family problems.
8. A punitive approach for children's behavioral problems is not productive.
9. Adolescents need special care by pediatricians, and their problems are often difficult to deal with and can be life threatening.
10. The pediatrician needs to see beyond the teenager's provocative behavior, which is usually defensive and is not personal. Confidentiality is essential.
11. It is most helpful for pediatricians to maintain contact with dying children and their families for the benefit of all.

OBSTETRICS/GYNECOLOGY

The obstetrics/gynecology specialty has a number of elements that make it very appealing. It provides an opportunity for a practitioner to participate in what is generally an extremely joyful and fulfilling event: the birth of a child. It also provides a physician with the practice opportunity of treating women through both medical and surgical means. Obstetrician/gynecologists treat women throughout the life cycle, which provides a fascinating view of the changes that both puberty and menopause bring. The other side of the equation is that the practice of obstetrics and gynecology has a number of areas that are rife with strong emotions that can be very trying and difficult for the practitioner.

Obstetrics

Pregnant women must endure considerable physical discomfort. Some women experience strong psychic discomfort as well. The transition to motherhood can create enormous tension for some women. Additionally, the pregnancy itself can be experienced as being very unpleasant, if not terrifying, for some women having psychological difficulties. Typically, those whose own mothers were not able to provide them with sufficient emotional nurturance are going to question their own desire and ability to effectively nurture an infant. Some women who are unusually needful themselves may find it very difficult to provide a newborn with the nurturance and sustenance that he or she needs.

Example

Mrs. N. was pregnant with her first child. Throughout the pregnancy, she was upset and tearful but could not really articulate what was bothering her. She was referred for psychotherapy, where it was discovered that she was terrified about being able to adequately take care of a dependent and enormously needy baby. She did not think of herself as an adult and was locked in a dependency struggle with her mother. She had never felt that she was very capable and often deferred to her mother. Her own needs felt very intense, and she was not sure that she would be able to put them aside in order to take care of the consuming needs of an infant. Throughout her pregnancy she was frightened about her bodily changes and frequently called her doctor for reassurance. The doctor was sensitive to her concerns and was able to reassure her. In conjunction with her therapy, the patient was able to make it through the pregnancy without tremendous distress and continued to work on her unresolved issues after the baby was born.

This patient highlights a number of issues that can become manifest within pregnancy. She was strongly ambivalent about the pregnancy. She feared relinquishing the dependent role that she found stultifying yet gratifying. Her sense of herself did not include that of a competent adult. Rather she saw herself as adolescent, unprepared for motherhood. In fact, her experience of her pregnancy was reminiscent of a young girl's experiences of puberty. She felt unprepared for the rigors of adulthood and felt uncomfortable with bodily changes. Fortunately, she was able to get the psychological assistance that she needed. The physician also made herself available to the patient for reassurance. In this kind of situation, it is important that the physician take the correct line. Being overly sympathetic and accepting the patient's insistence on her incompetence will only recreate the mother-daughter struggle. Being appropriately empathetic while encouraging the healthy and adult side of the patient will assist her in recognizing her own hidden capabilities.

A popular and simplistic notion is that women are universally delighted with pregnancy. This is rarely completely true. Pregnancy brings forth a number of psychological issues that create ambivalent feelings. Many of these are relatively mild and expected. Wondering about one's capability of being a mother and being concerned about the sacrifices entailed in raising a child are quite common and are not problematic. Women often compare themselves, both consciously and unconsciously, with their own mothers, and pregnancy brings up old issues about their past mother-daughter relationship.

Example

Mrs. A. was exceedingly anxious throughout her pregnancy. She wished for a boy and seemed terrified that she might have a girl. She was not really cognizant of the reasons for her preference but seemed preoccupied with the gender of the child. She confided her concern to her physician who was able to help her identify the source of her severe anxiety. The patient and her mother had had a contentious and competitive relationship which was extremely painful, and she was very concerned that these feelings would emerge within a relationship with a daughter. Once she articulated her concerns, she felt much better, particularly after the doctor was sympathetic and reassuring.

In this instance, the doctor's perceptiveness and sensitivity helped the patient to feel better about a pervasive anxiety-arousing issue. Since the physician had no real knowledge of whether the patient and her new baby would have difficulties, false reassurances would not be realistic. The doctor helped the patient to voice her concerns and enabled her to see that help was available should the patient have difficulties with her feelings regarding her daughter. Pediatricians, nurse-practitioners, psychotherapists, and the obstetrician/gynecologist are all available resources for the patient who is concerned about proper child-rearing behavior.

Many patients, both potential fathers and mothers, have certain hopes and expectations for the gender of the baby. The reasons vary and are rarely problematic since most parents quickly adapt, at least on a more conscious level, to their baby's gender. However, there are some parents who have very definite expectations and become profoundly upset and even depressed when disappointed. Of course, this is potentially disastrous for the baby, who may grow up feeling unwanted, in general, and negative about his or her gender, in particular. At times, mothers are irrationally blamed for providing a baby of the "wrong" gender. Educating parents as to how gender is determined may mitigate some of this, but the psychological needs are usually of sufficient strength to override rationality. The reasons for this unfortunate situation vary. Fathers may put pressure on their wives for a boy to "carry on the family name" or because they are afraid of being a father to a girl. Some men view producing a male child as an indication of their manliness. Other men may be unconsciously worried about feeling competitive with a boy and hope for a girl. Some women may disparage girls and hope for a boy. This may reflect self-deprecating feelings toward themselves as females. Perhaps they have viewed being female as a definite disadvantage and want their child to have all the advantages possible. Some women who have been sexually abused wish for a boy so that their child presumably does not suffer as they have. Some women have hostility toward men and are afraid that they will not be able to love a boy. Regardless of the reason, intervention by the physician is necessary in order to help the parents to work through their disappointments so that the family relationships remain as healthy as possible. Helping the patients articulate and discuss their disappointments is beneficial. Encouraging reluctant fathers and mothers to hold and bond with their baby immediately can reduce disappointment. Some parents are able to put aside, at least temporarily, their disappointment in the face of a beautiful newborn.

In some sense, all infants represent a disappointment to new parents. They have formed a certain image of the expected child in their minds which their real newborn will not match. Most patients are quickly able to resolve such disappointment and become enraptured with their new baby. Many of those with strong unresolved reactions will need referral to a psychotherapist to assist them in understanding and working through the disappointment.

Ambivalence in pregnancy can also be seen in the occurrence of *hyperemesis gravidarum.* This is a condition where nausea and vomiting are more exaggerated and persistent than the usual early nausea and vomiting of pregnancy. The ambivalence toward the fetus is rarely conscious. Instead it becomes actualized within the physical symptoms. Such patients are often very needy and may be noncompliant. They are ambivalent about the pregnancy, and this manifests itself by the unconscious wish to expel it in some fashion. This wish is unacceptable and remains unconscious. It is important to remember that this is not the only wish present. Many of these women also wish for a healthy and thriving baby. The conflict between the two wishes can psychologically cause havoc. This condition is relatively rare, yet can be very difficult for physicians and other health care professionals. The patients need frequent appointments and reassurance that the baby is getting proper nutrition. Hospitalization, feeding tubes, or IV therapy are sometimes necessary to maintain adequate nutrition. The neediness of these patients may repel some physicians, particularly since they demand considerable time but do not seem to want to cooperate in order to improve their situation. Some "failure to thrive" infants may be the product of strongly negative feelings within the sense of ambivalence. Consequently, intervention is essential by referral to a mental health professional.

SUGGESTION. Ambivalence in pregnancy can take a number of different forms. Some parents question their abilities; others have expectations about gender. Some patients fear a repetition of their own difficult relationship with their parents. In all cases, a reassuring and available physician is extremely helpful. Referral for psychotherapy may be necessary with those whose fearfulness and negativity places the baby and family at risk.

One type of patient that often causes obstetricians grief is the patient who has developed a very definite birth plan that may be contrary to physician and hospital policies. Beyond this, many doctors resent being told what they can and cannot do, especially in the atmosphere of distrust that might be present.

Example

A patient, discussed in the section on "Oversuspiciousness" in Chapter 3, "blindsided" her doctor by refusing a labor-inducing medication, which resulted in a serious infection for her baby. The physician had thought that this had been settled earlier in the pregnancy. In response to a question, she informed the patient of her professional opinion concerning the advisability of using medication if the patient does not go into active labor following prolonged labor and/or premature rupture of the membranes. This particular patient had indicated some discomfort regarding medication during labor but had seemed reassured and agreeable to the doctor's recommendation. At term, the patient called the obstetrician when her membranes had ruptured but did not go to the hospital as requested. It was necessary for the physician to phone the parents and to emphatically request that they come to the hospital. Despite the doctor's advice, the patient refused all medications, resulting in an unfortunate and unnecessary infection.

This situation could not really be forestalled by the doctor. She had spoken with the patient about her expectations and they seemed to be in agreement. If she had known of the patient's plans, the doctor may very well have discontinued the professional relationship. This is always an option for the physician who feels that his or her professional judgment is being compromised. Prior to this rather drastic action, however, it is important to carefully explain the rationale for all procedures to ensure patient understanding and cooperation. Carefully encouraging patients to give voice to all beliefs and concerns is essential to minimize the possibility of this kind of situation occurring. Some patients are very suspicious of the medical establishment. They may not be able to be convinced otherwise, and the physician must maintain his or her professional judgment and not allow patients to overly control treatment.

SUGGESTION. Some patients feel the need to dictate the treatment. Physicians need to be explicit regarding their expectations and may need to decline participation if their professional opinions are compromised.

Teenage Pregnancy

Teenage pregnancy can be distressing to all involved. The notion of children raising children is frightening and often creates despair for caregivers. However, being judgmental about the fact of the pregnancy is never helpful or appropriate. These young people are often without adequate support systems and may need considerable active intervention from medical practitioners. These patients are often unmarried and their family may have abandoned them. It is often a source of worry for doctors since it is clear that many of these teenagers do not take adequate care of themselves and may not be able to care adequately for their baby.

Example

A young woman was rather blasé before her delivery, believing that she would not find it too difficult to care for a baby. At her 6-week postpartum visit, she indicated to the physician how surprised she was by how difficult and time-consuming it was to care for a baby. She had no idea of the emotional and physical demands.

It is essential that the practitioner establish a positive rapport with the patient. This is accomplished by listening carefully to her and to her story without being critical or authoritarian. Showing a genuine interest in the patient is essential. Rapport is not going to be quickly established or easily won. The patient is likely to have transferential feelings toward the physician that may mirror problematic relationship issues with the parent. Furthermore, teenagers are notoriously distrustful of adults. If rapport is not established, the patient is not going to allow herself to be helped.

Because of their often needy situation, pregnant teenagers require special intervention by the medical staff. They may need to be pointed to social service organizations to obtain the kind of assistance that they need. Some may be in abusive situations, and protective services may need to be notified. It is often hard to know if these young people are in abusive situations since they may deny their predicament. Continued concern and a sense of openness may result in eventual disclosure of abuse.

Older Pregnant Women

Women who are having their first children at a later age have some special problems that require attention. In some cases, fertility has been compromised and it may be more difficult for older women to get pregnant. Since their "biological clocks" are ticking, a sense of desperation is experienced.

There are many reasons why childbearing is delayed. Some women have not formed a positive and satisfying relationship with a man. Others have concentrated on their careers. Those who have had conflicts and ambivalence about being a mother are likely to experience considerable anxiety before and even after childbirth. Women who have not had children have become quite independent, as well as focused on their own needs, and may feel uncomfortable with the prospect of having their schedules controlled. Some older mothers are very unsure about their ability to be good mothers and may require reassurance from medical practitioners. Once pregnant, the ambivalence can cause considerable anxiety and worry. The obstetrician needs to be sensitive to these issues and to make himself or herself quite available to the patient.

Pregnancy Loss

Women who have suffered pregnancy losses have varied responses. Most often, miscarriage losses are not near as devastating as are intrauterine or neonatal deaths. However, each miscarriage loss is significant and can cause strong reactions. For those who have an infertility problem, miscarriages are devastating and a sense of depression and of hopelessness often results. Some women blame themselves for miscarriages, as well as for intrauterine and neonatal deaths, believing that these unfortunate occurrences were a result of some defect within themselves. Women who miscarry need to be reassured that they are normal, that miscarriages are quite common, and that they do not necessarily signify an enduring problem. Once the patient gets pregnant again, it is helpful for her to quickly initiate contact with the doctor. The medical staff can then be reassuring and help her to contain her anxiety until that first crucial trimester period is passed.

Intrauterine and neonatal deaths are, of course, a tragedy that will require considerable time and grieving. It is, again, important for the doctor to make himself or herself readily available to the patient for questions and comfort. Attending memorial and funeral services is often helpful to both. A death is also a blow to the physician who had anticipated a normal and healthy baby. Many physicians wonder whether they could have done something to prevent the death. This becomes particularly problematic when the patient blames the physician as well. It can precipitate an ugly encounter if the doctor gets defensive and, in retaliation, returns the patient's angry feelings. As difficult as it is, it is best for medical practitioners to try to absorb the patient's anger without retaliation. Some patients will leave the care of the doctor after a death, and the physician can try to understand how painful the association must be.

The obstetrician can try to help the patient with the loss by scheduling frequent visits in the first few months. Encouraging the patient and her husband to call with any questions can be helpful. Some patients may want to put together a scrapbook of mementos from the experience and may want to share it with the doctor. It is important that the physician make sure that sufficient time is scheduled. Some doctors want to escape the emotional pain by minimizing contact with the patient. This is ill advised and detrimental to both doctor and patient.

Some women decide to get pregnant soon after they experience a pregnancy loss. This is not particularly detrimental after a miscarriage but is ill advised after an intrauterine or perinatal loss. The parents need sufficient time to grieve. If sufficient time is not spent in the grieving process, the next baby will likely function as a "replacement baby" and will be burdened with unconscious parental expectations left over from the dead baby.

Example

> Mrs. T. entered psychotherapy feeling depressed and inadequate. She never felt that she achieved enough and had always felt that she was a disappointment to her parents. She was aware that her birth had occurred about 10 months after the death of a sister but had never realized the impact that it had had on her. Other than a different middle name, their names were identical. In life she competed against the fantasies and images of her long-deceased sister.

Encouraging patients to allow sufficient time for grieving will be helpful to mitigate this unfortunate situation.

SUGGESTION. Pregnancy loss is devastating for the patient. Physicians also experience a sense of loss and may blame themselves and become defensive. Absorbing the patient's anger without retaliation is the best approach. Frequent visits by the patient help the patient and the doctor to work through their disappointment and feelings of loss. Patients require a considerable period of time to work through their grief.

Depression and Pregnancy

In some situations, women are not able to resolve their feelings over pregnancy losses and may need referral to a mental health professional. When normal and expected feelings of grief and mourning do not abate, or they worsen, a referral is in order.

True postpartum depression is relatively rare. Many women experience some depressive feelings after childbirth.

Some of it may be hormonal, and some may be related to the loss of freedom and to the awesome responsibility of caring for an infant. In most cases, the depressive feelings abate over a period of a few weeks. If they do not, or if they increase, a more serious depression has formed. Some postpartum depressions are very serious, resulting in hospitalization. It is not unknown for severely depressed mothers to neglect the care of their children. The obstetrician should be on the lookout for mothers whose "baby blues" do not seem to resolve. Frequent visits and emotional support are important. Communicating with the family may be essential if the patient is not able to care for herself or for the baby.

Infertility

The inability to bear children is enormously distressing for both husband and wife. Each may blame themselves and each other, and terrible conflict can ensue. It is important that the practitioner be alert to these potential problems and initiate a referral to marital or individual therapy, if indicated. As mentioned, women and men often feel defective when they cannot produce a child. If a particular person is identified as having the problem, considerable blame can occur. Many marriages founder due to infertility problems, and marital therapy has been quite helpful in a number of cases.

Women struggling with infertility may get depressed after each period. It is difficult for them when friends or family members get pregnant. They want to feel happy for their friends or loved ones but their own pain and envy makes this difficult. The anger over their inability to get pregnant may also express itself as depression. At times, infertility problems may reflect ambivalence about becoming pregnant, and this can be reflected in infrequent intercourse.

For some couples, other psychological and marital problems become manifest as issues about pregnancy.

Examples

Mr. and Mrs. C. sought out the services of a psychologist when they could not agree as to whether to have a child or not. The husband was insistent on the wife getting pregnant. The wife was quite hesitant. Both had very hectic work schedules that neither wanted to compromise should they have a baby. The husband had recently and surprisingly become insistent about them having a baby, and this was perplexing to the wife. She strongly questioned her capability of being a good mother and was very reluctant to get pregnant. The husband described himself as being very depressed and unhappy. The husband had given the wife an ultimatum such that he would end the marriage if she did not agree to a pregnancy. They both refused further exploration and treatment.

Similarly, another couple sought out treatment because of marital difficulties. Again, the husband was adamant about his wife becoming pregnant despite her struggles with severe depression. He felt that he did not want to wait any longer and that he wanted to terminate the marriage if his wife was not prepared to accede to his wishes.

In both of these situations, serious psychological problems within both husband and wife were being expressed within the desire to get pregnant. It would be unfortunate if the obstetrician involved were to ignore the serious difficulties that were behind the wish to get pregnant.

There are certain warning signs that can alert a physician to psychological and/or marital problems within a pregnancy. Frequent phone calls with vague complaints, stomach problems, and other seemingly psychogenic complaints point to an underlying difficulty.

Example

A patient experienced considerable stomach problems during her pregnancy. Additionally, she was not communicative and seemed depressed and distracted. She would phone often but was never clear as to the reasons. She did not seem happy about the pregnancy. The doctor questioned her about her attitude but was put off. She wondered if the patient was being abused. About a year later the patient was able to tell the doctor that during the pregnancy she had discovered that her daughter was being sexually abused and could not bring herself to talk about it. She was pleased to know that the doctor had been so concerned.

It is important to question patients about an unusual manner or mood. Vague complaints, frequent phone calls, and psychogenic problems are red flags suggesting a psychological or family problem.

Patients who are unaccountably afraid of a vaginal delivery and who have trouble tolerating labor may have a history of sexual abuse. The association of a large object forcing itself through the vagina brings forth intensely painful memories of sexual violation.

SUGGESTION. Psychological problems may manifest themselves during pregnancy. These can relate to pregnancy losses, to marital and psychological difficulties, and to past sexual abuse. It is important for the practitioner to pursue subtle hints and to question patients about possible problems.

Entitlement

Some patients have a sense of entitlement that comes to the fore when they get pregnant. Typically, these women experience the pregnancy as being inordinately burdensome and believe that special treatment is deserved. At times they may desire work excuses for discomfort that does not seem out of the ordinary for pregnancy. They may be dissatisfied with their job situation and feel that their pregnancy makes it all the more unbearable, and they will demand time off. The physician will often first receive a number of phone calls complaining about vague and ill-defined complaints. This will often be followed by a visit in which the patient is accompanied by the husband or boyfriend whose presence is designed to verify the patient's inability to work. This sense of entitlement may irritate medical practitioners who are accustomed to working very hard and who may rarely take days off for minor ills. The best approach is to maintain a cool head and explain to the patients that the condition that they may be complaining about is a normal experience of pregnancy and cannot be considered a disabling disorder. Of course, a number of patients will not be satisfied with this answer and may get angry and/or may not give up their quest for time off.

Gynecology

Gynecological problems also carry heavy psychological weight because of the association with sexual functioning and feelings. A gynecological exam can be experienced as tremendously intrusive. Women with a history of sexual abuse are going to find such an exam quite difficult. Some fear the speculum, imagining that their vagina cannot accommodate what appears to be a large instrument. Other women are very uncomfortable with that area of the body, which they experience as dirty and mysterious. The proximity of the vagina to the anus has caused confusion to young girls, and this anatomical confusion can carry over to adults. Some patients need careful instruction as to their anatomy and physiology. Many women will not ask their doctor because of embarrassment, and the physician can ascertain any difficulties in these areas by patient hesitancy, discomfort, and confusion. Because of the sensitivity of the vaginal area, practitioners need to be inordinately sensitive to patient discomfort and emotional distress.

Adolescents

To assume that all adolescents create difficulties for gynecologists is inaccurate. Many of them are a delight, are cooperative, and enliven a practice with their enthusiasm. Others may present the physician with the difficulties that seem to be associated with adolescents. Many teenagers are sexually active and engage in unprotected sex with multiple partners. This dangerous behavior is likely to elicit a strong response from physicians, who may see their own children reflected in the faces of their young patients. Despite this provocation, it is important to establish a working alliance with the teenagers. This is accomplished by showing genuine interest and by being nonjudgmental. It takes time to gain their confidence. Letting the patient define the relationship by communicating that the doctor is there to help with her concerns establishes a sense of cooperation. It is essential that the teenager's concerns are addressed. If this is accomplished, discussion can ensue as to her needs and may lead in a direction where she is able to consider the wisdom of some of her actions.

At times, doctors may ascertain that the teenager is sexually active and will not pursue the patient for further information. Some teenagers are sexually active and may not want to be. The gynecologist can ask the patient whether she enjoys intercourse. If not, discussing alternatives can be very helpful.

It is essential to schedule considerable time with teenagers. If they are rushed, they are not likely to divulge information that is sensitive. Considerable conflict can exist between mothers and daughters, and the doctor can find himself or herself in the middle if not careful.

Example

A teenager was scheduled for an appointment with her mother's gynecologist because of the mother's concern about her child's sexual behavior. Upon arrival, the patient was extremely sullen and uncommunicative. She sat there looking angry and defiant. Knowing that the mother had made the appointment and realizing that the adolescent felt that she was there to satisfy the mother, the doctor told her that they did not have to proceed with the interview and/or the examination, and that whatever they did was up to the patient. She relaxed considerably and they talked comfortably.

The doctor's allegiance is to the patient, regardless of the age.

Confidentiality is a concern to the teenager, and they must be reassured that what they tell the doctor will remain confidential. Some teenagers who are sexually active have a higher percentage of abnormal Pap smears. Their high-risk behavior can have future health consequences, including reduced reproductive ability. Consequently, gaining their trust so that they pursue continued care is essential.

Some mothers want gynecologists to see their daughters once menarche begins. This is often ill advised since these youngsters still experience themselves as children and feel uncomfortable and threatened in an office specializing in care of adult women. If these children are turned off, it may be difficult for them to maintain good health in the future. Their first visit to a gynecologist should be a good one.

SUGGESTION. Adolescents often distrust physicians, and the doctor must earn their trust. Reassuring them as to their sense of control is essential, as is ensuring confidentiality. Establishing a positive relationship will create an atmosphere that will lead toward positive health behaviors in the future.

Dyspareunia, Vaginismus, and Pelvic Pain

Once medical causes are ruled out, these three disorders can be very difficult to successfully treat. They may point to sexual abuse or, at the very least, to considerable problems with sexual matters. Oftentimes other psychological problems accompany these disorders, and those having problems in this area do not seem very happy. Referral to a mental health professional is appropriate. Considerable patience is required by the physician since gynecological examinations are likely to take a long time and engender considerable emotional distress. Some women with dyspareunia and vaginismus fear being out of control. Consequently, their symptom ends up controlling their partners and, unfortunately, the doctor. It is easy but unfruitful to be insistent with these patients. The patient is, and always will be, in control, and that fact needs to be accepted. It is only when the patient feels comfortable that any progress will be achieved.

Unfortunately, some women with dyspareunia and pelvic pain go in search of a physical cause for what is most likely a psychological disorder. They tend toward doctor-shopping because they are looking for a particular physical diagnosis and treatment. They may thus end up with unnecessary surgeries.

Perimenopause

The process of going through menopause is akin to adolescence in reverse. It can be a frightening and frustrating experience for women. There are many bodily changes that women experience that seem abnormal but are not. Considerable emphasis must be given to educating women as to what is happening to their bodies. There are real physical effects that are disturbing. They often have bleeding problems, hot flashes, night sweats, and lubrication difficulties. Bloating and gas may occur and skin problems can emerge. Memory problems become evident. Some women have difficulty in accepting or recognizing these inevitable signs of aging and are certain that there is a serious medical problem. The aging process may very well feel like a betrayal of the body, resulting in anger and depression. The loss of fertility may feel like a loss for some women. To add insult to injury, just as these women are going through the perimenopausal process, many of their daughters may be going through adolescence.

Often patients want to blame a number of different problems on hormones. They may, in actuality, be depressed or have marital problems or have some other psychological problem that they want to consign to a hormonal problem. Other physicians may want to do the same thing when confronted with these women, resulting in the gynecologist feeling unreasonably burdened. The gynecologist then needs to help redirect the patient to the person or place where she can get the appropriate help.

SUGGESTION. Perimenopause creates distress for patients because of the varied bodily changes it causes. The reality of aging may be difficult to accept and there is the wish for medication to eliminate all discomfort. Other interpersonal and psychological problems may be wrongly attributed to perimenopause.

Hysterectomy

Hysterectomies get a varied response from women. Some who have been so uncomfortable from the symptoms that necessitated the surgery are delighted by the absence of pain and discomfort. Others experience a sense of loss. Younger women who are losing the ability to have children are strongly impacted and may suffer from profound feelings of distress. Even those beyond childbearing age may experience the removal of their uterus as a major loss. Being sensitive to the intense feelings created by the prospect of a hysterectomy can enable the physician to prepare the patient for these feelings. It is often helpful to initiate discussion about potential feelings of loss, since some patients will deny these feelings.

Since the uterus is involved in the orgastic response, its absence does have an effect on sexual functioning, and some women complain about the change. Informing patients prior to surgery of the possible changes is helpful. Opening an avenue of discussion enables patients to talk about any changes after the surgery. Many women are able to adjust to the changes, and their adjustment is enhanced by open communication.

Patients of all ages may have reactions to hysterectomies that are not anticipated.

Example

A 76-year-old woman underwent a vaginal hysterectomy along with a cystocele repair. An unfortunate consequence of the surgery was a foreshortening of the vagina. The husband came with the wife to her appointment the following year complaining of not being able to achieve complete penetration. He was very forthright about his concern. The doctor spoke with the couple and they decided to work with vaginal dilators. It was fortunate that the couple was able to approach the gynecologist with their concerns so that some remedy could be attempted.

One cannot always intuit patients' concerns. An open atmosphere that encourages questions is likely to promote the kind of discussion described in the example.

Conclusion

Obstetrician/gynecologists have the enviable opportunity of participating in one of the most pleasing, fulfilling, and joyous processes of medical practice: childbirth. The celebration can immediately turn to despair and grief should intrauterine or neonatal losses occur. The obstetrician needs to be comfortable in assisting patients in their grief and needs to address his or her own sadness and sense of loss. As the physician who handles reproductive issues, the obstetrician/gynecologist works with patients who have problems that bring forth intense emotions: infertility, pregnancy, and sexual functioning. To be of optimal help, the physician needs to be comfortable in dealing with the personal and marital problems that come with this territory. Obstetrician/gynecologists also have the privilege of working with the unique changes that only women encounter.

Summary

1. The transition to motherhood creates tension for some women. A new identity must be created, which requires a developmental leap. Some women experience pregnancy as being terrifying.
2. Some parents have definite expectations regarding the gender of their child, and disappointments can be highly detrimental if not worked through.
3. Ambivalence toward the fetus can be seen in *hyperemesis gravidarum*.
4. Inflexible and demanding obstetrical patients need to be dealt with as soon as possible, with the physician ensuring that professional standards are upheld.
5. Establishing and maintaining rapport is essential for the successful treatment of adolescents.
6. Pregnancy loss can create anger and blame toward the physician.
7. Physicians need to spend considerable time in helping patients with their loss and should encourage a substantial waiting period before another pregnancy is attempted.
8. Patients who cannot resolve their mourning or those with severe postpartum depression should be referred for psychotherapeutic treatment.
9. Frequent phone calls and psychogenic-type complaints may point to psychological and/or marital difficulties.
10. Gynecological problems have special psychological significance because of the association with sexual functioning.
11. Dyspareunia, vaginismus, and pelvic pain are often related to sexual conflicts, once physical causes are ruled out.
12. Menopause is often experienced as a betrayal of the women's body and is a concrete indication of the aging process.
13. At times, menopause is falsely implicated in a number of different complaints.

14. Hysterectomies can be wonderful for some women who have been suffering. It also represents an end to fertility and can be experienced as a loss for some patients.

DEATH AND DYING

Some practitioners may consider death to be the ultimate enemy within medical practice. This attitude ignores the reality of life—the inevitability of death. The physician's conflict between the desire to prolong life versus the continuous deterioration of the human body through aging and disease can cause great frustration. Consciously, physicians and other medical practitioners recognize their losing battle. Unconsciously, some pursue medical careers because of the unrealistic fantasy of being able to stave off death.

Example

Dr. K., for as long as he could remember, had wanted to be a physician. He had studied hard in college and had been a superb student in medical school. He excelled in his residency, and his career as a thoracic surgeon was promising. He rarely thought about his younger brother, who had died of leukemia at age 5, and certainly had no awareness that that tragedy could have had any motivating influence in his career choice. As Dr. K.'s career progressed, he became more and more depressed and moody. He experienced despair when he could not save a patient, even if he had performed competently. Because of his depression, he felt compelled to seek out psychotherapy. In that process he discovered that he had maintained the unconscious connection between his patients and his brother. Any "failure" brought back extremely painful feelings of loss and grief over his brother. When he was a child and he questioned his parents about his brother's death, under persistent questioning his parents informed him that his brother died when his heart stopped beating. His work as a heart surgeon was partly motivated by his impossible desire to save his brother.

Once the doctor was able to work through his unresolved feelings regarding his brother, he was more able to gain satisfaction from his work and became less devastated by patient deaths.

He no longer felt a patient death to be a personal failure to the extent that he did previously. It should be noted that it is understandable to question oneself when a death occurs and to have sad and grieving feelings. Those doctors who have unrealistic expectations and unconscious fantasies are the ones who have trouble accepting inevitable deaths.

If it is recognized and accepted that death is inevitable and does not necessarily represent physician failure, the doctor is more able to integrate this uncomfortable reality. The physician is able to gain satisfaction from his or her work and is likely to be able to maintain contact with the patient during the progression toward death. Those who cannot accept their own imperfections are likely to have difficulty with death and may abandon patients as they approach death. Some doctors who do this feel that they have failed and cannot tolerate their sense of blame as well as their feeling of loss.

Example

The oncologist had worked long and hard with a patient who suffered from stomach cancer. As it became clear that the cancer had metastasized, the doctor became less and less emotionally available. The patient felt puzzled and hurt, which exacerbated his sense of being alone. The oncologist had developed considerable feelings of closeness toward the patient and was having trouble tolerating her feelings of loss in regard to the patient.

If asked, the physician probably would not recognize her withdrawal. Nevertheless, it was perceptible and hurtful to the patient. These distancing maneuvers are subtle and are usually beyond conscious awareness. It is important to remember that withdrawing from patients is not only hurtful to the patient. The medical professional loses out on the opportunity to work through his or her own feelings about death in general and about the death of the patient, in particular.

Others are uncomfortable with the notion of their own death and want to distance themselves from that reality. It seems surprising that a person would become a physician if he or she fears death. One would think that a person with such an issue would avoid being near physical illness and death completely. However, some people become "counterphobic" as a defense against fears. That is, a person inordinately afraid of death becomes a physician as an unconscious attempt to deny and then to master the fear. Those whose motivations are counterphobic are often susceptible to emotional distress, since psychic processes put too much pressure on them for their defenses to work adequately.

It seems obvious that all people are afraid of death and that it is not unusual to want to distance oneself from that terrible reality. However, death is something that all must confront, and one's notion of death and the irrational fantasies associated with it can greatly increase fear and anxiety. Each death reminds us of our own, and one's image of death will determine how one approaches the death of others. Childhood experiences, fantasies, and family or religiously inculcated beliefs can create a notion of death that is awesome in its terror. Those who suffer from unresolved guilt feelings can imagine great tortures and punishment upon death. For that matter, physicians and patients who have such feelings will have enormous difficulties in dealing with death.

Example

Dr. K., mentioned earlier, had suffered the death of his brother when he was too young to be able to comprehend the true meaning of death. For a considerable time after his brother's death, the boy was terrorized by nightmares where he viewed his brother as being torn apart by demonic figures. This represented his conception of death. Additionally, like most people, the child had ambivalent feelings toward his brother and became terrified that his occasional hostile feelings might have contributed to his death.

Those who have suffered deaths of loved ones as children have an inordinate time dealing with death and disease as adults. They are all too often reminded of the earlier trauma, with the accompanying grief and the unconscious terrifying fantasies.

SUGGESTION. The inevitability of death can cause problems for medical professionals. Some are afraid of being blamed, others are reminded of losses within their own life, and still others are plagued by concerns about their own mortality. Guilt feelings also can wreak havoc with physicians' ability to deal comfortably with death. Withdrawal damages patients and doctors alike.

The Dying Patient

Patients will have an understandably diverse reaction to the fact of impending death. Each of us is intellectually aware of our mortality but often deny the reality of it. At first, patients will often deny the inevitability of their impending death. The notion of dying is an affront to a patient's sense of invulnerability and specialness. It is an assault on one's narcissism. The fact that a person has a finiteness to his or her life is a shock and feels like a betrayal. The person's body has let the individual down. It is not dissimilar to the difficulty that some people have in aging. Each decrease in functioning brings a sense of loss and can result in depression. The reality of aging is also a narcissistic injury. Much of the population of the United States is preoccupied with youth. Cosmetic and pharmaceutical companies make billions of dollars marketing medications designed to disguise the effects of aging. There is a constant push to try to reverse aging. Physicians are often expected to beat back the ravages of time, and patients can be infuriated with doctors' "incompetence."

This sense of hopelessness and lack of control increases exponentially with the reality of impending death. It brings forth the patient's wish for omnipotence. Patients develop fantasies about miracle cures and about mistaken diagnoses. The first response to news of serious or terminal illness is that of denial. The patient refuses to believe the physician's prognosis. As denial falls away, anger is often the next emotion to be experienced. The patient feels treated unfairly, and believes that a mistake has been made. Again, the sense of omnipotence and immortality is destroyed, resulting in feelings of inadequacy and compensatory rage. A sense of detachment from others may emerge. In some sense this is preparatory for the eternal detachment. It is also an angry detachment from those who still have their health. Envy of those not sick develops, and some become enraged with family and friends. Eventually, a sense of depression sets in as the patient begins to face the reality of death. The patient feels hopeless and alone. A great sadness may descend as the patient looks at disappointments in his or her life. The patient must face that future goals will not be met and that fantasies must be set aside. There may be a tremendous sense of failure as the patient recognizes his or her disappointments. In the best of circumstances, the patient comes to grips with his or her impending death and comes to accept reality, including disappointments. In these situations, a patient is able to die much more peacefully. Those who are not able to work through these feelings struggle through the dying process.

Families

A very sick or dying patient brings his or her family into the relationship with the physician. A number of varied responses can be expected.

Example

The patient was an elderly woman who was succumbing to a variety of ailments. She had lived a full and generally satisfying life and was prepared to die. She had requested not to be resuscitated. Unfortunately, her eldest daughter, who had been somewhat estranged from the family, was insistent that everything possible be done for her mother. She became quite upset with her mother, with the doctor, and with the rest of the family for "giving up." From this perspective, it seems obvious that the daughter's guilt over being relatively uninvolved in the family is generating her demandingness. Under the emotions of the moment and without adequate background information, the physician often does not have the whole picture available. The mother died in the midst of this contentiousness.

It would be simplistic and inaccurate to blame the daughter for all the contentiousness. This does not give justice to the complexity of this relationship and of relationships in general. Within family relationships, everyone has a perspective and should be given an opportunity to give voice to it. In some ways, the family objected to the daughter because, like always, she did not automatically go along with the family's decision. Her quest for independence, from her perspective, necessitated her distancing herself from the family. Her despair over her mother's inevitable death stemmed from her sadness that she and the mother could not forge a rapprochement. She was not ready to "give up" her quest to be able to maintain her independence yet have a satisfactory relationship with her mother. She also felt guilty about the estrangement. As is often the case, the nature of relationships persists throughout the lives of the participants, regardless of the circumstances. In fact, crises often exacerbate the problems because the intensity of the emotions generated stimulate the emergence of unresolved issues.

The physician may very well feel himself or herself to be in the middle. It is the patient's wishes that need to be adhered to, but conflicts can emerge that can be troubling. The medical practitioner should not allow himself or herself to be pulled into the particular family pathology of the dying patient. It is easy to be seduced by the seeming rationality of one position. It is important not to take sides, as if in an argument. If one feels emotionally drawn into the interaction such that intense and anxious feelings are experienced, it is a clear indication that one is being drawn into a family pathological interaction. It is best to allow all participants an opportunity to give voice to their opinion and to work out their difficulties, while being available as a consultant. There is a refreshing feeling of relief when one adopts a more neutral and facilitating position.

SUGGESTION. Family members continue their characteristic way of interacting throughout illness and death. It is important to maintain allegiance to the patient while not getting embroiled in family pathology. Each family member has a perspective which he or she feels is valid, and they should all have the opportunity to articulate it.

Families may have the expectation that relationships will change under the pressure of impending death. However, psychic processes are not governed by reality constraints, and the reality of death is not likely to alter long-entrenched family problems and relationships. Some family members are terribly disappointed when this does not happen. Feelings will run exceptionally strong when a family member is dying, and these emotions are not only sad and grieving ones. Tremendous anger and resentment emerge as the reality of impending death becomes evident.

Example

The brothers had always vied for the father's attention. He was a severe taskmaster who had never seemed pleased with either of his sons. As a consequence, they had developed intense rivalrous feelings that surfaced as their father was dying. Each tried to be in control, and the bitterness escalated into pushing and shoving. Hospital security had to be called to separate the brothers. Sadly, the brothers' real difficulty lay with the father and not with each other. They did not realize that their competitive feelings were the result of their unyielding father and that no success would have pleased him.

Hollywood endings rarely are the result in real life. These two brothers were continuing unto death the conflicts that were the result of their demanding and unhappy father. The father's impending death intensified the feelings as each brother felt his time to gain his father's acceptance waning. The frustration and anger that really belonged to the father was redirected, since it is often difficult to feel hostile toward a dying person.

SUGGESTION. Relationships generally remain constant despite impending death. Some participants are disappointed when their expectations for change are not met.

Ambivalence

All relationships engender mixed feelings. The notion of unconditional love is a fallacy. Human beings contain a multiplicity of feelings about everyone with whom they are intimately involved. In many cases, the positive feelings considerably outweigh the negative. In relationships that have been troubled, ambivalence reigns supreme. Those who have had conflictual relationships with their parents have an ambivalent tie that causes considerable distress when death occurs. There is much unfinished business that causes emotional pain. Furthermore, the ambivalence itself creates an intensity of feeling. The person feels a pull toward and a push away. Distance between the participants is rarely comfortable with a sense of overwhelming closeness or with the feeling of inconsolable distance. The physician can feel quite confused and overwhelmed by the intensity of feelings expressed within ambivalent relationships. Those with such feelings are likely to be extremely despondent and/or hostile within encounters with the physician. The feelings that they are experiencing are overwhelming and tend to get displaced onto the hospital staff. Maintaining equanimity in the face of such provocation is quite difficult but is helpful to all concerned.

SUGGESTION. Ambivalent feelings toward loved ones are normal. Conflicted relationships give rise to strongly ambivalent feelings, which cause intense emotions when one of the participants is dying. Some emotions may get displaced onto the medical staff, who need to remain calm in order to provide a stable focus for the patient and family.

Hospices

Hospice care has been in ascendancy in the last 20 years in the United States. In modern times, hospices were founded by Cicely Saunders, a British nurse turned physician. In hospice circles, she is revered. Hospice care's goal is toward the elimination of pain in dying patients. The elimination of pain includes physical, emotional, financial, and bureaucratic. Consequently, hospice care uniformly is approached with a team that consists of physicians, nurses, social workers, ministers, and bereavement counselors. Hospice care is designed to assist the terminally ill to address the many elements that come into play when one's life is ending. Nurses tend to be the primary caregivers within hospice care. They are with the patient on a continual basis and are often the professionals who are called upon once the patient dies. They deal with the body of the deceased and are often thrust into the emotionality of the family's struggles with the death. The emotional demands on nurses are considerable and they, more than any others, seem to bear the brunt of such a difficult endeavor. Social workers assist the families before and after the death in dealing both with bureaucratic issues and with emotional ones. They, too, have a very difficult job in dealing with the emotions engendered by dying patients and their families. Bereavement counselors and the clergy help assist the survivors in working through their feelings about the deceased. Of course, clergy also assist the dying in their spiritual needs. Most hospices are free standing; that is, not directly associated with a hospital, and most are not in-patient.

Physicians' main role is to control pain and physical discomfort through the administration of medication. Alexander Gotz (1996, personal communication), the medical director of a hospice, indicates that 80-90% of terminally ill patients experience severe physical pain and that physicians can effectively relieve 80-90% of the pain if proper treatment is administered. Gotz believes, as do many hospice physicians, that physicians are too conservative in pain relief and that morphine, "the gold standard" of pain relief, is inadequately prescribed. It is believed that most patients do not become psychologically addicted to the medication and that it can greatly enhance a dying patient's last hours. He asserts that physicians and families need to be educated on the benefits of aggressive pain relief. The problem of inadequate pain relief is even more profound in Third World countries. An article in the *New York Times* (DePalma, 1996) chronicles the difficulty in this regard in Mexico. Morphine, the pain relief medication of choice, is relatively inexpensive, yet trained physicians and restriction on availability results in inadequate pain relief. The article describes one woman whose pain was so severe from lung cancer that her screams caused a neighbor journalist to call the Mexican Secretary of Health and demand relief for the poor woman. The Secretary allowed the family to bring morphine in from the United States. The Mexican government is concerned that the United States government will oppose any attempt to increase morphine availability because of concern that it would be used illegally. The restrictions on morphine use throughout the world may be contributing to the increase in interest in assisted suicide.

Example

A 60-year-old woman with metastatic breast cancer is determined to contact Dr. Kevorkian, the suicide doctor. The hospice determines that her greatest fear is that of incapacitating pain. They suggest that she give an aggressive pain relief program a chance and assure her that she always has the freedom to contact Dr. Kevorkian. She agrees, and finds that she is able to maintain a reasonable quality of life, and loses interest in suicide.

A concern of many in the hospice community is that patients are not given adequate opportunity to explore their expectations of their disease, which may be unrealistic, as the preceding example attests. Hospice workers are very much concerned with pain relief, and for them a difficult patient is one with whom they have minimal success in relieving pain.

SUGGESTION. Pain relief is the major emphasis in hospice care. Hospice physicians tend to believe that most dying patients are undermedicated and that most patients can be relieved of substantial pain through judicious use of morphine.

Byock (1993) feels that most patients considering assisted suicide are inadequately treated with pain medication and/or antidepressants. He also asserts that assisted suicides are undertaken when the patient, family, and/or providers experience the patient as a burden. He feels that the burdens of the dying are an essential part of the human experience and should not be denied or not experienced. Deep sedation for terminally ill patients is seen as the viable alternative. Hospice physicians are generally opposed to assisted suicide.

Some patients have such emotional pain along with physical pain that they do not feel that life is worth living.

Example

> A patient suffered from amyotrophic lateral sclerosis, "Lou Geh-
> rig's disease," and was slowly dying a terrible death. A proud man,
> his level of incapacitation was unbearable and he pleaded for
> death.

This man could not be convinced that his "pain" could be
relieved, and he found his life to be intolerable. He could not
be persuaded that his dependency and the burden that he felt
he placed on his family was tolerable. He could only look forward to a life of increased incapacity and eventual death. Proponents of allowing one to have the choice of assisted suicide
believe that individuals should have control over their lives,
especially when they are suffering from a terminal illness. The
debate about the morality of assisted suicide creates intense
feelings and has the potential to polarize people, akin to the
abortion controversies.

As mentioned earlier, personality characteristics are enduring, and it is not expected that the dying process is going
to create changes in personality.

Example

> A 57-year-old man was dying of lung cancer. He was in considerable
> pain. He lived in a mobile home with his son, daughter-in-law, and
> their two children. The patient terrorized the wife with his temper
> and demandingness. The tasks of the hospice staff were multiple.
> The physician needed to help the patient with pain relief, the
> nurses with medication administration, evaluation of his condi-
> tion, and maintenance and care of bodily functions, and the social
> workers with family dynamics. The pain of this family was consider-
> able and the impact of the staff was not what they wished for. The
> death was very difficult and the relief was palpable.

The hospice staff needed to be satisfied with doing the best
that they could under very difficult circumstances. Many deaths
are difficult in terms of family disputes and bitterness. Hospice
staff are expert in working with and tolerating intense emotions. Many family members have expectations about the death

of loved ones. Some anticipate changes in relationships, others imagine relief, and still others are consumed by guilt. Hospice workers must be prepared to deal with any number of different and intensely emotional reactions and often realize that a great many compromises must be achieved prior to death. They try to achieve the best possible results under difficult situations.

Dying patients need to be given the opportunity to discuss their feelings about their disease, their impending death and about their lives. Some of those who are able to articulate their feelings and thus come to grips with their concerns can then die more peacefully.

Example

A woman was dying from metastatic breast cancer. She was self-described as a "bad mother" and had alienated her children by her inattention and neglect. As she lay dying, with the assistance of the hospice social worker she was able to articulate her feelings about her life, including her regrets. The social worker was able to assist her in a partial reconciliation, and she was able to die at some peace.

Unfortunately, patients who do not possess the ability to articulate their feelings prior to their illness are not likely to develop the ability when terribly ill. Hospice staff may need to make special efforts to help some of their patients to be able to express their feelings. This includes feelings about their lives, about the illness that is killing them, notions and fears about death, and concerns about family members.

SUGGESTION. Some family members expect dying patients to make substantial changes while dying. These expectations are often not met. Some patients are able to resolve their guilt and bitterness through the assistance of hospice workers.

Hospice workers sometimes complain that some physicians do not adequately prepare patients for their impending deaths. At times, patients on the verge of death are brought to the hospice by their families or by ambulance with the hospice given little opportunity to work with the patient and the families. This is usually a result of the physician avoiding informing the family of the impending death. Those who are uncomfortable in telling patients and families of the reality of the medical condition create terrible problems for themselves, for the patient, and for the hospice staff. These physicians may have tried to deny reality themselves, perhaps because of a concern over self-blame. This occurrence prevents patients and families from working through the impending death, and the mourning process becomes far more difficult for the family.

Another situation that is difficult for patients occurs when the treating physician "drops" the dying patient. Suddenly a relationship that was intense and, in some ways, close becomes cold and distant as the physician attempts to isolate himself or herself from the pain of losing a patient. Many patients develop strong attachments to their physicians and feel hurt and bewildered by the detachment. In all fairness, it is difficult for busy physicians to stay in contact with patients once they are under the care of hospice. Regardless, a considerable number of physicians do seem to distance themselves once the patient becomes a hospice patient. The unfortunate result for the physician is that he or she loses the opportunity to work through feelings of loss and disappointment. Eventually, a sense of hopelessness, frustration, and even depression can develop if physicians continue to isolate themselves from their feelings.

SUGGESTION. Physicians who do not adequately prepare patients and families for impending death are reinforcing denial and are probably operating out of a feeling of failure. Those who have difficulty in maintaining relationships with dying patients are hurting patients and themselves.

One group of patients whose families may have difficulty with their death are those dying of AIDS. Some families have rejected the patient if he contracted the disease through homosexual contact. These patients have to contend with dying a terrible death while estranged from families. Fortunately, most families are able to reconcile with the AIDS sufferer under the cloud of death. Sadly, the homosexual's lover is often ostracized by the family and has to bear his grief alone.

Those suffering from AIDS or any other supposed "lifestyle" disease are entitled to the same care and concern as those dying from any other, more "legitimate" disease. It was not that long ago that cancer was viewed with great shame. People who shun those with any particular condition are trying to distance themselves from their own frightened feelings. They take some pleasure in imagining that they are safe from this dread disease because they do not engage in homosexual sex, use drugs, or engage in other unsafe behaviors. This belief is untrue, misguided, and short-sighted. It is also an attempt to look at others in a negative way in order to elevate oneself. Those working in such situations have a difficult task in helping families to reconcile. It is essential that the medical staff be sensitive and sympathetic to all points of view while attempting to help the family to come to grips with the patient's condition.

Conclusion

Death is the opponent that always wins. Some physicians are able to accept the inevitability of death and understand that acceptance of death can enrich life and can assist in working through feelings of loss. Others are terribly afraid of death and may feel blame for losing a patient. Death is a threat to feelings of omnipotence and narcissism, and the reality of death can lead to feelings of hopelessness and despair. Those who work through these feelings can approach death more peacefully.

Summary

1. The physician's conflict between the desire to prolong life and the reality of eventual death can be terribly frustrating and depressing.
2. Some physicians have unrealistic fantasies about their ability to stave off death.

3. Doctors uncomfortable with their own mortality have difficulty accepting the reality of death.
4. Those who have suffered losses through deaths as children may have difficulty in accepting death as adults.
5. Physicians may find themselves in the middle of family conflicts and should make every attempt to remain neutral and facilitating if possible.
6. Relationships do not typically change under the threat of death. Similarly, patient's personalities tend to remain constant as well.
7. Dying patients vary in their responses to their prognosis. Commonly, they first feel denial, then anger, followed by hopelessness, and then acceptance.
8. It is important that patients be given the opportunity to explore their feelings about death, about their disappointments, and about their sadness.
9. Hospices have been a most welcome development in recent years, which has resulted in patients and famlies receiving tremendous assistance in death and dying.
10. Hospices utilize a team approach with physicians, social workers, nurses, clergy, and bereavement counselors.
11. Physicians' main job in hospice work is pain relief. Hospice doctors believe that morphine use should be increased for pain relief.
12. Hospice physicians are typically against "assisted suicide."
13. The cause of a patient's disease is irrelevant and all dying patients should be treated compassionately.

8

The Practitioner's Difficulties

The term "difficult patients" is a bit unfair and negative toward patients. In some ways it represents a distancing maneuver to suggest that the difficulties that health care professionals have with patients are generated by irrational and uncooperative patients. This approach ignores the contribution that health care professionals and that the health care delivery system make toward practitioner-patient problems. It is more accurate to view the relationship between health care professionals and patients as a system wherein a perturbation in one aspect can cause distortions and difficulty in the entire system. This is the same approach taken in apprehending psychosomatic disorders.

A systems approach removes fault and blame and sees the participants as coequal, with each bearing responsibility for both the success and the failure of the interaction. It emphasizes the relationship between the participants such that a positive and cooperative relationship is likely to contribute to a successful interaction. However, there are many problems that can emerge from the provider side of the equation that can negatively affect the relationship.

COUNTERTRANSFERENCE

Countertransference is a term that has evolved in its meaning. Originally it was used to describe feelings, thoughts, and behaviors that a therapist would have toward his or her patient that were generated by therapist psychopathology. It was viewed as being undesirable and as something to be avoided. Those who had countertransference reactions toward their patients were seen as needing self-analysis or psychological treatment to ascertain the origins of the difficulty. Presently, countertransference is viewed from a much broader perspective and refers to the feelings that are experienced by the professional within the patient-practitioner encounter. It does not refer to the benign, expected feelings but to those of sufficient intensity to suggest that a meaningful and important interaction is occurring.

Examples

A medical resident was viewed by most of his peers and by his supervisors as being competent and efficient. For one staff member, however, the resident was seen as being incompetent and sloppy. There was nothing that the resident did that was correct as far as the attending staff member was concerned. Despite being in the minority, he was certain that the other physicians were blind to the resident's ineptitude. The attending staff member was rude and discourteous to the young physician, making his life miserable. The latter was quite relieved when he reached a level where his contact with his supervisor was minimal.

Another resident was also competent but was generally disliked by both her cohorts and by the attending staff. She presented herself as a "know-it-all" and was demeaning to others whose opinions differed from hers. She was convinced others were jealous of her extraordinary abilities.

A patient was in psychotherapy for a variety of difficulties. She was often mad at the therapist for any behavior which, in her mind, indicated a lack of caring for her. The therapist would often become aware of her angry feelings by recognizing a sense of irritation that he would feel toward her. He would question the patient as to whether she was angry, and she would invariably acknowledge that she was.

These are three of many possible examples of countertransference. The first is an example of an individual's psychopathology creating strong feelings and inappropriate behavior toward another person. The unfortunate resident had no idea that he reminded the staff member of his despised brother. In fact, even the staff physician was unaware of the stimulus. As far as he was concerned, the resident was incompetent. The source of his animosity was unconscious.

The second example is one that is quite common. This particular resident, because of her own psychopathology (feelings of inadequacy), communicates derision to others. It is quite understandable that she is disliked. Unfortunately, the resident was also unaware of her provocative behavior. This is an example of a countertransference (or transference, depending on the view), wherein most people would react negatively to a particular person's manner. The terms transference-countertransference are used depending on the perspective taken. They developed out of psychotherapy experiences, and countertransference usually refers to the transference experienced by the therapist, often in relation to the patient. The terms can be effectively used to explain and understand qualities of interaction in many other relationships. In the preceding example, the resident's transference to fellow physicians was negative and demeaning, and the countertransference of her colleagues was one of dislike and hostility.

The third example is where the countertransference is used by the therapist to help him and the patient to understand an aspect of the latter that is not readily available to articulation. The patient was not really aware of her anger since it felt painful and forbidden. She could only communicate it to the therapist via the use of projective identification. The therapist experiences the patient's anger and is then able to reflect it back to the patient for further analysis and exploration. Once the therapist draws it to her attention by asking the patient if she is angry, she is able to talk about her angry feelings. A feeling of relief ensues, and discussion proceeds along new and important avenues. The therapist uses his feelings as a guide to the patient's feelings. In general, a therapist uses his or her judgment as to whether to divulge to the patient the fact of and the content of his or her feelings. The therapist will decide whether to communicate directly his or her feelings or to use them as a source of information to be silently processed. In the preceding example, the therapist used his feelings to enable him to identify the patient's feelings and to question her about them. Other approaches can also be used.

Example

The therapist found himself not listening to the patient, drifting away. He realized that this was becoming a relatively common occurrence. He decided to communicate his difficulty in listening to the patient and then asked her her thoughts. Initially the patient's feelings were hurt. After some time, she was able to talk about her own sense of being unfocused and how she had spent much of her life searching for her sense of self. The therapist's communication of his countertransference opened up a whole new and crucial arena for exploration.

Countertransference that is useful in understanding patients can take several different forms. The preceding example explicates an aspect of the patient that she was aware of in some vague sense but that had never been articulated. The therapist is experiencing an unacknowledged aspect of the patient. This also applies to the earlier example, with the irritated therapist indicating an angry patient. Another aspect of countertransference is where the practitioner acts out a part in the patient's past life, unwittingly.

Example

A physician finds herself feeling irritated prior to a visit by a particular patient. The patient would complain incessantly about her various ailments but would never follow the doctor's recommendations. The tension between the two would become palpable, and both would feel frustrated and unsatisfied. This interaction reflected the patient's typical interaction with her mother, whereby *she* was never listened to. The most effective approach would be for the physician to identify the tension and to hope that the patient would be able to use the information to lessen the intensity of her emotions.

In medical practice, the concept of countertransference is useful in understanding difficulties medical practitioners have in dealing with patients.

SUGGESTION. Countertransference is a concept that describes practitioner feelings toward patients. It can be useful in understanding patient feelings and beliefs. It can also represent problematic practitioner feelings, beliefs, and behaviors.

Countertransference can be appropriate and informative or inappropriate and detrimental, depending on its source and its expression.

Transference and countertransference are often referred to as a dyad, emphasizing their interpersonal nature and suggesting that interpersonal difficulties reflect contributions from both participants. There are times, however, when inappropriate practitioner behavior exists independent of patient provocation or participation. This would be the case in speaking of alcoholism, drug abuse, sexual acting out, inappropriate medical care, and general disregard for patients. Thus, countertransference can be considered as a generally expectable emotional reaction to patient provocation (the patient's drama) or can be seen as a practitioner reaction to a patient that is primarily motivated by practitioner psychopathology (the practitioner's drama).

The Patient's Drama

Each patient has a drama that he or she enacts or tries to enact with those significant in his or her life. These dramas are typically unconscious, although an insightful person may have some sense of his or her conflicts and issues. These issues are of lifelong duration and reflect the patient's typical way of relating, based on family preferences and training, and also reflect the patient's "unfinished business." Communication difficulties between doctor and patient may very well reflect idiosyncratic communication patterns that are discordant.

Example

The surgeon was very decisive in his recommendations. He had the habit of saying to patients, "I want you to do . . ." and said it in a way that communicated a command. Most patients were a bit intimidated by him, and his reputation was so stellar that they did not react strongly to his mildly authoritarian manner. Mr. J., however, reacted very negatively and would resist the doctor's recommendations, but always in a rather oblique and hidden way. The physician found himself becoming furious with the patient and became even more authoritarian, which the patient reacted to by becoming less compliant. The patient had been raised in a very strict and rigid family and had driven his father crazy with his passive-aggressive behavior. This was being enacted within the doctor-patient relationship, with the doctor unwittingly playing the role of the father. Neither was aware of the drama that was being played out, although each knew that there was conflict present. To break the impasse, either participant needed to speak about the conflict to allow a "clearing of the air." Unfortunately, the patient had never had the experience of talking about problems; he acted them out instead.

The patient's life experiences caused him to react negatively to an aspect of the physician that most others would brush aside. The countertransference of the doctor was partly a measure of his propensity toward authoritarianism but was also stimulated by the patient's obstinance. To deal more effectively with this situation, the doctor needs to examine his own reaction to the patient, to tone down his behavior, and also to learn to talk to the patient.

Dishonest Patients

Patient transferences and the countertransference reactions elicited are endless in their variety. Dishonest patients can evoke strong feelings from practitioners.

Example

Mr. K. requested that his physician alter the medical records to reflect that the onset of his ulcer condition did not occur until his insurance went into effect. His physician became very accusing and angrily told his patient that he would not conspire to cheat the insurance company. The patient felt angry and accused and soon switched physicians.

In a sense, this is a countertransference reaction since the doctor need not react in such an angry and accusatory way. It alienates the patient and accomplishes nothing. It is far better simply to refuse the suggestion or even to indicate that such behavior would be fraudulent. Those that suggest such illegal actions tend to rationalize their behavior and probably do not think that they are doing something wrong, or think that they are somehow justified in their actions. A measured refusal may give such patients cause to consider their behavior without affording them the opportunity of righteous indignation.

Helpless Patients

Another drama that is often enacted is that of the "incompetent" or helpless patient. This reflects a patient who is intelligent enough to understand the doctor's explanations and directions but continues to portray himself or herself as not being capable of comprehending the situation. Such patients tend to evoke in the doctor an angry and dismissive reaction, or the physician may play into the patient's "helplessness."

Example

Ms. B. was overweight, although the heart disease in her family suggested the wisdom of regular exercise and weight reduction. Her internist made several suggestions as to exercise regimens and spoke about nutritional issues. The patient seemed interested but spoke about the difficulty in getting exercise time in with her busy schedule. Each time the doctor made a suggestion, the patient spoke about how overwhelmed she was and implied that she was incapable of making any changes. The physician felt quite sympathetic to her, called and scheduled appointments with a nutritionist, and encouraged the patient to call with any problems. The patient expressed tearful appreciation, and the doctor ended up feeling very proud of himself for being so understanding and supportive. Despite her claims, this patient was far from helpless. She was an extremely successful attorney. She had difficulty in accepting responsibility for herself and tended to induce in others "rescue fantasies." The doctor's behavior was not going to help the patient to become more responsible for her problematic behavior.

The patient was inducing in the physician a countertransference reaction that ultimately was not very helpful. Of course, some patients are not that capable, are overwhelmed, and may need special care, yet the physician needs to be careful not to feel too gratified by helping out patients. The existence of self-aggrandizing feelings should suggest to the physician that he or she is acting in an overgratifying manner. The physician is playing out the part of being a rescuer, which reinforces and unhealthfully gratifies the patient's needs. The patient disavows responsibility for much of what occurs in her life and can continue to act in any manner she desires since she is obviously "helpless" and "incompetent." This practitioner feels very special and kind since it is obvious that he is having an important impact on her behavior. Imagine his surprise and eventual anger when he discovers that the patient will effectively thwart any suggestions that the doctor makes. In reality, a patient such as this is very controlling and angry, albeit secretly so. Furthermore, the practitioner may be feeding into the patient's dependency needs and is getting gratified by the patient's intense feelings toward him. He feels important and essential to the patient, which is pleasurable. Unfortunately, the patient remains dependent and "helpless" and does not begin to take charge of her life. It is far better for doctors to be suspicious of any extremely pleasurable feelings that they have toward a patient. It usually indicates that something is amiss. It is certainly appropriate to have positive and affectionate feelings toward patients, even strong ones. However, intensely positive feelings along with a sense of being embroiled in the patient's life should suggest caution. In the preceding example, the physician needs to maintain some sense of neutrality and equanimity while encouraging patient independence. An independent and healthy lifestyle is the goal, after all.

Some doctors will not become embroiled in the affairs of "helpless" patients. Rather, they become distant and disapproving. These physicians are averse to overdependency, probably because of a refutation of their own dependency needs. As a consequence, they become cold and distant toward such patients, resulting in hurt and angry feelings and an exacerbation of the helplessness. The patient does not know how to process the rejection and falls back upon familiar and familial ways of coping, regressing and becoming more "incompetent." This angry and dismissive attitude is a countertransference reaction as well and should be avoided. Whether governed by psychopathology or not, the patient is doing what he or she can under the circumstances and should not be condemned. The practitioner's efforts should be directed at helping the patient to become more independent.

SUGGESTION. "Helpless" patients may evoke either intense rescue fantasies or reactions of anger and rejection. Neither is beneficial, and a neutral attitude with an aim of increased competence and independence is most appropriate.

The Manipulative Patient

While the preceding patients are, in a sense, manipulative, others may be more blatant in their manipulations and often become furious when the health care practitioner resists their manipulations or confronts them.

Example

The patient complained to his internist about the treatment he received at the endocrinologist. He indicated that the doctor was rude and unsympathetic and that he seemed unconcerned about his thyroid problems. The patient seemed quite upset and sincere, and the doctor became angry at the specialist for treating him so shabbily. He mentally made a note not to refer to that physician again. He happened to run into the endocrinologist in the hospital soon thereafter, and the internist brought up the patient's experience, somewhat accusatorily. The endocrinologist told a different story, in which the patient was late and demanding and the doctor had to chastise the patient because of his extreme rudeness to the receptionist. The story did seem to ring true, and the internist felt embarrassed and chagrined for having been taken in by the patient. On the next visit, he recounted the endocrinologist's story and the patient, after some hesitancy and defensiveness, admitted the essential truth of the story as the specialist had recounted it. The doctor felt betrayed and angry.

Certainly, being angry at the patient is understandable. One should be careful to maintain a healthy skepticism about what one is told, especially from those with whom one is unfamiliar. In the preceding example the doctor should have ascertained the endocrinologist's version before taking sides. Even if he did ascertain some veracity in the patient's account, it is still better to remain calm and nonaccusatory. There may be extenuating circumstances of which the practitioner is unaware. In this situation, a simple inquiry to the specialist would have cleared up the matter without intense emotions.

Patients wittingly and unwittingly drag practitioners into their lives. Since these forces operate at a hidden level, it is easy to get pulled into patient dramas. It is not a simple matter to assign responsibility for problematic situations. Oftentimes it is the patient and the doctor operating in concert that creates fiascos. The doctor cannot control the patient's maneuvering but can endeavor to stay neutral. The existence of strong and intense emotions is a tip-off that the doctor is becoming embroiled in a transference-countertransference encounter. Most often, simple awareness of the nature of the encounter frees the practitioner from the emotional pull to become involved. With extremely provocative patients, a calm discussion of the relationship problems can be very helpful.

Example

> The physician with the rescue fantasy was eventually able to figure out the source of his discomfort and was able to bring it to the patient's attention. In essence, the doctor told the patient that he had felt frustrated about making so many suggestions that the patient would then not follow. Furthermore, he felt that it was not helpful for the patient to cede so much control to the doctor, and that the patient had the wherewithal to handle many of these problems on her own. The patient became tearful and upset and felt rejected, but the discussion did encourage her to become more decisive. She told the internist that she had always been told as a child that she was not very competent and that she had developed that belief about herself as well, so that it was freeing to imagine that the doctor thought her competent.

SUGGESTION. Simply not becoming embroiled in transference-countertransference interaction often relieves practitioner discomfort. At times, calm discussion with the patient frees both participants.

The Hated Patient

Winnicott (1949) wrote about the inevitability of therapists feeling hatred toward their patients. In this article he pointed out that patients will exhibit parts of themselves to the therapist that are unlikable and that the patients themselves struggle with. Consequently, it is essential that this aspect of the person become manifest within the treatment. It is often found and identified within the countertransference. Being able to contain the rage and hatred is essential for the therapist in order to help patients to understand and come to grips with this part of themselves. This is no different within the doctor-patient relationship. Some patients elicit very intense negative feelings from their doctors. However, a doctor-patient relationship is considerably different than a psychotherapeutic relationship, and the basis of the encounter is not to work out patient psychopathology. Consequently, a health care professional needs to deal with his or her strongly negative feelings in a different fashion.

Example

The obstetrician felt herself to be a caring and concerned person and was dismayed when she found that she could barely tolerate Mrs. E. The patient had a certain way of complaining that set the doctor's teeth on edge. She found herself feeling unsympathetic to the patient's complaints. The patient picked up on the doctor's discomfort and felt hurt and angry. Eventually, they were able to confront the dilemma, and it was decided that the patient should seek out care from another physician.

To be sure, this is an undesirable situation, and the resolution transpired with considerable emotional pain and trauma. Neither participant left the encounter feeling particularly satisfied, and both were angry and upset. Nevertheless, the problem was alleviated without a larger problem occurring in the future.

It is important to recognize that strongly negative feelings are not necessarily inappropriate. What is essential is that the practitioner deal with these feelings in a way that is best for both participants.

SUGGESTION. Strongly negative feelings toward some patients are inevitable. It is essential that the practitioner acknowledge such feelings and deal with them in an appropriate manner by understanding and working them through or by transferring care before treatment is impacted.

The Practitioner's Drama

There are some transference-countertransference interactions that arise out of a confluence of the participants' pathologies. Nevertheless, a practitioner has a special obligation to maintain his or her professional manner and behavior regardless of patient provocation. A physician or other professional has a moral, and, at times, legal responsibility to act responsibly. The power differential between doctor and patient is a fact that cannot be denied, regardless of attempts at denial and rationalization. Health care professionals must act in a fashion to protect their patients and must operate in a manner that is in their patients' best interests. In the professional relationship, the physician or other professional must bear the brunt of responsibility for improprieties.

Countertransference difficulties that are discussed in this section are primarily a function of psychopathology. There is no reason to expect physicians or other health care professionals to be substantially emotionally healthier than any other segment of the population. In fact, the stresses and responsibilities of health care professionals are intense and can put pressure on coping abilities. Managed care pressures, malpractice concerns, and responsibility for others' care can create enormous stresses on physicians. Those whose psychological state is somewhat fragile may not be able to process the pressure and may act out inappropriately. Others may act in an inappropriate manner regardless of external events, due to the pressure of their internal psychopathological state. This chapter is, in part, designed to be cautionary to those health care professionals at risk for these countertransference reactions.

The Doctor as Patient

It is anecdotally well known that doctors are notoriously difficult patients.

Example

Dr. D. was hospitalized after a coronary. He was a successful ophthalmologist who had prided himself on being physically fit and healthy. He was a very precise, meticulous, and organized man whose life had always felt under control. In the hospital, he was outrageous. He was rude to the nursing staff, insisted on reviewing his medical chart, criticized his care, and was generally obnoxious and demanding. His heart attack was relatively mild, and his course of recovery was unremarkable.

Dr. D.'s behavior, and that of other physicians who find themselves in similar situations, is due to several variables. First, it is difficult for everyone, perhaps even more so for physicians, to accept the reality of mortality. Some physicians pursue the field of medicine as an unconscious, fantasized wish to ensure immortality. As the inevitability of aging occurs, many in the health care field experience their deterioration as a narcissistic injury and as an affront to their irrational wish for immortality. Their perceived sense of failure often gets projected onto those who take care of them. That is, the physician tries to blame others for his or her "failure" and for the unpleasant reality of mortality. Second, many physicians imagine themselves to be in control of themselves and of their lives. Disease and aging disabuses them of that notion. The reality of one's relative lack of control over some crucial life events leaves some practitioners angry and bitter. Third, doctors and other professionals pride themselves on their competence. Once in the hospital, with a physical problem in an area not in his or her expertise, doctors may feel incompetent. This feeling may get projected onto the hospital staff, including other physicians, as a way of protecting the patient from self-criticism. Last, doctors often want to portray themselves as being self-reliant and independent. A physical illness causes the patient to be quite dependent and needy, which may be a very uncomfortable feeling. Consequently, the doctor may act in such a way to ensure that no one feels sympathy and concern for him, which may help him obscure his dependency needs.

Of course, some physicians and health care professionals are wonderfully cooperative as patients. Those who take care of more difficult physician-patients should not lose sight that these patients are just as frightened as other patients, despite any posturing to the contrary. In fact, with their medical expertise, some health care professionals understand the disease process better than other patients and have a greater sense of their prognosis, which may leave them even more frightened than nonmedical patients. Consequently, they may not have the opportunity to gradually adjust to the reality of the disease.

Most physicians who are impossibly obnoxious in the hospital are acting out of anxiety and fear. The best way to approach this situation is to remain calm, sympathetic, and concerned despite the provocation. Additionally, recognizing that these health care professionals are frightened will enable those in the caregiver role to respond to these patients as one would to others. Patients of all stripes need warmth and nurturance. In more extreme cases, it may be helpful to communicate to the patient that it is understood how frightening and difficult it is to be in his or her situation.

SUGGESTION. Physicians and other health care professionals may react to physical illness as if it is an insult to their sense of competence. It may also force the patient to face mortality and one's lack of control over many events in life. Dependency needs may come to the fore that are difficult for those accustomed to independence. Those caring for physicians should remain aware of their fear, which may motivate difficult behavior. Remaining warm and caring despite the doctor's denial of need is important.

Angry and Arrogant Doctors

Some physicians seem unconcerned about how they relate to patients and to staff. At times, these doctors may be brilliant in their abilities and are often excused for their demeaning manner. Physicians often make more of an effort to be pleasant to patients but may be unnecessarily cruel toward residents and other hospital staff.

Example

Dr. M. was known as a brilliant thoracic surgeon. Unfortunately, he was also known as a terror to students, residents, staff, and those physicians that he felt were less talented than himself. His bedside manner also left something to be desired, being curt and seemingly unsympathetic to his patients and their families. He did not tolerate patients inquiring into his methods, insisting that they should unreservedly trust him. Everyone agreed that he was a superb surgeon and most seemed to forgive his arrogance, although he had no real friends. No one wanted to be on the receiving end of his sarcasm.

This situation is all too common. The surgeon had adopted a mode of relating that alienates others and results in a rather lonely life for himself. In his mind, he believes that sentiment would undermine his talent, that he needs to be totally focused on the difficult and crucial task confronting him, that of saving the patient's life. He believes that people should be satisfied with that and cannot understand why those close to him complain about his aloofness. To him, he shows his caring to his patients by being an excellent surgeon. To his family his caring comes through by the fact that he works so hard to provide for them. Of course, there are many equally capable physicians who do not feel the need to be so difficult and demanding. In reality this man may excel at the practice of medicine but greatly fears his ability to be able to relate interpersonally. He tries to turn his defective interpersonal skills into a positive attribute by demeaning those with more social skills as being "weak" and "spineless." This particular surgeon was always awkward and socially inept as a child and turned to his academic studies for pleasure and success. His father was a strict taskmaster and would belittle his son for perceived inadequacies. He always felt bad about his interpersonal difficulties, and yet, in some ways, has become the image of his sarcastic father. He is no longer inadequate; it is junior staff and those less talented who are to be ridiculed. A person with this particular pathology is strongly invested in being right and is not very amenable to criticism, even if proffered constructively. Many excessively authoritarian physicians would fall into this category. They are so uncertain of their sense of competence that they demand compliance to their dictates. They are terribly afraid of feeling powerless and thus demand obeisance. Powerlessness translates into weakness and inadequacy, which are intolerable attributes. Omnipotent strivings are also characteristic of such personalities. Their need to be perfect and all powerful is consuming and may leave helpless victims in their wake. There is a need to derogate those viewed as less capable and strong in order to feed their illusion of omnipotence. It is important that those in contact with such people not allow them to be successful in their derogation.

Those with such perfectionistic and arrogant personality characteristics are prone to depressive reactions as they age. They may become aware of the emptiness of their lives and begin to realize the futility of their quest to feel adequate by demeaning others and by interpersonal isolation. Intervention at this point may be successful in helping them to widen their perspective and to gain satisfaction from other areas of their lives. Also, inevitable failures in their profession tend to be humbling and may require a reconsideration of their personality style. Some of those whose omnipotent strivings are particularly strong can become extremely depressed when faced with failure. Failure, inevitable or not, feels like an expression of inadequacy, and the physician's self-punitiveness can be profound. One can sometimes see a spiraling of intensity of perfectionism when a person is faced with perceived failure. The person becomes more and more driven to be all-powerful and perfect. This is a prelude to an emotional crisis.

There can be a number of reasons for a person to have a difficulty in anger modulation. Some have not learned how to cope with frustration, since they have not developed internal ego strength that allows them to successfully process frustration. Those prone toward angry outbursts have a certain ego weakness. They may function perfectly well under most circumstances, but under pressure may not have the internal wherewithal to deal comfortably with difficult problems. Health care professionals are under pressure which, at times, can tax ego structures. When combined with family or personal pressures, a potent mix can result. These individuals often have a low tolerance for frustration. This very difficulty may have partially motivated their interest in the sciences, which can seem so exact and unambiguous. In reality, medical practice is highly variable, with a multitude of uncertainties.

Others with anger problems may suffer from feelings of inadequacy, similar to the arrogant physician described in the example. They also have difficulty in processing disappointment and have trouble tolerating imperfection. Their internalized self-critical faculty is intense, and they become extremely self-punitive. When this occurs, they can project this sense of "badness" outward and become blaming and accusatory.

Being the recipient of angry outbursts is often quite difficult. It is usually most helpful to try to maintain equanimity in the face of attack. Allowing oneself to be drawn into a conflagration is not beneficial. This is not to say that one should necessarily allow oneself to be falsely accused or to "turn the other cheek." One should defend oneself when being attacked, but it is best to not retaliate in the same fashion.

SUGGESTION. Angry and arrogant people are those who struggle with feelings of inadequacy that they often project onto others. They often have difficulty in processing intense emotions, and responding to their provocations is not helpful.

Sexism, Racism, and Ageism

Assumptions made about a person without truly knowing the person is the basis of discrimination. Discrimination goes beyond the commonly acknowledged racism and sexism. Prejudices are based on many personal characteristics that are different from these possessed by the one standing in judgment. The key feature of prejudice is difference. Those viewed negatively are seen as being different from, inadequate in relation to, the perceiver. As such, prejudice represents an attempt to feel better about oneself by undermining and demeaning someone else. Bias exists on the basis of age, weight, height, physical looks, foreignness, skin color, ethnic identity, education, and wealth. These prejudices are pervasive, yet may manifest themselves in a very subtle fashion.

Example

The elderly black man was being seen for a routine physical in a clinic specializing in geriatric patients. He was dressed casually in jeans and work shirt. The new geriatric fellow was eager to be of service to the patient and was thorough in his examination and in his questions. He did seem to focus on the patient's financial status and made sure that the patient understood what he was being told. He felt quite chagrined when he discovered that the patient was a retired physics professor.

The fellow made assumptions about the patient based upon stereotypes that he held regarding African Americans. He immediately assumed that the patient was uneducated and of poor financial means. The patient was a bit put off.

These kinds of assumptions objectify patients and cause them to feel that the care that they are receiving is impersonal at best. Endless stories abound about patients who are treated rudely and poorly because they are obese, because they are on government assistance, or because they are uneducated. Such attitudes exist because the person holding them is trying to distance himself or herself from their own perceived inadequacies, which get projected onto the patients. No one is without prejudice. Most importantly, a health care practitioner needs to be careful not to let his or her prejudices affect the treatment and care of patients, regardless of his or her beliefs.

Example

An exceedingly obese woman was complaining of her husband's lack of sexual interest. The internist silently thought it was not surprising, considering the patient's obesity. The husband was also a patient of the doctor, and yet she did not think to question him on his lack of libido during his next visit. The husband did bring it up and indicated that he was concerned about it. He did talk about some recent job problems and his concern about his children. The doctor asked him whether his wife's weight bothered him and he was surprised. "There's just more to love," the patient said. The physician was then able to focus on helping the patient to deal with his disappointments and to run other tests to rule out a physical etiology.

Assumptions like these can cause physicians to overlook possible medical causes for conditions. Prejudices can obviously alienate patients and in extreme cases contribute to malpractice actions. A positive relationship with a patient can go a long way toward minimizing the possibility of lawsuits should there be an adverse result. Clearly, prejudicial attitudes and feelings are detrimental to patient and practitioner alike. Ignorance of different cultures and discomfort with foreignness can also result in overly critical attitudes. It is more helpful to express curiosity about unfamiliar cultures and habits than to be judgmental.

A judgmental posture may reflect prejudicial beliefs. Regardless of its source, judgmental behaviors usually have little place in the examining room.

Example

Mrs. T. moved to a new city and sought out a pediatrician for her two young children. During the discussion, she told the doctor that she was a working mother and that the children were in day care. The physician informed her that it would be far better for her children if she were to stay home, "where she belonged." The mother became upset, confused, and felt criticized. She felt that she and her husband were doing the best that they could to juggle their career needs along with providing a good upbringing for their children. She decided to find another pediatrician.

The attitude of the doctor was in no way helpful. The patient needs support and understanding, not condemnation. Besides which, the doctors knows nothing of the patient's circumstances and is in no position to decide what is best for her and her family. He does not suggest that her husband share responsibility for child care. All the responsibility and blame is placed on the mother. Those who hold such beliefs and who then communicate them to patients, subtly or otherwise, might want to consider the reasons for their existence. Prejudicial beliefs are not rationally held, even if those holding them try to insist they are.

SUGGESTION. Prejudicial beliefs are based on the projection of one's own inadequacies onto those who differ. At times, it may also reflect ignorance about different cultures. Judgmental attitudes are not helpful and are presumptuous.

Sadism

Sadism can be defined as one taking pleasure in another's pain. The use of the word *sadistic* to describe some health care practitioner's behavior may seem too extreme. Unfortunately, sadism does exist in all areas of human experience, including medical practice. This is not to say that health care practitioners are necessarily cruel and hostile, yet sadistic feelings do seem to intrude upon proper medical care, at times.

Example

> The internist was sick and tired of his patient continually bothering him with minor complaints. He did not particularly like the patient and disapproved of his alcoholism. When the physician examined the patient, he was unnecessarily rough and thought to himself that perhaps this would teach the patient not to trouble him with such trivial problems. As he was slightly more rough than he would normally be, he felt some satisfaction.

Of course the doctor's roughness was not going to teach the patient anything. It was simply a desire to be punitive, and the doctor gained some satisfaction by being hurtful. This behavior is inappropriate but is probably not that uncommon. Besides being problematic for the patient, most who act out in such a way toward a patient are likely to feel guilty afterwards, consciously or not. It is important to remember that psychic needs are paramount and that those with an active conscience are not going to be able to escape later self-condemnation for inappropriate behavior. This consequent need for punishment may not always be apparent and can manifest itself in many ways.

The physician in the preceding example later found himself being unaccountably irritable with his wife and provoked an argument that was very unpleasant for him.

Sadism can easily masquerade. Those physicians who do unnecessary surgery may have sadistic impulses operating. They are causing pain to their patients and gaining satisfaction from it, financially or from the pleasures of performing surgery. The desire to hurt others when one is hurt is an unfortunate human characteristic, but is one that need not be acted upon. Those with sadistic tendencies are those who have been hurt a great deal as children and who have interpreted that hurt as being intentional and malicious. They are very thin-skinned people who feel the need to retaliate. They tend to be self-absorbed and, at times, have trouble seeing situations from other perspectives.

Since the tendency toward some sadistic impulses is ubiquitous, it is naive to assume that such tendencies can be easily conquered or eliminated. Rather, those working in the helping professions need to be vigilant in not allowing themselves to take satisfaction from others' pain or misfortune. In more extreme forms, those who find themselves behaving inappropriately in satisfying sadistic needs should seek out psychotherapeutic treatment to receive help in conquering this deep-rooted difficulty.

SUGGESTION. Sadism is gaining satisfaction from another's pain. Sadistic behavior can range from mild to severe and reflects an individual with narcissistic difficulties. Sadistic behavior is usually disguised, and the perpetrator is likely to be oblivious of its existence. Self-examination is important in its identification and elimination.

Drug and Alcohol Abuse

Drug and alcohol abuse are rampant in our society, and it has been well documented that health care professionals are not exempt. There is even more of an emphasis on keeping such behaviors secret since the ramifications of admitting substance abuse are intense. Furthermore, physicians and other health care professionals may have expectations that they are beyond the frailties of others and may find the weakness of addiction to be shameful and embarrassing. Most physicians have worked very hard to reach the position that they have achieved and are often loath to admit to weaknesses. A physician's reputation is going to suffer if it is discovered that he or she has a substance abuse problem. Licensing officials will take a special interest in a health care professional with such difficulties because of the threat it poses to patient welfare. Consequently, it is very difficult for physicians to acknowledge that they have difficulties in controlling their intake of alcohol or of controlled substances.

The reasons that physicians become addicted are no different from those of people in the general population. Severe stress combined with personal difficulties in coping with external and internal psychological pressure are typically the reasons that physicians overimbibe.

Example

The radiologist was under extreme personal stress engendered by a divorce. He felt tremendous stress from his work since he had considerable pressure to read a number of different images, all accurately, of course. He felt lonely and isolated at home and found himself mixing himself a drink after work. Gradually, the drinks increased in strength and frequency. His sleep became impaired, and he arrived at work looking haggard and tired. At a department social function he became intoxicated and was embarrassed by his behavior. A friend on the staff approached him and asked him about his drinking. He did admit to some of his difficulties, and his friend suggested that he obtain some sort of psychological treatment. The radiologist fortunately agreed and was helped by appropriate treatment.

Many in the profession tend to turn their heads at clear evidence that their colleagues are having a difficulty. It is most appropriate to approach a colleague whom one suspects of having a substance abuse problem. Without a doubt, this takes considerable courage and may result in considerable rage and denial by the accused. Nevertheless, ignoring what is an obvious problem puts both patients and the health care professional at risk. Going to the department head or supervisor with one's concern may also be effective, since the position offers some protection to the supervisor should a confrontation be necessary. States and professional groups have developed resources for impaired health care professionals that are confidential.

Because of access, physicians are prone to the abuse of psychoactive medication. The use of such medications are more easily hidden because the effects of overuse are not readily apparent. Any physician who is self-prescribing psychotropic medications is acting unwisely, and this includes the use of antidepressants. If a doctor feels the need for medication, he or she should obtain a referral to an appropriate mental health professional.

SUGGESTION. Health care professionals may be at a higher risk than the general population for substance abuse because of intense pressure, high personal expectations, and availability of medications. Confronting colleagues is extremely difficult but may be essential to protect patients and the professional.

Sexual Improprieties

Health care professionals have a special responsibility in their relationships with patients. The power differential between doctor and patient is such that it is inevitably an unequal relationship, and any sexual relationship that ensues is problematic and inappropriate. Typically, those physicians who engage in sexual relationships with patients do so with those who have a history of exploitative relationships. It represents a confluence of patient and provider psychopathology, a transference-countertransference interaction. Regardless of the patient's provocation, responsibility for any sexual relationship lies with the professional. By the virtue of their respective positions, the physician or other health care professional is deemed to be in a parental role, that of operating in the best interests of the patient and not being exploitative. The patient is in a one-down position, not fully capable of deciding what is or is not best for him or her.

Example

The physician was always attracted to pretty young women. While married, he never felt that his wife was sufficiently appreciative of his unique abilities. She was not as responsive sexually as he would have wished. His patients, on the other hand, seemed to worship him. After a particularly bad fight with his wife, he propositioned a young woman patient who was susceptible to his charms. He and the woman patient started an affair that lasted about 3 years. He eventually insisted that they terminate the relationship after she became more demanding of his time.

The psychological dynamics of a physician who operates in this fashion are not substantially different than those of one who abuses women sexually. It is an exploitative relationship that is designed to elevate the physician's feelings about himself while treating the woman in a demeaning fashion. He did not really care for her as a person; she was only used to reinforce his lofty image. Furthermore, the betrayal of his relationship to his wife also points out his hostility toward her, and toward women in general. Men who use their position to obtain sexual gratification are insecure and inadequate and cover this by seducing unsuspecting women. The patients are at a disadvantage because of the power differential implicit within the doctor-patient relationship. Practitioners who engage in such behavior are plagued by persistent questions about their masculinity and feel the need to boost themselves by imagining themselves to be irresistible. However, this self-image is obtained only within the confines of an exploitative relationship. They do not value themselves in other ways and imagine that women only appreciate their sexual prowess. Their self-absorption is evident, and they are usually suffering from a narcissistic disorder. Men who become involved in these abusive relationships are likely to fear and hate women. Their backgrounds may include mothers who were overseductive and/or overcontrolling. Fathers who have been demeaning and undermining may also contribute to their underlying sense of vulnerability and fragility, which can be boosted by seducing women.

Typically, those women who become subject to the seduction are those who have suffered some sort of sexual abuse or discrimination in the past. The transference-countertransference drama is such that the exploiter looks for one who is prepared to be exploited. In no way is this an attempt to indict those women who find themselves embroiled in this kind of relationship. The ultimate responsibility for this violation of the doctor-patient relationship lies with the physician. Women who do not have difficulties in this area are not likely to be attracted to the charms of the seducer. Those who have been abused in the past are working out of their own intrapsychic drama and presumably are looking for a nonexploitative relationship but unconsciously choose an exploiter as a partner. This is a reflection of the repetition compulsion, whereby the patient repeats in the present traumas of the past as an attempt to master them and rework them. As always, these attempts are doomed to failure, and once again the women find themselves involved in an exploitative relationship with a man who has no real interest in them.

Although the predominance of such relationships occur between male health care professionals and women patients, exploitation can occur within other combinations as well. Although certainly not nearly as common, women can become exploitative both with men and with other women. Similarly, male homosexual exploitative relationships also occur.

Seductive behavior does not always culminate in a sexual relationship. An undercurrent of sexual tension can exist within a doctor-patient relationship that still undermines the professionalism of the encounter. There are many feelings that physicians and other professionals feel toward their patients which need to be dealt with in an appropriate manner. Sexual feelings are no different. Being attracted to a patient is commonplace and is not necessarily problematic. It only becomes a problem when these feelings become manifest within the relationship, acted upon or not. A health care professional who feels himself or herself becoming uncomfortably attracted to a patient needs to take some action to maintain a professional relationship. Self-restraint is essential. If the professional finds that to be too difficult or to be impossible, consultation with a colleague or mental health professional would be essential.

Although admittedly very difficult to do, transfer of the patient to a colleague would be in the best interests of all concerned.

Some people have tried to circumvent the ethical shakiness of doctor-patient relationships by terminating the professional relationship and then continuing the personal relationship. This is a dubious solution because the patient participant was in a less powerful role, and this dynamic is likely to continue to be acted out.

SUGGESTION. Sexual activity within the doctor-patient relationship is inappropriate and is damaging to both participants. It represents a problematic transference-countertransference interaction, yet the ultimate responsibility lies with the health care professional. Those who become sexually involved with patients are being exploitative and have problems with feelings of adequacy and competence. Consultation with a mental health professional is advised should one become tempted toward violating the professional barrier.

Incompetent Doctors

Unfortunately, there are physicians and other health care professionals that do not function at a level of competence that is acceptable. Presumably, if one has been able to succeed in educational programs, one should be able to perform at an adequate level on the job in that occupation. This is not always the case, however. This section focuses on those professionals who are not working up to their abilities because of psychological difficulties. It does not touch upon those whose incompetence is based on lack of intellectual capability or some other attribute that is not caused by psychological factors or is not amenable to psychological remediation.

Example

Dr. G. was a surgeon who had a stellar reputation in the public's eyes but was not as well thought of within the medical community. Other doctors as well as nurses knew that he was prone toward carelessness. Furthermore, he did not seem to be in control of his patients. That is, his need to please his patients caused him to allow them to call the shots. Consequently, surgical decisions were made more on his need to be liked than on sound medical decision making.

This physician's need to be liked by his patients caused him to make decisions that were of questionable validity. He was not really aware that his decisions were less than medically sound. He felt quite confident that he was doing what was best for the patient and he was very proud of the fact that he was so liked. It made him feel that he was a good and caring physician, unlike some of his stiffer and more formal colleagues. In point of fact, his carelessness and poor judgment contravened his belief in his being a caring physician. A caring health care professional puts his or her patients' needs first. At best, this physician was confused about what constituted a competent physician. At worst, his disregard of proper medical decision making was an indication of underlying hostility toward his patients since his actions were potentially hurtful. In this situation, his self-absorption and possible hostile wishes were compromising his ability to function in a competent manner.

There are many potential reasons for incompetence and carelessness. Self-absorption (narcissism), drug and alcohol abuse, lack of caring and concern (sociopathy), or high levels of anxiety, depression, and other psychological disorders are all plausible reasons. Physicians whose personality organization is at the borderline personality disorder level are going to find it difficult to be effective physicians. Similarly, doctors with other internal psychological conflicts may find these difficulties intruding upon competence. One such conflict would be that of discomfort with success. It is not unusual for individuals to view success in a competitive fashion, as if their success means another's failure. This is related to early competitive feelings with parents that engender fear and anxiety. Consequently, the individual does what he or she can to thwart success since it is so threatening. This is basically a neurotic issue, and one that can be seen in those who seem to always be snatching defeat from the jaws of victory.

The idea that one is not operating at a sufficiently capable level is a very difficult one to accept. Many people want to believe that they are competent and are highly resistant to recognition of less than optimal functioning. Supervisory personnel are usually best equipped to deal with such physicians by helping them to recognize their inadequate performance and by suggesting means toward improvement. The discomfort of this and the wish to deny the reality of a friend's or colleague's incompetence often results in such behavior being ignored. If one is going to confront a colleague, it can be done in such a way as to minimize extreme emotional responses. Any discussion should take place privately and should be explicit as to what behaviors are inadequate and what changes are necessary. Questions as to extenuating circumstances should be asked. It is also helpful to give at least equal weight to those positive qualities exemplified by the physician in question.

SUGGESTION. Physicians and other health care professionals who operate in a questionable manner may be struggling with psychological issues that are likely to require intervention. Most deny that they are working at a less than optimal level, and colleagues often collude in the denial. Confrontation by a senior or supervisory person may work best, and emphasis should be on concrete problems and solutions, while reinforcing the individual's positive qualities.

Criminal Acts

There are some practitioners in the health care field who are dishonest and who engage in criminal acts. Some of those who commit such acts are sociopathic; that is, without care or remorse. The vast majority of those who commit criminal acts cannot simply be consigned to the sociopathic diagnostic category. People are rarely all one way or another. There is an admixture of positive and negative qualities. Those who commit criminal acts can be motivated by several different needs. Most often, though, physicians who engage in criminal acts have the overriding feeling that they do not have enough. Despite the capability of making a nice living from the practice of medicine, some have a consuming greed that cannot be satiated. No matter how much they have, they want more. Typically, they overspend as well, resulting in debt and a need to garner more money. Perhaps they felt in some way deprived as children and are determined to fill the emptiness through accumulation of money. Regardless of the underlying reason, these physicians have lacunae in their self-critical faculties. These emotional needs feel all consuming and are hard to resist. Some who commit crimes have an underlying feeling of being fraudulent and act out this feeling in their behavior. Physicians and other health care professionals are no different psychologically from the rest of the population and are going to be tempted by possibilities of "easy money." It is hoped that those so tempted are reminded of the satisfactions that are achieved from their practices, which will be lost under the greed and guilt of criminal enterprise.

SUGGESTION. Most of those who engage in criminal activities are not truly sociopathic, although gaps in their self-critical faculties are evident. Greed represents an underlying feeling of not having enough, despite reality. Criminal activity ruins the satisfaction achieved in medical practice.

CONCLUSION

Countertransference can be both vexing and helpful. It often provides useful information to the practitioner of patient issues, yet also engenders intense and often unpleasant emotions. Patients and practitioners can become embroiled in a transference-countertransference stalemate, wherein past issues from each are being played out in the present. These encounters are very "sticky" and difficult to extricate oneself from.

Although many transference-countertransference difficulties arise out of joint difficulties, it is primarily the practitioner's responsibility to remain rational and above the fray. Patients do bring in their dramas and then attempt to draw the physician onto the stage. Despite the provocation, it is important that practitioners maintain their equilibrium.

Practitioners have their own problems that can impede successful medical treatment. At times, these dramas drag patients onto the stage, which is disastrous and inappropriate. As the more responsible party, physicians and other professionals have a moral and legal burden beyond that of the patient. Temptations abound which need to be resisted, understood, and worked through in order to maintain a professional attitude and to ensure continued satisfaction.

SUMMARY

1. The term "difficult patient" neglects the contribution of health care professionals' psychopathology in patient-practitioner problems.
2. Countertransference can represent an expectable, intense emotional reaction to patient provocation or can indicate a practitioner's psychological problems.
3. Countertransference can represent an enactment of either the patient's or the practitioner's drama.
4. Many patient provocations stimulate strong feelings from the practitioner that are usually best not acted upon.
5. Strongly negative feelings toward patients are not inappropriate and only become a problem when the physician feels a need to retaliate.
6. Health care professionals are under considerable pressure, which can exacerbate underlying psychopathology.
7. Physicians and other health care professionals have a special obligation to protect the patient despite provocation.
8. The patient-practitioner relationship is unequal, and sexual activity between the two is inappropriate and exploitative.
9. There are many psychological variables that impede physician competence. These include self-absorption, drug and alcohol abuse, lack of caring and concern, anxiety, depression, and other psychological disorders.
10. Inappropriate practitioner behavior, besides being illegal or unethical, greatly reduces job satisfaction and may engender self-destructive behavior because of guilt, conscious and unconscious.

9

Conclusion

Clearly, a major emphasis of this book has been on the importance of maintaining a positive practitioner-patient relationship. The quality of relationships will affect the satisfaction that one is able to achieve in life. Similarly, positive and gratifying practitioner-patient relationships will enhance both patient and practitioner sense of well-being.

The nature of early childhood relationships with parents is the single most important factor in determining psychological health. A healthy-parent child relationship will enable a person to have the resources to deal with the vagaries of life. This kind of upbringing creates a strong and capable ego, so that one is able to deal with stresses and strains without undue distress. Furthermore, those with a strong ego and healthy background are likely to make good choices in terms of their relationships. Contrary to popular belief, substance abuse and emotional problems do not visit themselves upon unsuspecting victims. These difficulties are a result of individuals' difficulty in coping with internal and external stresses, which inevitably relate to early childhood difficulties. The conclusion reached is that early formative relationships presage both psychological health and satisfying interpersonal relationships. The quality of practitioner-patient relationships will depend on the participants' level of psychological health.

The quality and nature of past important relationships directly affects the treatment relationship. Transference will impinge upon the practitioner-patient relationship, for better or for worse. When considering the nature of transferential reactions, it is necessary to realize that they operate with great complexity and subtlety. This can create a confusing mélange of intense and painful emotions. Patients unconsciously try to re-enact troublesome relationships from the past, which can quickly and easily ensnare an unwary practitioner. The repetition compulsion serves several masters. It is a wish to undo, to redo, some painful occurrence from the past, with a better result hoped for. There is also an attempt to master the past trauma, which causes it to be replayed again and again. Finally, past traumatic and difficult relationships imprint themselves on people, causing them to see the world through the lens of the trauma and to forever relive the trauma from innumerable perspectives. A traumatized person will play out any number of roles and fantasies, switching positions precipitously. This propensity is very confusing to all those involved, including the patient. Many of these traumas have profound effects on the one traumatized, including creating bodily sensations that are not available for verbal understanding. Attempting to discuss troublesome emotional reactions may be met by intense affects, tears, and an inability to articulate the patient's thoughts and feelings. The patient is not being contrary; rather, he or she may not have the words available to describe that which is transpiring. This can be quite frustrating for those who are trying to understand.

Disruptions in the treatment or working alliance are often the result of psychological problems interfering with the establishment and maintenance of a positive transference. A negative transference emerges that mirrors past difficult and unpleasant relationships. Those who have significant psychological problems are more likely to be troubled by negative transferences. In general, the best policy is to confront negative transferences as soon as they are detected. Negative transferences that are ignored or denied will often intensify and create more problems as time goes on.

Past troublesome relationships can become manifest in a variety of psychological and behavior problems. Psychological symptoms are signals of emotional distress. Symptoms do not usually exist in isolation. The individual's personality structure is intimately tied in to the individual's psychological problems. Treatment aims not only to eliminate the overt symptom but to identify and work through the underlying causes. Consequently, easy resolution of psychological difficulties is not possible. This can be perplexing and frustrating for medical practitioners, who may hope and expect psychological problems to have clear-cut solutions.

The form that psychological problems can take are varied. The psychiatric and psychological fields have developed a taxonomy that can be helpful but also misleading. The emphasis on diagnosis can oversimplify psychological problems and can create a sense of the impersonal. The diagnostic system gives only a rough approximation of the nature of the patient's psychological functioning. An emphasis on the behavioral manifestations of the disorder ignores the more crucial underlying personality structures that create the symptoms. The form of the symptom is important and can provide important information. In the details of the person's thoughts, feelings, and fantasies is where a true understanding of the patient is obtained.

The frequent appearance of psychological problems within medical practice can be disconcerting to a medical practitioner, who is understandably more comfortable in working with physical disease. Psychological problems are ubiquitous and will impact practitioner-patient relations as well as compliance with medical regimens. The level of the patient's psychological health will have an effect on how he or she deals with physical disease. A view of the individual as possessing a self-regulating mechanism suggests that perturbation in the physical, in the psychological, or in the social arena can affect any aspect of the individual. Physical diseases do not exist in isolation and will have an effect on the patient's psychological health. Conversely, psychological disorders have an effect on the physical side of the patient, contributing both positively and negatively to the curative process. Even beyond that, psychological variables can have a major causative effect on physical disorders such as heart disease and gastrointestinal disorders. Probably most frustrating to physicians and other medical practitioners are hypochondriacal disorders, where obsessive worry is the predominant feature. It is often difficult to understand patients who seem to want to be ill. It is more useful to think of somaticizing and hypochondriacal patients as those who do not have access to verbal means to communicate their distress.

Each medical specialty brings both problems and pleasures. Practitioners do not end up in their particular specialty by chance. There is a self-selection process that helps to lessen mismatches between patient and practitioners. For example, a pathologist has certain personality characteristics and practice expectations that differ from a pediatrician. Despite personality proclivities and preparation, each specialty has problems that bedevil practitioners. Pediatricians must deal with overbearing and overcontrolling parents. Obstetricians are fortunate to be able to participate in the joys of childbirth but must also deal with perinatal deaths along with the various emotional consequences that accompany the workings of the reproductive system. Death is the opponent that all in the health care field struggle against. It is an adversary that always wins the battle, ideally later rather than sooner. Each physician must learn to deal with failure and death without undue self-recrimination. Every death should precipitate some sense of loss and grief for the medical practitioner. Those that isolate themselves from such feelings are at risk for the development of psychological difficulties and also remove themselves from an important and meaningful aspect of medical practice.

Practitioners and patients each make their own contribution to interactional difficulties, although one participant's pathology may be provoking the difficulty to a greater degree. Patients and practitioners both have family dramas that exert pressure for expression. In the best situations, these dramas remain hidden or are sublimated through alternative modes. In some situations, patients, practitioners, or both actualize their emotional traumas within their relationship. The worst situation occurs when patient and practitioner work in concert to establish a troublesome transference-countertransference dyad. Practitioners need to be aware that strong and intense emotions toward a patient are a signal that a process is occurring that needs attention. Physicians are not immune from psychological problems, and these problems can intrude upon medical practice. Psychological help is available and practitioners should avail themselves of it for any psychological distress, but especially in situations where their practice is affected.

There are a multitude of pressures on medical practitioners. Being responsible for the well-being of others is tremendously burdensome. The reality of managed care, capitation, and other attempts to control medical practice are enraging and discouraging. Despite this, far and away most physicians continue to gain satisfaction in their practice. In most cases, it is the relationship with the patient that is most satisfying. Practitioners who continue to understand and to nurture such relationships are those that are going to find the greatest contentment in medical practice.

References

American College of Obstetricians and Gynecologists. (1995, August). *Technical Bulletin 209,* 1–9.

American Psychiatric Association. (1994). *Diagnostic and statistical manual of mental disorders* (4th ed.). Washington, DC: Author.

Anderson, B. L., Kiecolt-Glaser, J. K., & Glaser, R. (1994). A biobehavioral model of cancer stress and disease course. *American Psychologist, 49,* 389–404.

Brenner, C. (1991). A psychoanalytic perspective on depression. *Journal of the American Psychoanalytic Association, 39,* 25–43.

Byock, I. (1993). Consciously walking the fine line: Thoughts on a hospice response to assisted suicide and euthanasia. *Journal of Palliative Care, 9*(3), 25–28.

Cameron, K., & Gregor, F. (1987). Chronic illness and compliance. *Journal of Advanced Nursing, 12,* 671–676.

DePalma, A. (1996, June 19). For Mexicans, pain relief is both a medical and a political problem. *New York Times* (International Edition), *50,* 463.

Fonagy, P. (1991). Thinking about thinking. *International Journal of Psycho-Analysis, 72,* 650–656.

Francis, C. (1991). Hypertension, cardiac disease and compliance in minority patients. *American Journal of Medicine, 91* (Suppl. A), 29s–36s.

Freud, S. (1955). Mourning and melancholia. In J. Strachey (Ed. and Trans.), *The standard edition of the complete psychological works of Sigmund Freud* (Vol. 14, pp. 243–258). London: Hogarth Press. (Original work published 1917)

Friedman, H. S., Tucker, J. S., Schwartz, J. E., Tomlinson-Keasey, C., Martin, L. R., Winogard, D. L., & Criqui, M. H. (1995). Psychosocial and behavioral predictors of longevity, the aging and death of the "Termites," *American Psychologist, 50,* 69–78.

Gabbard, G. (1991). Technical approaches to transference hate in the analysis of borderline patients. *International Journal of Psycho-Analysis, 72,* 625–637.

Gatchel, T., & Blanchard, J. (Eds.) (1993). *Psychophysiological disorders: Research and clinical applications.* Washington, DC: American Psychological Association.

Gluhoski, V. L. (1994). Misconceptions of cognitive therapy. *Psychotherapy, 31,* 594–599.

Greenson, R. (1965). The working alliance and the transference neurosis. *Psychoanalytic Quarterly, 34,* 155–181.

Greenson, R. (1967). *The technique and practice of psychoanalysis* (Vol. 1). New York: International Universities Press.

Kagan, N. (1984). The physician as therapeutic agent: Innovations in training. In C. Van Dyke, L. Temoshok, & L. Zegans (Eds.), *Emotions in health and illness: Applications to clinical practice* (pp. 209–226). Orlando, FL: Grune & Stratton.

Killingmo, B. (1989). Conflict and deficit. *International Journal of Psycho-Analysis, 70,* 65–79.

Krystal, H. (1988). *Integration and self-healing: Affect, trauma, alexithymia.* Hillsdale, NJ: Analytic Press.

Lange, M. H., Heins, J., Fisher, E., & Kopp, J. (1988). Empirical identification of techniques useful for counseling patients with diabetes. *Diabetes Education, 14,* 303–307.

Langs, R. (1976). *The Bi-personal field.* New York: Aronson.

McDougall, J. (1989). *Theaters of the body: A psychoanalytic approach to psychosomatic illness.* New York: Norton.

McFarlane, J., Parker, B., Soeken, K., & Bullock, L. (1992). Assessing for abuse during pregnancy. Severity of injuries and associated entry into prenatal care. *Journal of the American Medical Association, 267,* 3176–3178.

Mintz, I. (1983). Psychoanalytic descriptions: The clinical picture of anorexia nervosa and bulimia. In C. P. Wilson, C. C. Hogan, & I. Mintz (Eds.), *Fear of being fat* (pp. 83–113). New York: Aronson

Novick, J., & Novick, K. K. (1991). Some comments on masochism and the delusion of omnipotence from a developmental perspective. *Journal of the American Psychoanalytic Association, 39,* 307–338.

Psychotherapy: Does it work? (1995, November). *Consumer Reports, 60,* 734–739.

Schell, B. (1996). Chronic disease and psychotherapy, part II. *Psychotherapy Bulletin, 31*, 60–65.

Shapiro, D. (1965). *Neurotic styles.* New York: Basic Books.

Shapiro, D. (1981). *Autonomy and rigid character.* New York: Basic Books.

Slochower, J. (1987). The psychodynamics of obesity: A review. *Psychoanalytic Psychology, 2*, 145–158.

Stern, D. (1985). *The interpersonal world of the infant.* New York: Basic Books.

Taylor, G. (1993). Application of a dysregulation model of illness and disease: A case of spasmodic torticollis. *International Journal of Psycho-Analysis, 74*, 581–596.

Twaddle, V., & Scott, J. (1991). Depression. In W. Dryden & R. Rentoul (Eds.), *Adult clinical problems: A cognitive behavioural approach* (pp. 56–85). London: Routledge.

Wickramasekera, I. (1989). Enabling the somaticizing patient to exit the somatic closet: A high risk model. *Psychotherapy, 26*, 530–544.

Winnicott, D. W. (1949). Hate in the countertransference. *International Journal of Psycho-Analysis, 30*, 69–74.

Winnicott, D. W. (1960). The theory of the parent-infant relationship. *International Journal of Psycho-Analysis, 41*, 585–595.

Winokur, G., & Clayton, P. (1994). *The medical basis of psychiatry* (2nd ed.). Philadelphia: Saunders.

Index

375